Pam Schiller • Douglas Clements • Julie Sarama • Rafael Lara-Alecio

Teacher's Edition B

A Division of The McGraw·Hill Companies

Columbus, Ohio

www.sra4kids.com

SRA/McGraw-Hill

A Division of The **McGraw·Hill** *Companies*

Send all inquiries to:
SRA/McGraw-Hill
8787 Orion Place
Columbus, OH 43240-4027

Printed in the United States of America.

ISBN 0-07-572190-2

1 2 3 4 5 6 7 8 9 WEB 07 06 05 04 03 02

WELCOME TO

THE DLM EARLY CHILDHOOD EXPRESS

The DLM Early Childhood Express . . . Your Route To Learning Success!

The DLM Early Childhood Express is a holistic, child-centered program that nurtures each child by offering carefully selected and carefully sequenced learning experiences. It provides a wealth of materials and ideas to foster the social-emotional, intellectual, and physical development of children. At the same time, it nurtures the natural curiosity and sense of self that can serve as the foundation for a lifetime of learning.

The lesson format is designed to present information in a way that makes it easy for children to learn. The cycle is modeled on knowledge gained from the latest neuroscience research. Intelligence is, in large part, our ability to see patterns and build relationships out of those patterns, which is why ***The DLM Early Childhood Express*** is focused on helping children see the patterns in what they are learning. It builds an understanding of how newly taught material resembles what children already know. Then, it takes the differences in the new material and helps the children convert them into new understanding.

Every aspect of ***The DLM Early Childhood Express*** is designed to make learning instinctive. Circle Time at the beginning and end of each day helps children focus on the learning process, reflect on new concepts, and make important connections. The practice portions of the lessons are designed to allow children to apply what they have learned.

Neuroscience research reveals that unless knowledge is applied within twenty-four hours of its introduction, it will probably have to be relearned.

The early years, birth to age six, are the most fertile years in an individual's life for developing language skills. So lessons in The DLM Early Childhood Express are focused on language acquisition and those all-important early reading skills. With the right foundation, reading success is only a matter of maturation.

For children to grow intellectually, they must feel confident in their abilities and secure in their relationships with teachers, family members, and peers. ***The DLM Early Childhood Express*** addresses social-emotional development in a number of ways. It is included in every lesson (via positive reinforcement), built into content connections (via interactive activities), and inherent in the way families are actively involved in ***The DLM Early Childhood Express*** classrooms.

Welcome to ***The DLM Early Childhood Express***. Add your own ideas. Mix and match activities. Our program is designed to offer you a variety of activities on which to build a full year of exciting and creative lessons. Happy learning to you and the children in your care!

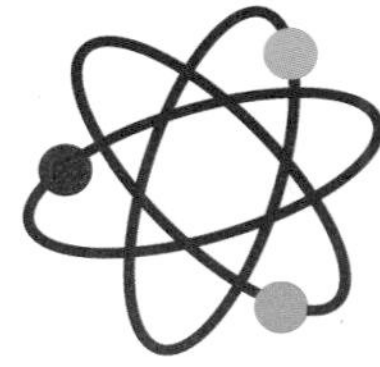

Key Findings in Brain Research

The knowledge gained from recent brain research makes it possible to give children the strongest possible foundation for learning. Here are some important facts:

- At birth each child has already developed a complex brain circuitry. The way the circuitry is "wired" depends upon such external forces as nutrition, environment, and degree of sensory stimulation.
- Early experiences contribute significantly to the structure of the brain and its capabilities. Children learn in the context of relationships. Early interactions are critical.
- Brain development is not a step-by-step process. It is more like a spiral with waves or windows of opportunity. Certain periods of a child's development are especially conducive to developing specific skills.

During the first three years of life, a child forms an estimated one thousand trillion synapses. However, neuron connections form only when a child interacts with his or her environment. The richer the child's environment is and the more he or she interacts with it, the more neuron connections the brain will create.

Young children are biologically predisposed to learn. With ***The DLM Early Childhood Express***, they can do it more effectively than ever before.

Your Day Takes Shape

When it comes to scheduling, flexibility is key. With ***The DLM Early Childhood Express***, it's easy to fit lessons into your day.

These suggested schedules can (and should) be altered to reflect:

- Lunch, recess, and other assigned periods
- Your individual teaching style
- The length of your day (half or full)

Both of these sample schedules begin with a Morning Circle. Beginning your day this way:

- Helps you and your class settle in and get organized
- Allows children time to adjust to the transition from home to school
- Provides an opportunity for building a sense of community

TYPICAL FULL-DAY SCHEDULE

8:00 – 8:30	Morning Circle: Begin the Day & Literacy
8:30 – 9:00	Literacy Learning Centers
9:00 – 9:15	Story Circle: Reading Together
9:15 – 9:30	Music and Movement
9:30 – 10:00	Group Activity: Math
10:00 – 10:20	Active Play (outdoors if possible)
10:20 – 10:40	Group Activity: Content Connection or Story Circle
10:40 – 11:15	Learning Centers
11:15 – 12:00	Lunch
12:00 – 12:15	Story Circle: Reading Together
12:15 – 12:45	Rest
12:45 – 1:00	Music and Movement
1:00 – 1:30	Group Activity: Revisit Literacy Lesson or Content Connections
1:30 – 2:20	Learning Centers
2:20 – 2:45	Active Play (outdoors if possible)
2:45 – 3:00	Closing Circle: Reflect on the Day

THE DLM EARLY CHILDHOOD EXPRESS

TYPICAL HALF-DAY SCHEDULE

8:00 – 8:30	Morning Circle: Begin the Day & Literacy
8:30 – 9:00	Literacy Learning Centers
9:00 – 9:15	Story Circle: Reading Together
9:15 – 9:30	Music and Movement
9:30 – 10:00	Group Activity: Math
10:00 – 10:20	Active Play (outdoors if possible)
10:20 – 10:40	Group Activity: Content Connection or Story Circle
10:40 – 11:15	Learning Centers
11:15 – 11:30	Closing Circle: Reflect on the Day

A Typical Weekly Lesson Plan

To help you understand how the weekly lesson plan is organized, each section of the lesson is defined and the location of specific activities within each lesson is described.

Day	Morning Circle	Learning Centers	Storytime	Group Activity	Learning Centers	Music & Movement	Closing Circle
Monday	Begin the Day Literacy Focus and Develop	Literacy Practice	Literacy Reflect "What Makes Me Happy?" /¿Cómo te sientes hoy?	Math Lesson Focus, Develop, Practice & Reflect	Math Practice Theme Centers Content Connection: Science	"The Wonderful Thing About Tiggers" from *Four Baby Bumblebees* CD	Reflect on the Day
Tuesday	Begin the Day Literacy Focus and Develop	Literacy Practice	Literacy Reflect "The Many Faces of Me"/ "La muchas caras de mi persona"	Math Lesson Focus, Develop, Practice & Reflect	Math Practice Theme Centers Content Connection: Health & Safety	"If You're Happy and You Know It" and "Vamos a cantar"	Reflect on the Day
Wednesday	Begin the Day Literacy Focus and Develop	Literacy Practice	Literacy Reflect "Keiko's Good Thinking"/ "El buen pensamiento de Keiko"	Math Lesson Focus, Develop, Practice & Reflect	Math Practice Theme Centers Content Connection: Literacy/Social Studies	*Making Music with Thomas Moore* CD	Reflect on the Day
Thursday	Begin the Day Literacy Focus and Develop	Literacy Practice	Literacy Reflect *Itsy Bitsy Spider/ La araña pequeñita*	Math Lesson Focus, Develop, Practice & Reflect	Math Practice Theme Centers Content Connection: Fine Arts	Hopscotch	Reflect on the Day
Friday	Begin the Day Literacy Focus and Develop	Literacy Practice	Literacy Reflect *How Happy I Would Be!/Me gustaria tener*	Math Lesson Focus, Develop, Practice & Reflect	Math Practice Theme Centers Content Connection: Science	Circle 'Round the Zero Circulo alrededor de cero	Reflect on the Day

Circle: Literacy or Math

These are whole-group activities that include songs, poems, stories, and part or all of a Literacy or Math lesson. Notice that there are several Circle activities for each day. The first Circle of the day, or Morning Circle (see suggestions on page 1), helps children organize their day, get focused, and make that all-important transition from home to school. The Closing Circle lets children recap their day and reflect on applications of what they have learned.

Group Activity: Literacy or Math

This may be a whole- or small-group activity (depending on your preference and the nature of the activity). You can find group activities in Literacy or Math lessons – or use suggestions from Content Connections (see pages xiv and xv).

Learning Centers

These are small-group activities that provide time for practicing skills and concepts taught in the lessons. Suggestions for learning center practice are found in each Literacy and Math Lesson as well as in the Content Connections. The Learning Centers presented on the first pages of theme and are intended to remain open for the entire week. These centers provide the opportunity for children to explore a wide range of curricular areas.

Music/Movement

This section recommends large- or small-group games and dances from the Teacher Resource Anthology, or songs and dances from the program's Music CDs.

Second Language Learners

This section includes suggestions for ways to adapt the lessons to the specific needs of second language learners.

School/Home

Ideas to help tie a lesson to the home come from the Home Connection feature in the lesson.

SRA understands the important role families play in the learning process. By keeping them informed and involved, ***The DLM Early Childhood Express*** helps to reinforce what is taught in the classroom.

Tools for Teaching

The DLM Early Childhood Express is packed full of the components you'll need to teach each theme and enrich your classroom. The Teacher Resource Package is the heart of the program, because it contains all the necessary materials. Plus, the Anthology contains all the fun components that you'll love to teach. You'll find letters, bears, puppets, and instruments in the Manipulative Package to connect learning skills with play.

Teacher Resource Package
This package contains all the essential tools for the teacher. It includes the Teacher's Resource Anthology, 550 pages of the things you love most about teaching Early Childhood, such as songs, patterns, finger plays, and feltboard stories. This package also contains Teacher's Editions, CDs and other resources no teacher would want to be without.

Teacher's Edition A
Teacher's Edition B
Teacher's Edition C
Teacher's Edition D
Teacher's Resource Anthology
Resource Guide, CD ROM & Pattern Blocks – Math
Resource Guide – Phonics (English)
Resource Guide – Phonics (Spanish)
Photo Library
Photo Library User's Guide and CD-ROM
Resource Guide – Home Connections
3 English CDs (1 Instrumental)
Alphabet Wall Cards
Sequencing Cards
Oral Language Development Cards

Manipulative Package
Rhythm band instruments, counters, puppets, and more to be used in lessons as well as to enhance learning center activities.

Uppercase Letters, 42/Set
Lowercase Letters, 44/Set
Spanish Letters, 18/Set
Dinosaurs Counters, 108/Set
Light Brown, Plush Bear Puppet with Shirt
Dark Brown, Plush Bear Puppet with Shirt
1 Set Wood Maracas
4 Hand Bells
1 Drum

Hurray for Pre-K!
Available in English and Spanish

Sara Sidney – The Most Beautiful Iguana in the World
Available in English and Spanish

Humpty Dumpty Dumpty
Available in English and Spanish

Listen to the Rain
Available in English and Spanish

In ***The DLM Early Childhood Express*** the Big Books support the literacy lessons, offer storytime suggestions, and are often used in content connections. The Listening Center Package puts books directly into children's hands.

With ***The DLM Early Childhood Express***, children can feel the excitement of turning the pages themselves as they follow along with the story that is being read on the audiocassette.

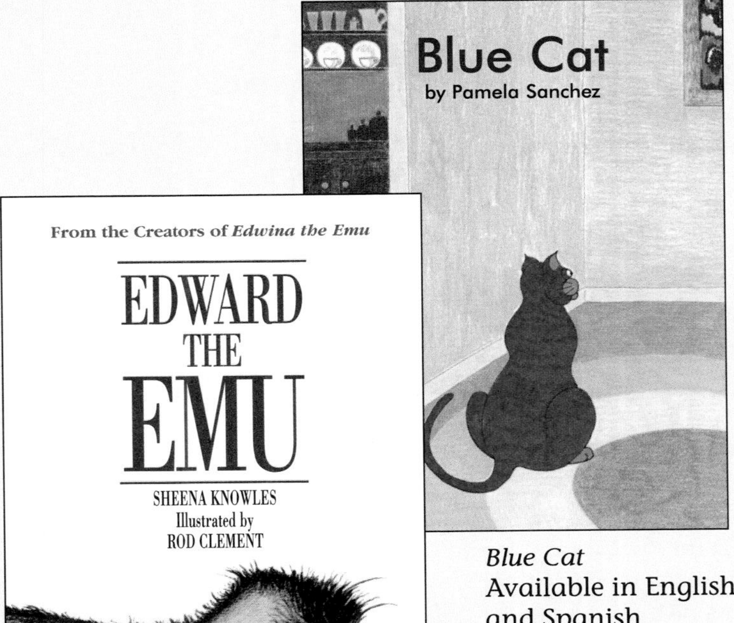

Blue Cat
Available in English and Spanish

Edward the Emu
Available in English and Spanish

SRA Alphabet Book
Available in English and Spanish

Fish Wish
Available in English and Spanish

Listening Center Package

This package puts books in the hands of children, allowing them to turn the pages themselves as they listen to the stories.

73 Little Books (2 copies of each title)
18 Audiocassettes

Big Book Package

Big Books offer read to and sharing reading experiences for children.

37 Big Books

The ***DLM Early Childhood Express*** program is also available in an English/Spanish edition.

Themes That Help Children Grow

Theme	CORE LITERATURE		
	English	Spanish	Author
School Days	Hurray for Pre-K!	¡Qué viva el preescolar!	Ellen B. Senisi
Physical Me	Here Are My Hands	Aquí están mis manos	Bill Martin Jr
Thinking and Feeling Me	How Happy I Would Be!	Me gustaría tener...	Alma Flor Ada
My Family	A Birthday Basket for Tía	Una canasta de cumpleaños para Tía	Pat Mora
Fall/Autumn	Fall	El otoño	Maria Rius
Friends	Ginger	Jengibre	Charlotte Voake
Pets	Sara Sidney: The Most Beautiful Iguana in the World	Sara Sidney: la iguana más bella del mundo	Pam Schiller and Tamera Bryant
Opposites	Sing a Song of Opposites	Canta una canción de opuestos	Pam Schiller
Color, Shape, and Size	The Color Bear	El oso de colores	Barbara Brenner
Color, Shape, and Size	Blue Cat	Gato azul	Pamela Sanchez
Things That Go Together	Wordsong	Canto de palabras	Bill Martin Jr
Under Construction	Animals That Build Their Homes	Animales que construyen sus nidos	Robert M. McClung
Growing Things	The Tortilla Factory	La tortillería	Gary Paulsen
Food and Nutrition	Martí and the Mango	Martí y el mango	Daniel Moreton
Nursery Rhymes	Humpty Dumpty Dumpty	Humpty Dumpty Dumpty	Thomas Moore and Pam Schiller
Sound and Movement	This Old Man Is Rockin' On	Este viejito tiene mucho ritmo	Tracy Moncure and Pam Schiller
Music	Animal Orchestra	La orquesta de los animales	Scott Gustafson
Winter	Flannel Kisses	Besos de franela	Linda Crotta Brennan
Community Workers	Guess Who?	Adivina quién...	Margaret Miller
Traditional Tales	The Little Red Hen	La gallinita roja	Retold by Rebecca Allen
Traditional Tales	A Bicycle for Rosaura	Rosaura en bicicleta	Daniel Barbot
Cowgirls and Cowboys	The Cowboy Mouse	El ratón vaquero	Beverly J. Irby and Rafael Lara-Alecio
Travel	Little Rabbit's Journey	El viaje del conejito	Beverly J. Irby and Rafael Lara-Alecio
Travel	The Zebra on the Zyder Zee	Una aventura en alta mar	Pam Schiller
Celebrations	¡Fiesta!	¡Fiesta!	Ginger Foglesong Guy
Spring	De Colores	De colores	traditional from Mexico
Weather	Listen to the Rain	Escucha la lluvia	Bill Martin Jr
Real and Make-Believe	The Dragon's Coming After You	El dragón te está persiguiendo	Sally Farrell Odgers
Bugs	Insect Picnic	El picnic de los insectos	Anne Rockwell
Bugs	The Itsy Bitsy Spider	La araña pequeñita	Retold by Tracy Moncure and Pam Schil
Animals	SRA Book of Animals	SRA El libro de los animales	
Zoo Animals	Edward the Emu	Eduardo el emú	Sheena Knowles
Farm Animals	The Farm	La granja	traditional from Mexico
Ocean Life	Fish Wish	Deseos de un pez	Bob Barner
Big Things	Who Is the Beast?	¿Quién es la bestia?	Keith Baker
Summer Fun	The Little Ants	Las hormiguitas	traditional from Mexico

Young children love to learn about themselves. But as they grow, their interests expand to include family, friends, their communities, and the wider world.

Anthology Stories

"I Like School"/"Me gusta la escuela" action story
"I Can, You Can!"/"¡Yo puedo, tú puedes!" flannel board story
"Keiko's Good Thinking"/"El buen pensamiento de Keiko" flannel board story
"Mi abuelo"/"My Grandfather" flannel board story
"The Fall of the Last Leaf"/"La cáida de la última hoja" action story
"Mr. Wiggle and Mr. Waggle"/"Señor Wiggle y Señor Waggle" action story
"A Pet of my Own"/"Mi propia mascota" flannel board story
"El burrito enfermo"/"My Sick Little Donkey" flannel board story
"Rafita and Pepita: Dance of Opposites"/"Rafita y Pepita: un baile de opuestos" action story
"The Color Song"/"Los colores" flannel board story
"Freddie the Snake"/"Braulio, la culebra" flannel board story
"Animal Homes"/"Hogares de animales" flannel board story
"This Is the House That Jack Built"/"Esta es la casa que Juan construyó" flannel board story
"A Special Surprise"/"Una sorpresa especial" prop story
"Let's Pretend to Bake a Cake"/"Pretendamos como que horneamos un pastel" action story
"Little Miss Muffet"/"La Señorita Mufete" flannel board story
"Tortoise Wins a Race"/"La tortuga gana la carrera" flannel board story
"The Traveling Musicians"/"Los músicos viajeros" flannel board story
"The Snow Child"/"La niña de nieve" listening story
"My Father Picks Oranges"/"Mi papá recoge naranjas" listening story
"Henny-Penny"/"Gallinita-Nita" flannel board story
"The Little Red Hen"/"La gallinita roja" flannel board story
"Little Annie Oakley"/"La pequeña Annie Oakley" flannel board story
"Wheels On the Bus"/"Ruedas del bus" flannel board story
"Roll On, Roll On"/"Rueda, rueda" flannel board story
"La piñata"/"The Piñata" action story
"A Spring Walk"/"Una caminata en primavera" action story
"Sing Me a Rainbow"/"Cántame un arco iris" flannel board story
"Candy Land Journey"/"Un viaje a la tierra del dulce" action story
"Ms. Bumblebee Gathers Honey"/"La avispa Zumbi lleve miel" prop story
"Las hormiguitas"/"The Little Ants" flannel board story
"Dog: A Mayan Legend"/"Perro: Una leyenda maya" flannel board story
"Party at Daisy's"/"Fiesta en casa de Daisy" flannel board story
"Old MacDonald"/"El viejo MacDonald" flannel board story
"Going On a Whale Watch"/"Vamos a mirar ballenas" action story
"Lion's Haircut"/"El corte de pelo del león" prop story
"Summer at the Beach"/"Verano en la playa" listening story

In ***The DLM Early Childhood Express***, lesson content is integrated into themes that reflect the world from children's evolving perspective. Organizing lessons in this way helps children to make connections and expand upon the knowledge and skills they have already achieved.

To find the topics that touch home with children the most, we turned to the real experts: their teachers. We held focus groups to learn what works in real Pre-K classrooms. We consulted national research studies and surveys on early childhood education, and we used our years of educational experience to bring it all together.

OVERVIEW

Developed with the Whole Child in Mind

With ***The DLM Early Childhood Express***, children develop concrete skills through experiences with music, art, storytelling, and teacher-directed lessons that, in addition to skills development, emphasize practice and reflection.

Literacy concepts, including:

- Listening Comprehension
- Vocabulary
- Verbal Expression
- Phonological Awareness
- Print and Book Awareness
- Letter Knowledge and Early Word Recognition
- Motivation to Read
- Developing Knowledge of Literary Form
- Written Expression

Math concepts, including:

- Number Concepts and Operations
- Patterns
- Geometry and Spatial Relations
- Measurement
- Classification and Data Collection

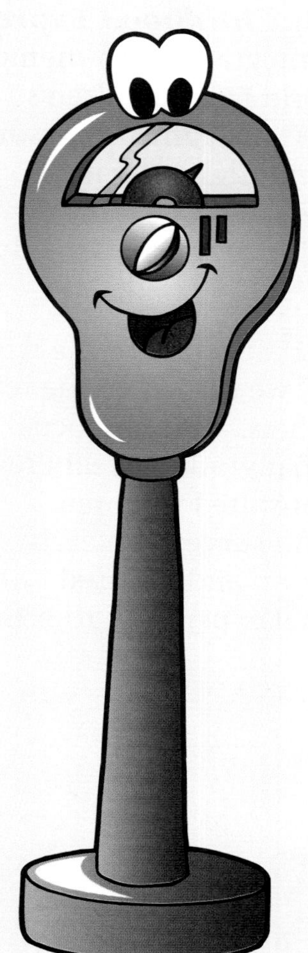

Theme
School Days
Physical Me
Thinking and Feeling Me
My Family
Fall/Autumn
Friends
Pets
Opposites
Color, Shape, and Size
Color, Shape, and Size
Things That Go Together
Under Construction
Growing Things
Food and Nutrition
Nursery Rhymes
Sound and Movement
Music
Winter
Community Workers
Traditional Tales
Traditional Tales
Cowgirls and Cowboys
Travel
Travel
Celebrations
Spring
Weather
Real and Make-Believe
Bugs
Bugs
Animals
Zoo Animals
Farm Animals
Ocean Life
Big Things
Summer Fun

Literacy Focuses		Math Focuses
Listening Comprehension		Classification and Data Collection
Listening Comprehension		Number and Operations
Vocabulary Print and Book Awareness	Verbal Expression Developing Knowledge of Literary Forms	Geometry and Spatial Sense
Vocabulary Developing Knowledge of Literary Forms Phonological Awareness	Verbal Expression Letter Knowledge and Early Word Recognition	Geometry and Spatial Sense
Verbal Expression Phonological Awareness	Listening Comprehension	Number and Operations
Verbal Expression Print and Book Awareness	Developing Knowledge of Literary Forms	Number and Operations
Phonological Awareness Vocabulary	Development of Knowledge of Literary Forms Verbal Expression	Number and Operations
Vocabulary	Listening Comprehension	Number and Operations
Vocabulary Verbal Expression	Listening Comprehension Print and Book Awareness	Geometry and Spatial Sense Classification and Data Collection
Phonological Awareness Speech Production and Speech Discrimination	Vocabulary	Geometry and Spatial Sense
Vocabulary		Number and Operations
Vocabulary		Geometry and Spatial Sense
Listening Comprehension		Number and Operations
Print and Book Awareness		Number and Operations
Phonological Awareness		Geometry and Spatial Sense
Verbal Expression Print and Book Awareness	Listening Comprehension Motivation to Read	Patterns
Vocabulary		Patterns
Verbal Expression	Phonological Awareness	Geometry and Spatial Sense
Listening Comprehension	Verbal Expression	Number and Operations
Developing Knowledge of Literary Forms		Number and Operations
Letter Knowledge and Word Recognition Developing Knowledge of Literary Forms	Verbal Expression Print and Book Awareness	Measurement
Verbal Expression	Listening Comprehension	Measurement
Verbal Expression	Vocabulary	Geometry and Spatial Sense
Vocabulary Verbal Expression	Listening Comprehension	Patterns Geometry and Spatial Sense
Verbal Expression Print and Book Awareness	Listening Comprehension	Number and Operations
Written Expression Speech Production and Speech Discrimination	Verbal Expression	Number and Operations
Phonological Awareness	Verbal Expression	Geometry and Spatial Sense
Developing Knowledge of Literary Forms	Verbal Expression	Number and Operations
Vocabulary; Letter Knowledge & Early Word Recognition Listening Comprehension	Developing Knowledge of Literary Forms Print and Book Awareness	Number and Operations
Developing Knowledge of Literary Forms Vocabulary	Verbal Expression Written Expression	Number and Operations
Motivation to Read Letter Knowledge and Early Word Recognition	Written Expression	Number and Operations
Print and Book Awareness Phonological Awareness	Written Expression	Classification and Data Collection
Phonological Awareness Developing Knowledge of Literary Forms	Listening Comprehension	Classification and Data Collection Patterns
Listening Comprehension Developing Knowledge of Literary Forms Verbal Expression	Vocabulary Phonological Awareness	Geometry and Spatial Sense
Listening Comprehension Developing Knowledge of Literary Forms	Vocabulary Written Expression	Geometry and Spatial Sense
Vocabulary Print and Book Awareness	Listening Comprehension	Geometry and Spatial Sense

Forging Connections in the

Objectives set the tone and direction for the lesson.

Vocabulary expands children's language capacity, giving them a better grasp of words.

A choice of **Activities** offers a variety of ways for children to build upon and enhance learning experiences.

A list of **Materials** makes preparation a snap.

Content Connection

Science

Objectives

To use one or more senses to observe and learn about objects, events, and organisms

To become increasingly sensitive to the sounds of spoken words

Vocabulary

drip-drop, pitter patter, splash, swoosh, swirl

goteo, golpeteo, salpicar, silbar, girar

DLM Materials

- *Teacher's Resource Anthology*
  "The Rain"/"La lluvia"
  "The Wind"/"El viento"

Materials to Gather

spray bottle, cookie sheet, water, sponge, baster, straws, paper plates, small paper sack

Activity 1

- Read "The Rain"/"La lluvia." Discuss the sounds of rain.
- Hand out a spray bottle, a cookie sheet, a tub of water, a sponge, and a baster. Invite the children to explore water sounds by spraying the water on the cookie sheet and into the tub. Challenge them to describe the sounds. Are the words they use examples of onomatopoeia? Encourage the children to splash the water and use the sponge and the baster to drip water.

  How does the water from the baster sound when it hits the surface of the water in the tub?

  ¿Cómo suena el agua cuando choca contra la superficie del agua en la bañera?

  Are the sounds examples of onomatopoeia (splish-splash, drip-drop, pitter patter)?

  ¿Los sonidos son ejemplos onomatopéyicos (plin plin, pun pun)?

Activity 2

- Read "The Wind"/"El viento." Discuss the sounds of wind.
- Provide a small sack, straws, paper plates, and a baster. Invite the children to make sounds that sound like wind. Challenge them to describe the sounds. Are the words they use examples of onomatopoeia? Encourage them to fill the bags with air and pop them. Have them fan the air with paper plates and blow through the straws.

World of Learning

Early learners are constantly making connections between what they know and what they have just learned. Cross-curricular connections are a powerful way to reinforce lesson concepts and expose children to the full spectrum of knowledge.

The challenge for teachers is to consistently integrate these connections into their lessons, and that can be a time-consuming task.

The DLM Early Childhood Express was designed to make it easy. Each lesson contains the most relevant cross-curricular Content Connections, presented as miniature lessons. You get everything you need to teach them effectively – all in one place.

Content Connection areas include:

Fine Arts:

Through art, children learn to express their thoughts, feelings, and ideas in symbolic ways.

Music & Movement:

Children learn to sing, play simple instruments, listen, and respond to music. They also begin to create and recreate moods and experiences in order to express their feelings through increasingly coordinated movement.

Science:

Science teaches children to observe, investigate, and draw conclusions about the world in a systematic way.

Social Studies:

Social studies teaches them to share, cooperate, and participate with others.

Health or Safety:

Lessons in health or safety help children make life choices that will enhance their physical well-being.

Physical Development:

Specially designed movement activities help children practice and improve their gross and fine motor skills as well as maintain personal space.

Personal and Social Development

Interwoven throughout the entire program, these activities enable children to develop a sense of who they are and their own capabilities to establish positive relationships with others.

Giving Children

Scaffolding Strategies

More Help Every child learns at a different pace, which is why flexible lesson plans are a must. This section offers suggestions, such as specific stories you can read, to help bring all children up to speed.

Extra Challenge Our ladder icons make scaffolding easy. Wherever they appear, you'll find strategies on how to adjust the pace or content of a lesson. When children are learning quickly, this section suggests additional activities to keep their interest engaged, such as thinking divergently about a specific topic (i.e., putting yourself in another person's place).

Teaching in a Diverse Classroom

Today's classrooms are diverse and exciting places to teach. Our children come from a range of ethnic and economic backgrounds and family situations. They bring to the classroom a wealth of culture and tradition.

As educators, we want all our children to see themselves in the activities we provide. The DLM Early Childhood Express:

Nurtures and celebrates children's cultural and ethnic heritages

Encourages children to share their traditions with each other

That is why we:

Actively support the continued development of children's home languages

Guide children as they learn English or Spanish as a second language

Make sure we are sensitive to all, so that every child feels comfortable in the classroom

a Sense of Community

There are many ways to create a positive home/school connection that will help support second-language learners. One is to let parents know how important it is to provide a rich language environment in their children's home languages. Encourage parents to talk, sing, read, and discuss books with their children in their home language – and to participate in community activities where the home language is spoken.

Another key strategy is to get parents (and families) involved in class activities. Take the time to get to know them. Listen to parents' ideas and share your positive comments about their children. Display the children's work, photos of them at school, and videotape the classroom activities to make parents feel at ease. Once they feel comfortable with you, parents can become powerful allies in addressing such issues as cultural conflict before they progress too far.

To effectively teach a second language, we must be able to make ourselves understood. In this, common sense is your best guide. Speak clearly at a natural pace. Use short, simple sentences, and pause between sentences to allow children to process your language. Link words and concepts with concrete objects, and paraphrase if children do not understand the first time around. Above all, remain alert and responsive to each child's needs. Acknowledge their attempts to communicate verbally or non-verbally in a conversational tone.

Diverse and multilingual classrooms are the way of the future. With the right approach, we can make them rich, supportive, and rewarding places to learn.

Teacher Editions That Simplify Your Day

The DLM Early Childhood Express Teacher Editions are easy to use. They provide a wealth of flexible and adaptable activities that help you customize lessons to fit the specific needs of your children.

Most themes are taught over a period of five days. Each day features circle group time that emphasizes Literacy and Math. Each Literacy and Math lesson is followed by a Content Connection that ties other curriculum areas, such as science, social studies, fine arts, physical development, health and safety, and personal and social

Every theme has an overview that provides a short description of what you and the children will encounter during the theme.

Each theme has three suggestions for Learning Centers that are intended to remain on-going for the duration of the theme. We often provide suggestions for altering the focus of children's play without altering the setup of the center.

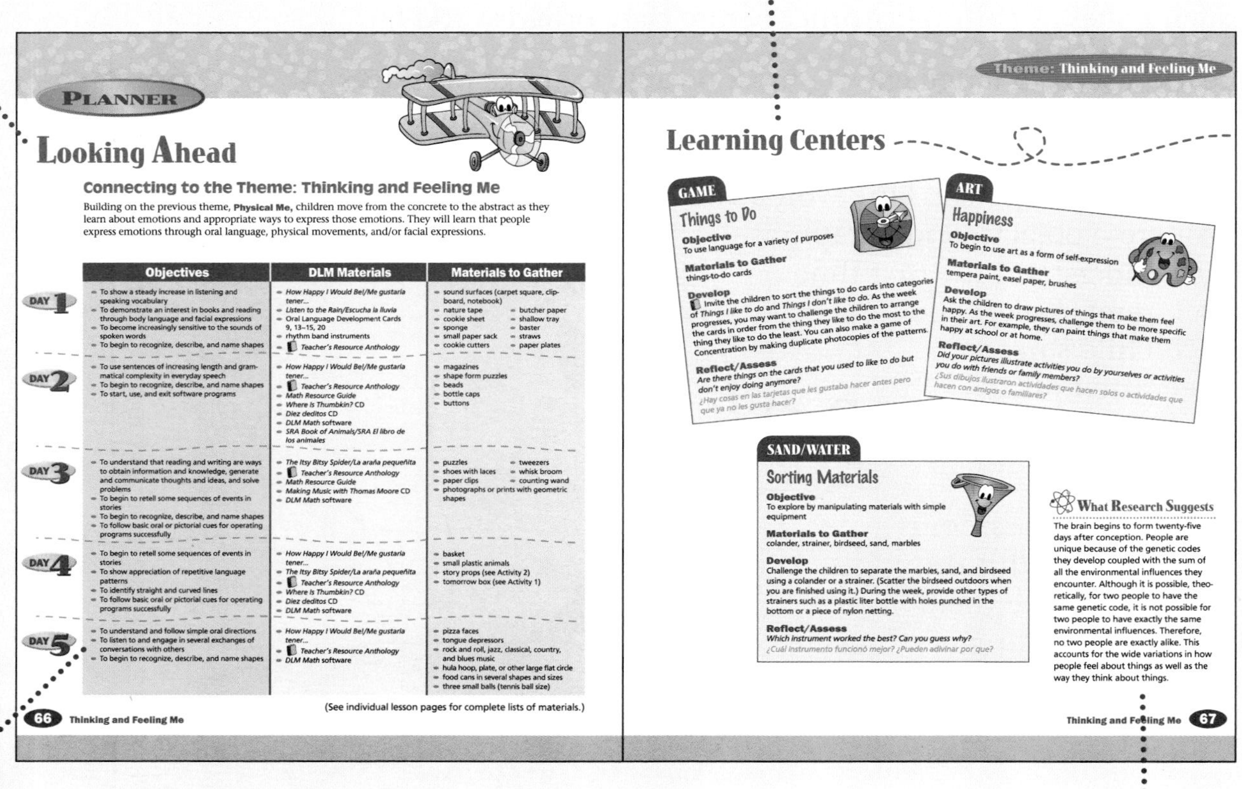

PLANNER

Looking Ahead

Connecting to the Theme: Thinking and Feeling Me

Building on the previous theme, **Physical Me,** children move from the concrete to the abstract as they learn about emotions and appropriate ways to express those emotions. They will learn that people express emotions through oral language, physical movements, and/or facial expressions.

	Objectives	DLM Materials	Materials to Gather
DAY 1	To show a steady increase in listening and speaking vocabulary To demonstrate an interest in books and reading through body language and facial expressions To become increasingly sensitive to the sounds of spoken words To begin to recognize, describe, and name shapes	*How Happy I Would Be!/Me gustaría tener...* *Listen to the Rain/Escucha la lluvia* Oral Language Development Cards 9, 13–15, 20 rhythm band instruments *Teacher's Resource Anthology*	sound surfaces (carpet square, clipboard, notebook) nature tape cookie sheet sponge small paper sack cookie cutters butcher paper shallow tray baster straws paper plates
DAY 2	To use sentences of increasing length and grammatical complexity in everyday speech To begin to recognize, describe, and name shapes To start, use, and exit software programs	*How Happy I Would Be!/Me gustaría tener...* *Teacher's Resource Anthology* *Math Resource Guide* *Where Is Thumbkin?* CD *Diez deditos* CD *DLM Math* software *SRA Book of Animals/SRA El libro de los animales*	magazines shape form puzzles beads bottle caps buttons
DAY 3	To understand that reading and writing are ways to obtain information and knowledge, generate and communicate thoughts and ideas, and solve problems To begin to retell some sequences of events in stories To begin to recognize, describe, and name shapes To follow basic oral or pictorial cues for operating programs successfully	*The Itsy Bitsy Spider/La araña pequeñita* *Teacher's Resource Anthology* *Math Resource Guide* *Making Music with Thomas Moore* CD *DLM Math* software	puzzles shoes with laces paper clips photographs or prints with geometric shapes tweezers whisk broom counting wand
DAY 4	To begin to retell some sequences of events in stories To show appreciation of repetitive language patterns To identify straight and curved lines To follow basic oral or pictorial cues for operating programs successfully	*How Happy I Would Be!/Me gustaría tener...* *The Itsy Bitsy Spider/La araña pequeñita* *Teacher's Resource Anthology* *Where Is Thumbkin?* CD *Diez deditos* CD *DLM Math* software	basket small plastic animals story props (see Activity 2) tomorrow box (see Activity 1)
DAY 5	To understand and follow simple oral directions To listen to and engage in several exchanges of conversations with others To begin to recognize, describe, and name shapes	*How Happy I Would Be!/Me gustaría tener...* *Teacher's Resource Anthology* *DLM Math* software	pizza faces tongue depressors rock and roll, jazz, classical, country, and blues music hula hoop, plate, or other large flat circle food cans in several shapes and sizes three small balls (tennis ball size)

(See individual lesson pages for complete lists of materials.)

66 Thinking and Feeling Me

Theme: Thinking and Feeling Me

Learning Centers

GAME

Things to Do

Objective
To use language for a variety of purposes

Materials to Gather
things-to-do cards

Develop
Invite the children to sort the things to do cards into categories of *Things I like to do* and *Things I don't like to do*. As the week progresses, you may want to challenge the children to arrange the cards in order from the thing they like to do the most to the thing they like to do the least. You can also make a game of Concentration by making duplicate photocopies of the patterns.

Reflect/Assess
Are there things on the cards that you used to like to do but don't enjoy doing anymore?
¿Hay cosas en las tarjetas que les gustaba hacer antes pero que ya no les gusta hacer?

ART

Happiness

Objective
To begin to use art as a form of self-expression

Materials to Gather
tempera paint, easel paper, brushes

Develop
Ask the children to draw pictures of things that make them feel happy. As the week progresses, challenge them to be more specific in their art. For example, they can paint things that make them happy at school or at home.

Reflect/Assess
Did your pictures illustrate activities you do by yourselves or activities you do with friends or family members?
¿Sus dibujos ilustraron actividades que hacen solos o actividades que hacen con amigos o familiares?

SAND/WATER

Sorting Materials

Objective
To explore by manipulating materials with simple equipment

Materials to Gather
colander, strainer, birdseed, sand, marbles

Develop
Challenge the children to separate the marbles, sand, and birdseed using a colander or a strainer. (Scatter the birdseed outdoors when you are finished using it.) During the week, provide other types of strainers such as a plastic liter bottle with holes punched in the bottom or a piece of nylon netting.

Reflect/Assess
Which instrument worked the best? Can you guess why?
¿Cuál instrumento funcionó mejor? ¿Pueden adivinar por que?

What Research Suggests

The brain begins to form twenty-five days after conception. People are unique because of the genetic codes they develop coupled with the sum of all the environmental influences they encounter. Although it is possible, theoretically, for two people to have the same genetic code, it is not possible for two people to have exactly the same environmental influences. Therefore, no two people are exactly alike. This accounts for the wide variations in how people feel about things as well as the way they think about things.

Thinking and Feeling Me 67

An overview of the theme's objectives and materials allows you to see at a glance what the children will be learning and the materials you will need to gather.

Each theme has a statement from emerging neuroscience research that connects or supports the lessons and activities the children will encounter as the theme unfolds.

development, to the lesson using theme and lesson objectives. The Connections provide meaningful context that helps children make sense of what they are learning.

In addition to the Teacher Editions, ***The DLM Early Childhood Express*** includes a **Teacher's Resource Anthology** with more than 500 pages of thematic songs, recipes, patterns, and finger plays. The DLM system is further enhanced by the Resource Guides–**Spanish Phonics**, **English Phonics**, **Math**, and **Home Connections**. See the ladder icon for simple **Scaffolding Strategies** that help you meet the individual needs of your children.

The **Second Language Learners** section offers teaching strategies that help children of all language backgrounds and abilities meet the lesson objectives.

Use the **Anthology Support** to find additional resources to enhance your lessons.

Our **Teacher Editions** are organized by theme and by day. **Objectives** set the direction of the lesson. **Begin the Day** gives children time to adjust to the environment and develop a sense of community with classmates. It also provides an opportunity for a daily literacy activity such as singing about the days of the week or writing the news of the day.

Each theme contains easy to follow literacy lessons that always follow the same four steps: Focus, Develop, Practice, and Reflect/Assess.

Our English/Spanish **Vocabulary** section highlights words that may be new. This helps expand children's ability to use both languages.

The **Materials** section tells you everything you need to gather (and assemble) in advance. No more last-minute surprises!

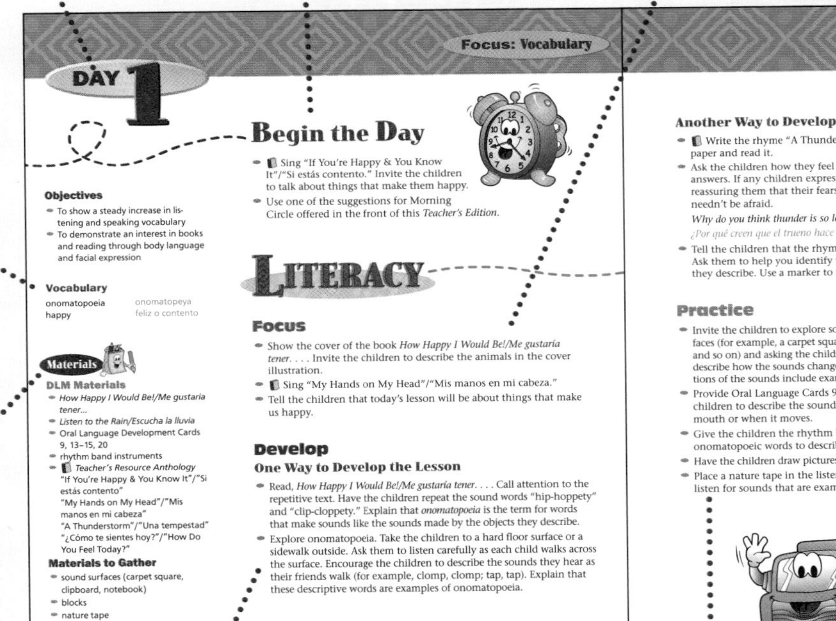

Focus: Vocabulary

DAY 1

Objectives

- To show a steady increase in listening and speaking vocabulary
- To demonstrate an interest in books and reading through body language and facial expression

Vocabulary

onomatopoeia — onomatopeya
happy — feliz o contento

Materials

DLM Materials

- *How Happy I Would Be!/Me gustaria tener...*
- *Listen to the Rain/Escucha la lluvia*
- Oral Language Development Cards 9, 13–15, 20
- rhythm band instruments
- *Teacher's Resource Anthology* "If You're Happy & You Know It"/"Si estás contento" "My Hands on My Head"/"Mis manos en mi cabeza" "A Thunderstorm"/"Una tempestad" "¿Cómo te sientes hoy?"/"How Do You Feel Today?"

Materials to Gather

- sound surfaces (carpet square, clipboard, notebook)
- blocks
- nature tape

Begin the Day

- Sing "If You're Happy & You Know It"/"Si estás contento." Invite the children to talk about things that make them happy.
- Use one of the suggestions for Morning Circle offered in the front of this *Teacher's Edition*.

LITERACY

Focus

- Show the cover of the book *How Happy I Would Be!/Me gustaría tener. . . .* Invite the children to describe the animals in the cover illustration.
- Sing "My Hands on My Head"/"Mis manos en mi cabeza."
- Tell the children that today's lesson will be about things that make us happy.

Develop

One Way to Develop the Lesson

- Read, *How Happy I Would Be!/Me gustaría tener. . . .* Call attention to the repetitive text. Have the children repeat the sound words "hip-hoppety" and "clip-cloppety." Explain that *onomatopoeia* is the term for words that make sounds like the sounds made by the objects they describe.
- Explore onomatopoeia. Take the children to a hard floor surface or a sidewalk outside. Ask them to listen carefully as each child walks across the surface. Encourage the children to describe the sounds they hear as their friends walk (for example, clomp, clomp; tap, tap). Explain that these descriptive words are examples of onomatopoeia.

68 Thinking and Feeling Me

Theme: Thinking and Feeling Me

Another Way to Develop the Lesson

- Write the rhyme "A Thunderstorm"/"Una tempestad" on chart paper and read it.
- Ask the children how they feel during thunderstorms. Explore their answers. If any children express fear of storms, discuss this calmly, reassuring them that their fears are natural. Emphasize that they needn't be afraid.

  Why do you think thunder is so loud?
  ¿Por qué creen que el trueno hace tanto ruido?
- Tell the children that the rhyme is full of examples of onomatopoeia. Ask them to help you identify the words that sound like the things they describe. Use a marker to underline those words.

Practice

- Invite the children to explore sounds by providing several different surfaces (for example, a carpet square, clipboard, notebook, piece of wood, and so on) and asking the children to tap on them. Encourage them to describe how the sounds change with each surface. Do their descriptions of the sounds include examples of onomatopoeia?
- Provide Oral Language Cards 9, 13, 14, 15, and 20. Challenge the children to describe the sounds that each animal makes with its mouth or when it moves.
- Give the children the rhythm band instruments. Have them think of onomatopoeic words to describe the sounds the instruments make.
- Have the children draw pictures of how they feel during thunderstorms.
- Place a nature tape in the listening center. Encourage the children to listen for sounds that are examples of onomatopoeia.

Preparation

- Prepare the "¿Cómo te sientes hoy?"/"How Do You Feel Today?" flannel board story.

Scaffolding Strategies

More Help Encourage children to think of sound words. Read some of the selections in the *Anthology* that use onomatopoeia such as "Six White Ducks"/"Los seis patos blancos" or "Clickety, Clickety, Clack."

Extra Challenge Brainstorm a list of words that illustrate onomatopoeia.

Second Language Learners

After children have sorted the things-to-do cards, ask open-ended questions. *Who reads to you at home?/¿Quién lee contigo en casa?* If children have a more basic level of second language proficiency, try using two choices: *Does Trinh or your mom read to you?*

Anthology Support

"Smart Cookie's Best Friend, Gabby Graham"
"Gabby Graham, la mejor amiga de Smart Cookie"
"Clickety, Clickety Clack"
"Old MacDonald"
"El viejo MacDonald"

Day 1 69

The **Preparation** section points out what needs to be done in advance of the lesson.

See the ladder icon for simple **Scaffolding Strategies** that help you meet the individual needs of the children.

The **Second Language Learners** section offers teaching strategies that help children of all language backgrounds and abilities meet the lesson objectives.

A choice of strategies allows you to adjust each lesson to fit your schedule. You can select the method that most appeals to you or use both for added support. If you teach in a dual-language classroom, teach one activity in each language. If you teach in a full day program, do one in the morning and the other in the afternoon.

Practice activities – vitally important to the success of our lessons – provide opportunities for children to apply the information they have just learned. You can choose which of these you want to use or try them all.

Visit **Anthology Support** for additional resources to enrich your lessons.

Teacher Edition

The DLM Early Childhood Express Teacher Editions are easy to use. They provide a wealth of flexible and adaptable activities that help you customize lessons to fit the specific needs of your children.

Some examples of items that will help customize your literacy lessons are shown on this spread.

Letter Knowledge addresses the first four weeks, when schoolchildren are introduced to the alphabet. Then, continuing with the fifth week's unit, there's a focus on individual letters.

Reflect/Assess questions help children think about possible applications of what they have learned in the lesson.

Teacher Notes provide special information about the lesson that may help you better understand its content or format.

Letter Knowledge provides suggestions for helping children learn to recognize the letters of the alphabet.

Reflect/Assess questions are part of every lesson.

Suggested Reading provides a list of books that tie to the theme or the objective of the day's lesson.

Teacher's Notes

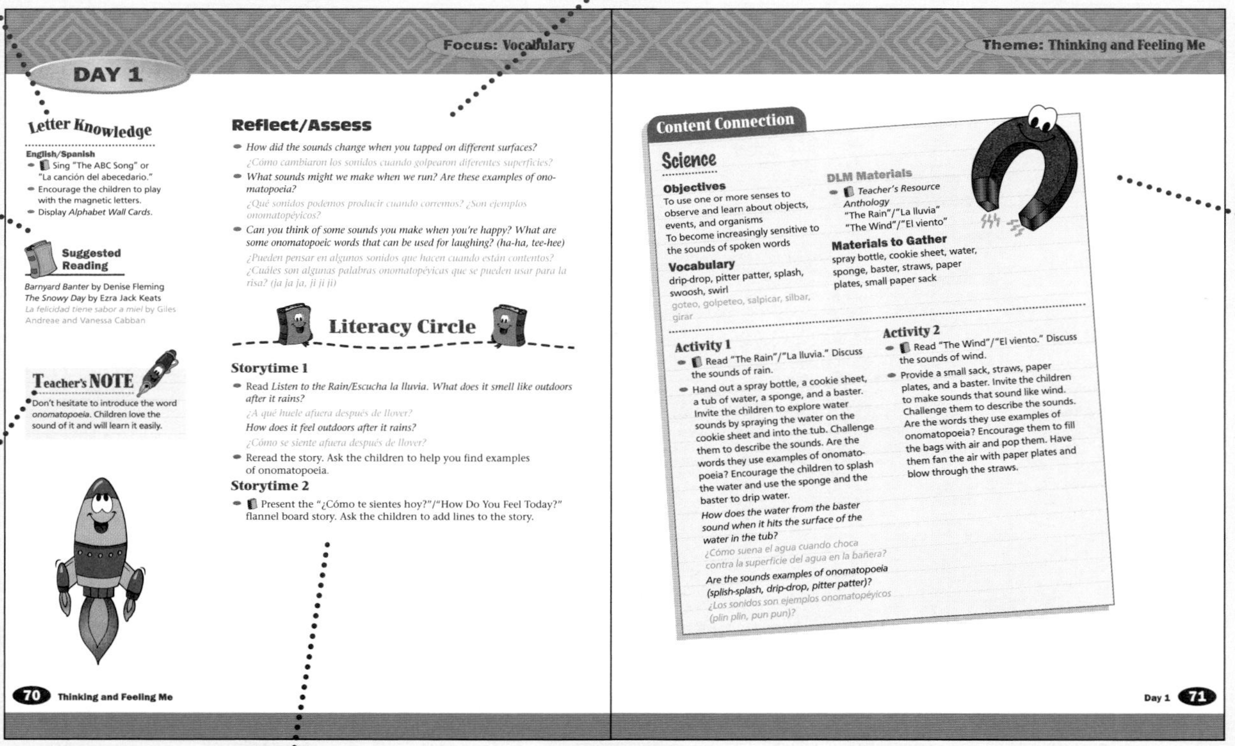

Content Connections are mini-lessons or center ideas that tie the lesson to other areas of the curriculum such as physical development, science, social studies and fine arts.

Focus: Vocabulary

DAY 1

Letter Knowledge

English/Spanish

- Sing "The ABC Song" or "La canción del abecedario."
- Encourage the children to play with the magnetic letters.
- Display *Alphabet Wall Cards.*

Suggested Reading

Barnyard Banter by Denise Fleming
The Snowy Day by Ezra Jack Keats
La felicidad tiene sabor a miel by Giles Andreae and Vanessa Cabban

Teacher's NOTE

Don't hesitate to introduce the word *onomatopoeia*. Children love the sound of it and will learn it easily.

Reflect/Assess

- *How did the sounds change when you tapped on different surfaces?*
  ¿Cómo cambiaron los sonidos cuando golpearon diferentes superficies?
- *What sounds might we make when we run? Are these examples of onomatopoeia?*
  ¿Qué sonidos podemos producir cuando corremos? ¿Son ejemplos onomatopéyicos?
- *Can you think of some sounds you make when you're happy? What are some onomatopoeic words that can be used for laughing? (ha-ha, tee-hee)*
  ¿Pueden pensar en algunos sonidos que hacen cuando están contentos? ¿Cuáles son algunas palabras onomatopéyicas que se pueden usar para la risa? (ja ja ja, ji ji ji)

Literacy Circle

Storytime 1

- Read *Listen to the Rain/Escucha la lluvia. What does it smell like outdoors after it rains?*
  ¿A qué huele afuera después de llover?
  How does it feel outdoors after it rains?
  ¿Cómo se siente afuera después de llover?
- Reread the story. Ask the children to help you find examples of onomatopoeia.

Storytime 2

- Present the "¿Cómo te sientes hoy?"/"How Do You Feel Today?" flannel board story. Ask the children to add lines to the story.

70 Thinking and Feeling Me

Theme: Thinking and Feeling Me

Content Connection

Science

Objectives
To use one or more senses to observe and learn about objects, events, and organisms
To become increasingly sensitive to the sounds of spoken words

Vocabulary
drip-drop, pitter patter, splash, swoosh, swirl
goteo, golpeteo, salpicar, silbar, girar

DLM Materials
- *Teacher's Resource Anthology*
  "The Rain"/"La lluvia"
  "The Wind"/"El viento"

Materials to Gather
spray bottle, cookie sheet, water, sponge, baster, straws, paper plates, small paper sack

Activity 1

- Read "The Rain"/"La lluvia." Discuss the sounds of rain.
- Hand out a spray bottle, a cookie sheet, a tub of water, a sponge, and a baster. Invite the children to explore water sounds by spraying the water on the cookie sheet and into the tub. Challenge them to describe the sounds. Are the words they use examples of onomatopoeia? Encourage the children to splash the water and use the sponge and the baster to drip water.
  How does the water from the baster sound when it hits the surface of the water in the tub?
  ¿Cómo suena el agua cuando choca contra la superficie del agua en la bañera?
  Are the sounds examples of onomatopoeia (splish-splash, drip-drop, pitter patter)?
  ¿Los sonidos son ejemplos onomatopéyicos (plin plin, pun pun)?

Activity 2

- Read "The Wind"/"El viento." Discuss the sounds of wind.
- Provide a small sack, straws, paper plates, and a baster. Invite the children to make sounds that sound like wind. Challenge them to describe the sounds. Are the words they use examples of onomatopoeia? Encourage them to fill the bags with air and pop them. Have them fan the air with paper plates and blow through the straws.

Day 1 71

Literacy Circle has two storytime suggestions. Choose one or use both.

Teacher Edition

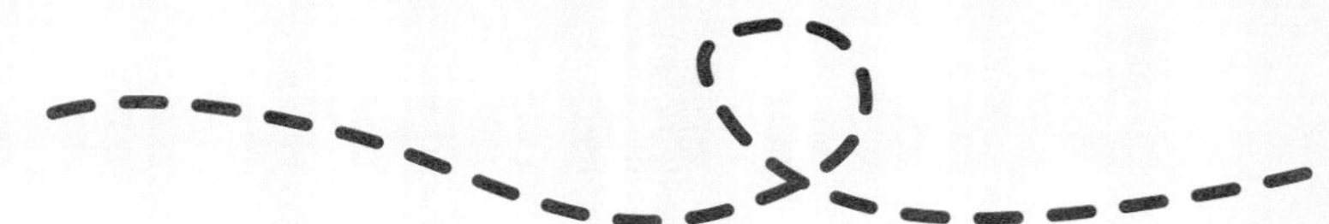

The content of Math lessons throughout the program is supported by research. To help plan your lesson further, **Objectives**, **Vocabulary** and **Preparation** tips are provided. And when new games and activities on the *DLM Math* software are introduced, suggestions for helping the children navigate the software appear in the **Develop** portion of the lesson.

Two suggestions for **Music and Movement** are offered for every day. You can choose one or both. **Content Connections** tie the math lesson to other areas of the curriculum, such as fine arts, science, social studies, health and safety, and physical development. And to finish up the lesson, **Reflect on the Day** helps the children recap the day, think about what has been learned, and discuss applications of the new information.

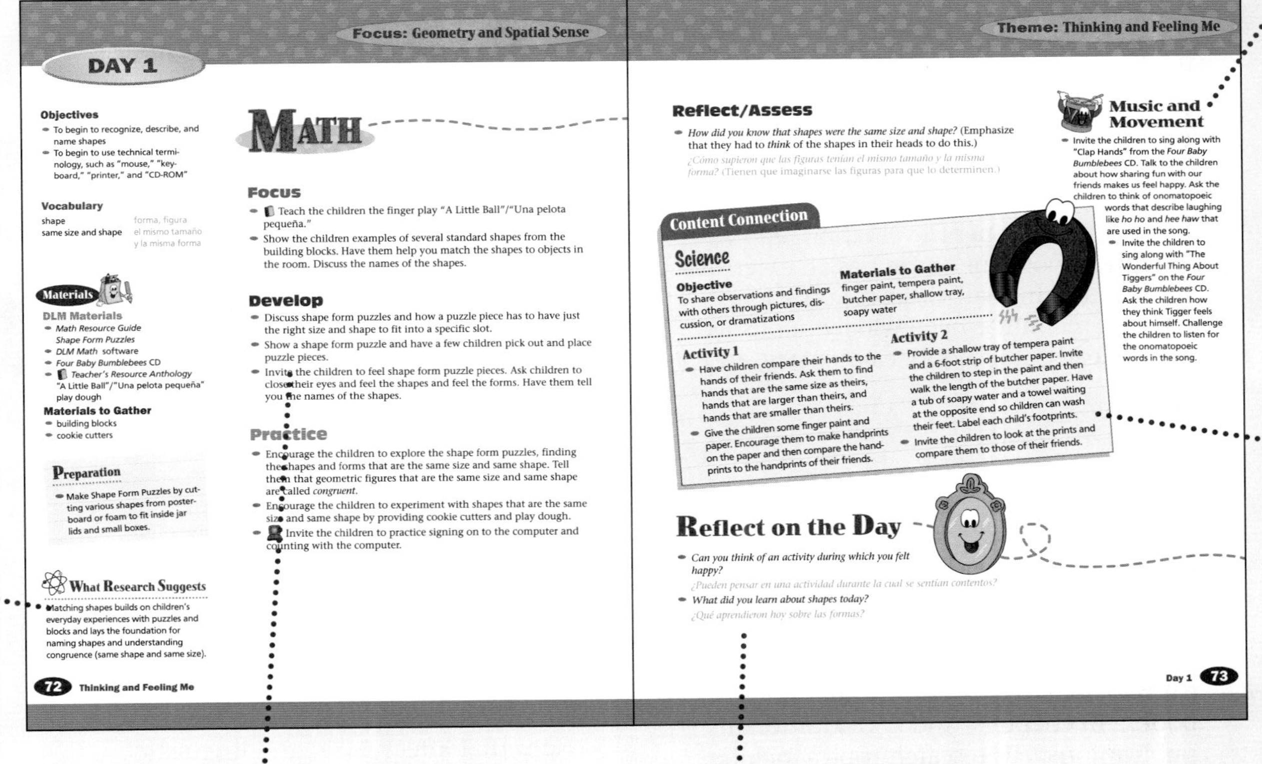

Focus: Geometry and Spatial Sense

DAY 1

Objectives
- To begin to recognize, describe, and name shapes
- To begin to use technical terminology, such as "mouse," "keyboard," "printer," and "CD-ROM"

Vocabulary

shape — forma, figura
same size and shape — el mismo tamaño y la misma forma

Materials

DLM Materials
- *Math Resource Guide* *Shape Form Puzzles*
- *DLM Math* software
- *Four Baby Bumblebees* CD
- *Teacher's Resource Anthology* "A Little Ball"/"Una pelota pequeña" play dough

Materials to Gather
- building blocks
- cookie cutters

Preparation
- Make Shape Form Puzzles by cutting various shapes from posterboard or foam to fit inside jar lids and small boxes.

What Research Suggests
- Matching shapes builds on children's everyday experiences with puzzles and blocks and lays the foundation for naming shapes and understanding congruence (same shape and same size).

MATH

Focus
- Teach the children the finger play "A Little Ball"/"Una pelota pequeña."
- Show the children examples of several standard shapes from the building blocks. Have them help you match the shapes to objects in the room. Discuss the names of the shapes.

Develop
- Discuss shape form puzzles and how a puzzle piece has to have just the right size and shape to fit into a specific slot.
- Show a shape form puzzle and have a few children pick out and place puzzle pieces.
- Invite the children to feel shape form puzzle pieces. Ask children to close their eyes and feel the shapes and feel the forms. Have them tell you the names of the shapes.

Practice
- Encourage the children to explore the shape form puzzles, finding the shapes and forms that are the same size and same shape. Tell them that geometric figures that are the same size and same shape are called *congruent*.
- Encourage the children to experiment with shapes that are the same size and same shape by providing cookie cutters and play dough.
- Invite the children to practice signing on to the computer and counting with the computer.

72 Thinking and Feeling Me

Theme: Thinking and Feeling Me

Reflect/Assess
- *How did you know that shapes were the same size and shape?* (Emphasize that they had to *think* of the shapes in their heads to do this.)
  ¿Cómo supieron que las figuras tenían el mismo tamaño y la misma forma? (Tienen que imaginarse las figuras para que lo determinen.)

Content Connection

Science

Objective
To share observations and findings with others through pictures, discussion, or dramatizations

Materials to Gather
finger paint, tempera paint, butcher paper, shallow tray, soapy water

Activity 1
- Have children compare their hands to the hands of their friends. Ask them to find hands that are the same size as theirs, hands that are larger than theirs, and hands that are smaller than theirs.
- Give the children some finger paint and paper. Encourage them to make handprints on the paper and then compare the handprints to the handprints of their friends.

Activity 2
- Provide a shallow tray of tempera paint and a 6-foot strip of butcher paper. Invite the children to step in the paint and then walk the length of the butcher paper. Have a tub of soapy water and a towel waiting at the opposite end so children can wash their feet. Label each child's footprints.
- Invite the children to look at the prints and compare them to those of their friends.

Reflect on the Day
- *Can you think of an activity during which you felt happy?*
  ¿Pueden pensar en una actividad durante la cual se sentían contentos?
- *What did you learn about shapes today?*
  ¿Qué aprendieron hoy sobre las formas?

Music and Movement
- Invite the children to sing along with "Clap Hands" from the *Four Baby Bumblebees* CD. Talk to the children about how sharing fun with our friends makes us feel happy. Ask the children to think of onomatopoeic words that describe laughing like *ho ho* and *hee haw* that are used in the song.
- Invite the children to sing along with "The Wonderful Thing About Tiggers" on the *Four Baby Bumblebees* CD. Ask the children how they think Tigger feels about himself. Challenge the children to listen for the onomatopoeic words in the song.

Day 1 73

Music and Movement

The research that supports the content of ***The DLM Early Childhood Express*** math lessons is provided throughout the program.

Content Connections tie the Math lesson to other areas of the curriculum.

The **Develop** portion of the Math lesson provides information, demonstrations, and activities to help teach the lesson objectives.

Reflect on the Day appears every day.

Bring Experience and Research

Dr. Pam Schiller

Dr. Pam Schiller is Senior National Early Childhood Consultant for SRA/McGraw-Hill and a past president of the Southern Early Childhood Association. She is the author of numerous award-winning teacher resource materials and children's books. Her areas of expertise include applications of neuroscience research, charter education, and curriculum development. She shares her extensive knowledge through workshops, radio and television interviews, and keynote speeches.

Dr. Rafael Lara-Alecio

Dr. Rafael Lara-Alecio is Associate Professor and Director of the Bilingual/ESL Programs in the Departments of Educational Psychology and Teaching, Learning, and Culture at Texas A&M University. His primary areas of expertise in bilingual/ESL education include methodologies, biliteracy, assessment/evaluation, and parental involvement. He has an extensive background in mathematics and science education and has been widely published. Dr. Lara-Alecio is an experienced early childhood, elementary, and secondary school teacher.

Dr. Douglas Clements

Dr. Douglas Clements is Professor of Mathematics and Computer Education at the University at Buffalo, The State University of New York. A veteran of Pre-Kindergarten and Kindergarten classrooms, Dr. Clements has published over 90 refereed research studies, four books, 40 chapters, and 250 additional publications. His research topics include the early development of mathematical ideas, the effects of social interactions on learning, and the use of computer applications in mathematics education. He is currently working on several National Science Foundation projects.

Dr. Julie Sarama

Dr. Julie Sarama is an Assistant Professor of Mathematics Education at the University at Buffalo, The State University of New York. She is currently the Principal or Co-Principal Investigator for projects funded by the National Science Foundation on professional development, research-based materials development, and Pre-Kindergarten math. Dr. Sarama has taught mathematics enrichment classes at the Pre-Kindergarten and Kindergarten levels. She is also co-author of the award-winning *Turtle Math*.

Thomas Moore

An early childhood educator and musician, Dr. Thomas Moore has successfully blended his interests as former coordinator of the North Carolina Head Start Collaboration Project, on-camera consultant with the Early Childhood Professional Development Network, and president of Thomas Moore Records. He has produced numerous children's learning tools, including eight educational albums and tapes. He delivers his message in words, music, print, and practice.

Dr. Leo Gómez

Dr. Leo Gómez is Associate Professor of Bilingual-Bicultural Education and the Assistant Dean of the College of Education at the University of Texas Pan American. He has focused his research on the curriculum, assessment, and language issues that affect racial and linguistic minority populations. Dr. Gómez has been extensively involved in the development, implementation and assessment of two-way bilingual education programs in Texas.

Into Your Classroom

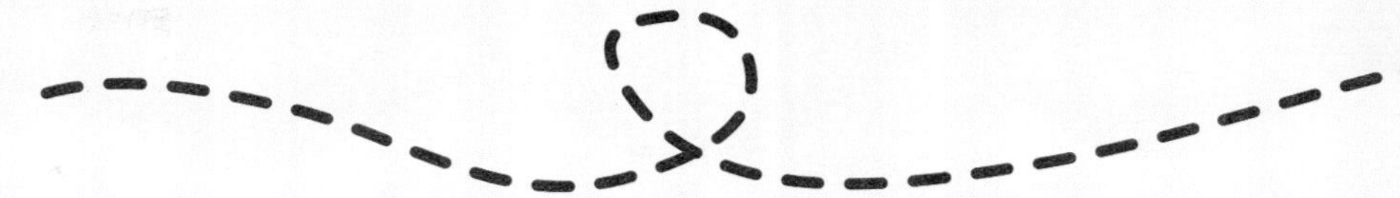

Dr. Beverly J. Irby
Dr. Beverly J. Irby is Professor and Director of the Center for Research and Doctoral Studies in the Department of Educational Leadership and Counseling at Sam Houston State University. She has held several leadership positions in bilingual education. In her research, writing, and presentations, Dr. Irby has explored issues in administration, curriculum development, and gifted and early childhood education.

John Funk
John Funk is Adjunct Professor of Children's Literature at the University of Utah. He has extensive teaching expertise in Pre-Kindergarten, Kindergarten, and Grades 1 and 2. He is past president of the Utah Association for the Education of Young Children, and in 1996 he became the first Kindergarten teacher to be named Utah Teacher of the Year.

Dr. Patricia Phipps
Dr. Patricia Phipps is the Executive Director of the California Association for the Education of Young Children. She has served as a faculty member in the Graduate School of Education at George Mason University and the College of Education at the University of Houston. Her areas of expertise include multiple intelligences, brain research implications, multicultural and cross-cultural issues, and family/school/community connections in the early childhood field.

Contributing Writers

Dr. Amie Mitchell Beckett
Dr. Amie Mitchell Beckett is a Professor of Early Childhood Education at the University of Texas at San Antonio. She has served as an early childhood specialist at the state and national levels, with the Texas Education Agency, the U.S. Department of Education, and various professional organizations.

Maria Galindo
Maria Galindo has served as a teacher, educational psychologist and assistant principal in Mexico. She is now Early Literacy Specialist in the Head Start program at Houston's Aldine Independent School District.

Dr. Linda Rodriguez
Dr. Linda Rodriguez has been an educator for 16 years, and for the past four years she has served as principal of a Pre-Kindergarten school in Houston's Aldine Independent School District. Her areas of expertise include curriculum alignment and the early identification of talent among Pre-Kindergarten children.

Dr. Alma Flor Ada
Dr. Alma Flor Ada is Director of Doctoral Studies for the Multicultural Program, School of Education, University of San Francisco, California. She received her doctorate from Pontificia Universidad Catolica del Peru, Lima, Peru. Dr. Ada was the founder and the first Editor-in-Chief of the Journal of the National Association for Bilingual Education. She is a widely published author and frequent speaker about topics concerning bilingual education.

Program Reviewers

Sue Bredekamp - Council for Professional Recognition, Washington, DC • **Mary Carr-Wilt** - Director of 21st Century Grant, Longview, WA • **Peggy Freedson-Gonzalez** - University of Texas, Austin, TX Center for Reading and Language Arts • **Charlotte Hollarn** - Director, Center for Early Childhood Professional Development, Moore, OK • **Jodi Martin** - Children's World, CO • **Nancy Mayes** - Richardson ISD, Richardson, TX • **Cherene McDonald** - Channelview ISD, Houston, TX • **Ruth Meza** - Dallas ISD, Dallas, TX • **Lizette Rodriguez** - Judson ISD, San Antonio, TX • **Gail Rowe** - Program Director of Head Start Programs Dayton, OH • **Robin Stephenson** - Director, The Association for Christian Schools International, Colorado Springs, CO

TABLE OF CONTENTS

Teacher's Edition 

Morning Circle Suggestions

Below are a few suggestions for the Begin the Day Morning Circles. You might use them on a rotation basis, or use one of them for a while and then change to a new approach. You might also want to develop your own strategy by mixing and matching the suggestions below.

#1 Ask the children what day of the week it is. When they respond, tell them that you are going to write a sentence that tells everyone what day of the week it is. Print "Today is Monday" on a piece of chart paper or on a chalkboard. Look on your Helper Chart to find the name of today's helper. Let the children help you locate the name. Print another sentence: "Today's helper is Miguel." Ask the helper to come forward and find the magnetic letters that spell his or her name.

As the year progresses, you might want to have the helper find the magnetic letters that spell the day of the week. Eventually some children may be able to copy the entire sentence with magnetic letters.

When writing your sentences, you might want to make capital letters that begin sentences green (to indicate that they start the sentence) and periods red (to indicate that they stop the sentence).

#2 Print "Today is ______" on the chalkboard or on a piece of chart paper. Ask the children to help you fill in the blank. Print the day of the week in the blank. Invite the children to look at a calendar to determine today's date. Write the date under the sentence that tells what day of the week it is. Invite the children to clap out the syllables of both the sentence and the date.

#3 Make happy- and sad-face puppets for each child by cutting yellow circles from construction paper and drawing happy and sad faces on them. Laminate the faces, and glue them to tongue depressors. Cover two large coffee cans. On one can glue a happy face, and write the sentence "I feel happy today." Glue the sad face to the second can, and write the sentence "I feel sad today."

Give each child a happy- and a sad-face puppet. Encourage the children to tell how they feel today and to hold up the appropriate puppet. Encourage the children to come forward and place their puppets in the can that represents their feelings. For example, if Gabrielle says she feels happy today, she will place her puppet in the can with the happy face. Later in the year you can add puppets to represent other emotions.

You can vary this activity by using a graph titled "How I Feel Today"/"Cómo me siento hoy." Have the children place their puppets in the appropriate column on the graph instead of in the cans.

#4 Print the words to the "Days of the Week Song"/"Los días de la semana" on a piece of chart paper. Sing it with the children. Ask a volunteer to tell what day of the week it is. As the children become more familiar with the written days, you can ask the volunteer to show you on the chart what day of the week it is.

#5 Provide a large calendar. Ask the children what day of the week it was yesterday. When they respond, ask them what day it is today. Place a seasonal sticker on today's date. Have the children follow your lead and recite: "Yesterday was Monday, September 12. Today is Tuesday, September 13. Tomorrow will be Wednesday, September 14."

Ask the children how many days are in the month of September. Count the squares on the September calendar. You may want to use a Weather Wheel with this activity and sing "The Weather Song"/"La canción del tiempo."

You can also sing "Months of the Year"/"Los meses del año."

Looking Ahead

Connecting to the Theme: Color, Shape, and Size

The lessons in this theme continue to examine the relationships among color, shape, and size. As several activities allow children to cut out various shapes, children will continue to develop their fine motor skills. Children should begin to develop an awareness of street signs, local buildings, and other symbols.

	Objectives	DLM Materials	Materials to Gather
DAY 1	• To begin to engage in dramatic play with others • To utilize a variety of materials, to create original work • To begin to develop pincer control in picking up objects • To begin to identify rhymes and rhyming sounds in familiar words, participate in rhyming games, and repeat rhyming songs and poems • To gather information using simple tools such as a magnifying lens and an eyedropper	• Rafita and Pepita puppets • *Fall/El otoño* • *Blue Cat/Gato azul* • Oral Language Card 64 • *Teacher's Resource Anthology*	• purple items • tracing paper • purple markers and crayons • index card
DAY 2	• To refine and extend understanding of known words • To begin to identify rhymes and rhyming sounds in familiar words, participate in rhyming games, and repeat rhyming songs and poems • To begin to offer explanations, using his or her own words	• *The Tortilla Factory/La tortillería* • Oral Language Card 66 • *Teacher's Resource Anthology*	• black items • paint • sand • index card • black markers and crayons • white crayons • black paper
DAY 3	• To produce speech sounds with increasing ease and accuracy • To begin to identify rhymes and rhyming sounds in familiar words, participate in rhyming games, and repeat rhyming songs and poems • To begin to develop pincer control in picking up objects	• *The Color Bear/El oso de colores* • Oral Language Card 67 • *Teacher's Resource Anthology*	• white items • white chalk • shaving cream • contact paper shapes • index card
DAY 4	• To refine and extend understanding of known words • To participate in creating and using real and pictorial graphs	• Oral Language Cards 6, 30 • Life Span sequence cards • *Teacher's Resource Anthology*	• small, medium, and large items • sorting mats
DAY 5	• To show a steady increase in listening and speaking vocabulary • To begin to perform simple investigations	• *Blue Cat/Gato azul* • "This Is the Circle That Is My Head" • *Teacher's Resource Anthology*	• shape blocks • surprise package • construction paper shapes

(See individual lesson pages for complete lists of materials.)

Learning Centers

DRAMATIC PLAY

Clothing Comparisons

Objective
To begin to engage in dramatic play with others

Materials
dress-up clothes

Develop
Provide a variety of dress-up clothes. Place orange things in the center on Monday, black on Tuesday, and white on Wednesday. On Thursday place obviously big and little clothes in the center. On Friday include clothing accessories of different shapes such as bracelets, hats, heart or star pendants, and so on.

Reflect/Assess
Is it easy or difficult for you to share? Why?
¿Para ustedes es fácil o difícil compartir? ¿Por qué?
How do you feel when you wear black? Orange?
¿Cómo se sienten cuando llevan ropa negra? ¿Anaranjada?

FINE MOTOR

Play Dough Shapes

Objectives
To begin to develop pincer control in picking up objects
To reproduce shapes such as circles, squares, triangles, and rectangles

Materials
play dough, tongue depressors, cookie cutters, bottle caps, small sturdy box lids, pipe cleaners

Develop
Mix play dough in a variety of colors and provide accessories. Encourage the children to make cookies or to roll and shape circles, squares, triangles, hearts, stars, and rectangles. Have them use tongue depressors, bottle caps, box lids, and pipe cleaners to make shapes in the play dough.

Reflect/Assess
Do you like the shapes you made? Why or why not?
¿Les gustan las formas que hicieron? ¿Por qué sí o por qué no?

ART

Making Collages

Objective
To utilize a variety of materials to create original work

Materials
tissue paper, small boxes, newspaper, wallpaper, magazines, bottle caps

Develop
Encourage the children to make a variety of collages. Suggest geometric-shape collages with multiple colors and monochromatic colors, textured collages, three-dimensional collages, and torn paper collages. Show them how to crumple paper for their collages, tear paper shapes, and use templates to create specific shapes. Emphasize color, shape, and size vocabulary.

Reflect/Assess
What type of collage did you make? Why?
¿Qué tipo de collage hicieron? ¿Por qué?
Why did you choose to use those colors?
¿Por qué decidieron usar esos colores?

What Research Suggests

Intelligence is, in large part, a person's ability to see patterns and build relationships using those patterns. Size has multidimensional patterns that make it a difficult concept to understand. A person can categorize items by size. Yet within each category there are differences in size. Size is relative and changes over time. A child's understanding of size grows as he or she experiences the variations and seeming contradictions related to size.

Begin the Day

- Introduce the "I Like Purple"/"Me gusta el morado" cheer.
- Use the suggestions for Morning Circle offered in the front of this *Teacher's Edition*.

Objectives

- To begin to identify rhymes and rhyming sounds in familiar words, participate in rhyming games, and repeat rhyming songs and poems
- To begin to create or re-create stories, moods, or experiences through dramatic representations

Vocabulary

blue	azul
red	rojo
orange	anaranjado
purple	morado

DLM Materials

- Rafita and Pepita puppets
- *Fall/El otoño*
- *Blue Cat/Gato azul*
- Oral Language Development Card 64
- *Teacher's Resource Anthology*
  "I Like Purple"/"Me gusta el morado"
  story map
  Purple Cow Milkshakes
  "The Great Big Turnip"/"El nabo gigante"

Materials to Gather

- basket of purple items
- tracing paper
- purple markers and crayons
- index card

LITERACY

Focus

- Point out the purple items in your basket. Invite the children to name purple items. Ask: *What kinds of fruit are purple?*
  ¿Hay tipos de frutas son moradas?
- *Do shoes come in purple?*
  ¿Hay zapatos de color morado?
- Have the bear puppets ask each other what their favorite purple food is.
- Tell the children that today we will be learning about the color purple.

Develop

One Way to Develop the Lesson

- Display Oral Language Card 64. Use the suggestions on the back of the card to stimulate conversations about the color purple.

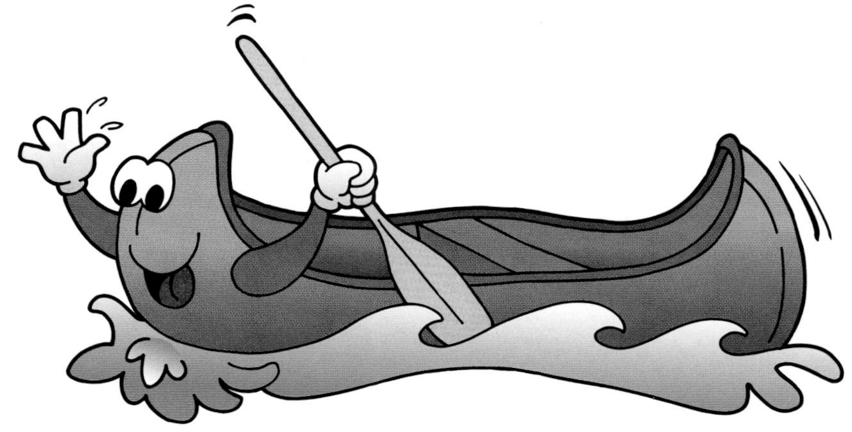

Another Way to Develop the Lesson

- Ask the children to recall the "The Great Big Pumpkin"/"La calabaza gigante" flannel board story. Tell them that you have a similar story to tell them today. Ask them to listen for the one thing that is different in today's story.
- Present the "The Great Big Turnip"/"El nabo gigante" flannel board story.
- Find out what the children know about turnips. *What color are turnips?*

  ¿De qué color son los nabos?

  Are they the same color inside?

  ¿Son del mismo color por dentro?

  How big are they?

  ¿De qué tamaño son?

  Have you seen turnips as big as the turnip in the story?

  ¿Han visto nabos tan grandes como el nabo del cuento?
- Use one of the suggested patterns for story maps. Encourage the children to make story maps for both "The Great Big Pumpkin"/"La calabaza gigante" and "The Great Big Turnip"/"El nabo gigante." *How are the stories alike and different?* *¿En qué se parecen y en qué se diferencian los cuentos?*

Preparation

- Gather purple items, placing them in a basket.
- Make "The Great Big Turnip"/"El nabo gigante" flannel board story.
- Gather milk, ice cream, and grape juice for Purple Cow Milkshakes.

Practice

- Invite the children to add pages for purple to the color books they started last week.
- Write *purple* on a 4" × 6" index card with a purple marker or crayon. Add this to the other color word cards in the Writing Center. Provide tracing paper and encourage the children to trace the new color word.
- Help the children make Purple Cow Milkshakes.
- Place "The Great Big Turnip"/"El nabo gigante" flannel board story in the Language Center. Encourage the children to retell the story.

Scaffolding Strategies

More Help Serve purple grapes or grape juice.

Extra Challenge Discuss what it means when a person says someone is turning purple.

Second Language Learners

Before sharing "The Great Big Turnip"/"El nabo gigante" story, bring in a turnip to show to the children. Describe its color inside and out, smell, feel, and taste. Pantomime the story, and then tell it using the figures. Ask: *What did he do then?/¿Qué hizo entonces?* Some children may pantomime while others use verbal language. Both indicate that they understood the question.

DAY 1

Letter Knowledge

English

- Read "Frank" from the *English Phonics Resource Guide.*

Spanish

- Introduce the letter *m* using the story "Mario" from the *Spanish Phonics Resource Guide.* Encourage the children to stretch the beginning sound /m/ and rub their stomachs with their hands as if they have just eaten something good.

Suggested Reading

Harold and the Purple Crayon by Crocket Johnson
Color by Ruth Heller
Color Dance by Ann Jonas
El reino de la geometría by Alma Flor Ada

Anthology Support

"Los colores en mi mundo"
"The Colors in My World"
"The Color Song"
"Los colores"

Reflect/Assess

- *Which color do you think is the most like purple? Why?*
  ¿Cuál color es más parecido al morado? ¿Por qué?
- *What famous dinosaur is purple?*
  ¿Cuál dinosaurio famoso es morado?

Literacy Circle

Storytime 1

- Read *Fall/El otoño.* Discuss the foods mentioned in the book.

Storytime 2

- Reread *Blue Cat/Gato azul.* Encourage the children to read with you. *Which animal is purple?*
  ¿Qué animal es morado?

Content Connection

Science

Objective
To gather information using simple tools such as a magnifying lens and an eyedropper

Vocabulary
blue, red, purple
azul, rojo, morado(a)

Materials to Gather
eyedroppers, food coloring, egg cartons, tempera paint

Activity 1

- Provide bowls of red and blue food coloring and an egg carton with all the crates half full of water. Have the children move the food coloring from the bowls into the egg carton crates using an eyedropper. Ask them to mix the red and blue food coloring. *What happens when you put the food coloring in the egg carton crates?*
  ¿Qué pasa cuando ponen el colorante de comida en el cartón de huevos?

Activity 2

- Distribute blue and red tempera paint and encourage the children to mix the colors. *What happens when you mix red and blue paint?*
  ¿Qué pasa cuando mezclan pintura roja con pintura azul?

DAY 1

Objectives

- To describe similarities and differences between objects
- To start, use, and exit software programs

Vocabulary

rectangle	rectángulo
square	cuadrado
vertical	vertical
horizontal	horizontal
parallel	paralelo

DLM Materials

- *Math Resource Guide*
  Shape Step/Paso de figuras
- *DLM Math* software
- *Teacher's Resource Anthology*
  Follow the Leader/Sigue al líder
  Pumpkin Roll Relay/Carrera de calabazas
  Catch the Pumpkin/Agarra la calabaza

Materials to Gather

- picture frame or other large rectangle
- attribute blocks or construction-paper shapes (see previous week)
- rectangular blocks (see previous week)
- sticky notes
- small pumpkin or ball

Preparation

- Tape construction-paper shapes to the floor with masking tape.
- Trace faces of rectangular boxes.

MATH

Focus

- Review vertical, horizontal, and parallel with the children by playing Follow the Leader/Sigue al líder. Give directions using the terms. Ask them to hold their arms up so they are vertical. Then, ask them to hold their arms out horizontally in front of them.
- Show the children a large rectangle, such as a picture frame, and ask them to name the shape. Ask a child to point to a horizontal side. Then ask him or her to point to the parallel horizontal side. Without turning the rectangle, ask a child to point to a vertical side. Then ask him or her to point to the parallel vertical side. Turn the rectangle a bit and ask the children to find the parallel slanted lines.

Develop

- Have the children play Shape Step/Paso de figuras. Ask them to step on a rectangle on the floor. Acknowledge the children who step on a square by saying *Good for you. You remembered that a square is a rectangle, too.*

  Muy bien. Recordaron que un cuadrado también es un rectángulo.

  Remember that all squares are rectangles, but only rectangles with all 4 sides equal in length are squares. If the children skip any rectangles, such as a very thin one, step on it yourself and ask why it is okay to do that. Repeat the activity, asking children to step only on squares.
- Introduce and demonstrate Mystery Toys, Level 2. At this level, children must choose the shape for which the character asks.

Practice

- Encourage the children to continue to play Shape Step/Paso de figuras, stepping on rectangles with an attribute such as the color red.
- Invite the children to match the boxes to the traced rectangles.
- Encourage the children to find rectangles throughout the classroom. Provide sticky notes so they can mark the rectangles they find. Challenge them to count the rectangles they marked.
- Have the children work on Mystery Toys, Level 2.

Reflect/Assess

- *How do you know which shapes to step on when I ask you to step on the rectangles?*
  ¿Cómo saben qué figuras pisar cuando les digo que pisen los rectángulos?

Music and Movement

- Play Pumpkin Roll Relay/Carrera de calabazas.
- Play Catch the Pumpkin/Agarra la calabaza.

Content Connection

Personal and Social Development

Objectives
To begin to show self-control by following classroom rules
To begin to share and cooperate with others in group activities

Materials to Gather
ball, shape manipulatives or cutout construction-paper shapes

Activity 1

- Use masking tape to make a triangle, a square, and a rectangle on the floor. Make enough so the whole group is included. Have the children sit at the corners of each shape and roll a ball to each other so that the shape is formed as the ball is rolled.

Activity 2

- Have a shape hunt. Hide shape manipulatives or cutout construction-paper shapes and encourage the children to find them.

Suggested Reading

The Silly Story of Goldie Locks and the Three Squares by Grace Maccarone
Bear in a Square by Stella Blackstone
What Is Square? by Rebecca K. Dotlich
Round and Square by Janet Martin
There's a Square by Mary Serfozo

Reflect on the Day

- *What did you learn about colors and shapes? What was your favorite activity?*
  ¿Qué aprendieron hoy sobre los colores y las figuras? ¿Cuál fue su actividad favorita?
- *Look for orange shapes today when you go home. Tomorrow, I will ask you what you found.*
  Fíjense en figuras anaranjadas cuando se vayan a su casa. Mañana les preguntaré qué encontraron.

Home Connection

- Remind the children to wear black tomorrow.
- Let families know that you are collecting coat hanger tubes, oatmeal boxes, and coffee cans for an activity next Monday.

Begin the Day

- Introduce the "I Like Black"/"Me gusta el color negro" chant.
- Have the children tell you about the orange shapes they found after school yesterday.
- Use the suggestions for Morning Circle offered in the front of this *Teacher's Edition.*

Objectives

- To refine and extend understanding of known words
- To begin to identify rhymes and rhyming sounds in familiar words, participate in rhyming games, and repeat rhyming songs and poems

Vocabulary

orange	anaranjado
black	negro(a)

Materials

DLM Materials

- *The Tortilla Factory/La tortillería*
- Oral Language Development Card 66
- *Teacher's Resource Anthology*
  "I Like Black"/"Me gusta el color negro"
  "Miss Mary Mack"/"La señorita María Marao"
  black play dough
  "The Color Song"/"Los colores"
  "My Sick Little Donkey"/"El burrito enfermo"

Materials to Gather

- basket of black items
- sand
- index card
- black markers and crayons
- white crayons
- black paper

LITERACY

Focus

- Display the black items in your basket. Invite the children to name other black items. Ask: *Which animals are black?*
  ¿Qué animales son negros?
  Do cars come in black?
  ¿Hay carros negros?
- Sing "Miss Mary Mack"/"La señorita María Marao." What color does Miss Mary Mack wear?
  ¿Qué color de ropa lleva La señorita Marao?
- Tell the children we will be learning about black today.

Develop

One Way to Develop the Lesson

- Show Oral Language Card 66. Use the suggestions on the back of the card to stimulate discussions about the color black.
- Ask the children to point out black things in the classroom.
- Encourage them to think of words that rhyme with *black/negro(a).*

Another Way to Develop the Lesson

- Ask the children if they have seen plowed land ready to be planted. Invite those who have had experiences with crops and farmland to share their experiences with the others. Tell the children that you are going to tell them a story about the earth turning from mostly black to vibrant colors.
- Read *The Tortilla Factory/La tortillería.*

  What color is the earth in the spring?

  ¿De qué color es la tierra en primavera?

  What happens to the earth in the summer?

  ¿Qué le sucede a la tierra en verano?

  What happens after corn is harvested?

  ¿Qué pasa después de recoger la cosecha de maíz?

Practice

- Invite the children to add the color black to their color books.
- Write *black* on a 4" × 6" index card with a black crayon or marker. Provide tracing paper and encourage the children to trace the word *black* with black markers or black crayons in the Writing Center.
- Give them black play dough. Have them shape black objects.
- Place *The Tortilla Factory/La tortillería* book and tape in the Listening Center.
- Invite the children to write on the chalkboard or to use white crayons on black paper.

Preparation

- Gather black items, placing them in a basket.
- Mix black play dough.
- Make "The Color Song"/"Los colores" flannel board story.

Scaffolding Strategies

More Help If the soil in your area is black, take the children outdoors and let them dig up small amounts of topsoil.

Extra Challenge Encourage the children to think of black things that they enjoy eating.

Second Language Learners

Place posterboard in front of an overhead projector so you cannot see what is on the glass. Using familiar objects with clearly defined shapes, place an item on the projector (scissors). Have children guess the item from its shadow. Reinforce vocabulary (shadow/sombra) by saying: *Yes, this is the shadow of scissors.*

Sí, ésta es la sombra de las tijeras.

Repeat for each item.

Anthology Support

"The Zebra"

"La cebra"

"Two Little Blackbirds"

"Dos mirlos"

The Zebra on the Zyder Zee

DAY 2

Letter Knowledge

English

- Make a sandpaper *e*. Invite the children to trace the letter with their fingers as they repeat the sound /e/. Have them copy the letter in a sand or salt tray.

Spanish

- Make a sandpaper *m*. Invite the children to trace the letter with their fingers as they repeat the sound /m/. Have them copy the letter in a sand or salt tray.

Suggested Reading

Ten Black Dots by Donald Crews
El libro grande de Spot, colores, formas, números by Eric Hill
Inch by Inch by Leo Lionni
Mi pequeño libro de los colores by Susan Amerikaner

Teacher's NOTE

In American culture, there are negative connotations of the word *black* (for example, *blackball, black mood,* or *black Tuesday*). Help the children make positive associations with *black* such as *black belt* or *black tie*.

Reflect/Assess

- *What does the saying "it's as black as night" mean?*
  ¿Qué significa decir "tan negro como la noche"?
- *Think of something black that you like, and tell me about it.*
  Piensen en algo que les guste que sea de color negro y descríbanmelo.

Literacy Circle

Storytime 1

- Present the "My Sick Little Donkey"/"El burrito enfermo" flannel board story. *What is black in the story?*
  En el cuento, ¿qué objeto es de color negro?
- Invite the children to sequence the story using the My Sick Little Donkey sequence cards.

Storytime 2

- Present "The Color Song"/"Los colores" flannel board story. Invite the children to write a verse for black.

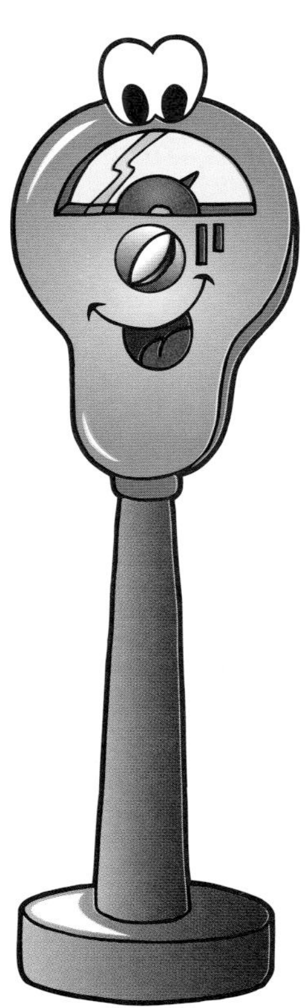

Content Connection

Science

Objective
To begin to offer explanations, using his or her own words

Vocabulary
shadow/sombra

Materials to Gather
light source

Activity 1

- Invite the children to dance between a light source, such as an overhead projector or flashlight and a bare wall. Encourage them to make dancing shadows on the wall. *How are shadows created?* *¿Cómo se forman las sombras?*

Activity 2

- Place an object in a window so that the sun casts the object's shadow on the wall. Encourage the children to watch the shadow change. *Does the shadow become shorter, taller, or longer?* *¿La sombra se hizo más corta, más alta o más larga?*

DAY 2

Objectives

- To sort objects into groups by an attribute and to begin to explain how the grouping was done
- To match objects that are alike

Vocabulary

hexagon	hexágono
large	grande
small	pequeño
thick	grueso
thin	delgado

DLM Materials

- *Math Resource Guide*
  Memory Game: Geometry cards (Set A)
  Memory Game: Geometry version/Juego de memoria: versión geométrica
- *DLM Math* software
- *Teacher's Resource Anthology*
  Shadow Games/Juegos de sombras

Materials to Gather

- attribute blocks or manipulatives with 2 or more attributes
- construction-paper hexagons
- black streamers

Preparation

- Make several copies of Memory Game: Geometry cards (Set A).Two copies combine to make a playing set. Each playing set should be a different color.
- Cut hexagons in various shapes and sizes from construction paper.

MATH

Focus

- Spread out and discuss the attributes of the blocks or construction-paper shapes. Name the shapes with the children. Talk about the different colors and sizes, keeping in mind that size can be large or small and, if using blocks, thick or thin. Include hexagons.

Develop

- Introduce the Memory Game: Geometry version/Juego de memoria: versión geométrica. Separate one playing set of Memory Game: Geometry cards into 2 piles with each pile containing one of every shape. Arrange each pile into separate arrays facedown. Flip over one card from each array. If they don't match, flip them back facedown. (For easier play, flip only one card.) Continue until all matches are found.
- Demonstrate how to print toys from Mystery Toys, Level 2.
- Review how to play Memory—Geometry, Level 1.

Practice

- Provide sets of Memory Game: Geometry cards for the children to play the game individually or in pairs.
- Encourage children to play freely with the attribute blocks or construction-paper shapes. Challenge them to describe the shapes.
- Have the children work on Mystery Toys, Level 2. Invite them to print their toys when they have finished. Encourage the children to work on Memory—Geometry, Level 1 after they complete Mystery Toys.

Reflect/Assess

- *Show two different attribute blocks or construction-paper shapes. How are these two shapes different?*

  Muestren dos bloques de atributos geométricos diferentes o figuras de cartulina. ¿En qué se diferencian estas dos figuras?

- *What toy did you make on the computer? What shapes were in the toy?*

  ¿Qué juguete hicieron en la computadora? ¿Qué figuras había en el juguete?

Music and Movement

- Dance with black streamers.
- Play Shadow games/Juegos de sombras.

Suggested Reading

Mouse Paints by Ellen Walsh
So Many Circles, So Many Squares by Tana Hoban

Content Connection

Fine Arts

Objectives

To begin to show an interest in the artwork of others
To use a variety of materials to create original work

DLM Materials

SRA Photo Library software

Materials to Gather

black construction paper, white paper, glue

Activity 1

- Encourage the children to look for shapes in the structures on the *SRA Photo Library* software.

Activity 2

- Invite the children to use black construction-paper shapes to build a city skyline on white paper. Have them glue down their best arrangement.

Reflect on the Day

- *What did you learn about colors and shapes? Which activity was your favorite?*

  ¿Qué aprendieron sobre los colores y las figuras? ¿Qué actividad fue su favorita?

- *Look for black shapes today when you go home. Tomorrow, I will ask you what you found.*

  Fíjense en figuras negras cuando se vayan a su casa. Mañana les preguntaré lo que encontraron.

Home Connection

Remind the children to wear white tomorrow.

What Research Suggests

Sorting and describing shapes not only helps children learn *classifying* skills, it is also one of the ways children learn about *attributes* of shapes.

Begin the Day

- Introduce the "I Like White"/"Me gusta el blanco" cheer.
- Ask the children to tell you about the black shapes they found after school yesterday.
- Use the suggestions for Morning Circle offered in the front of this *Teacher's Edition*.

Objectives

- To produce speech sounds with increasing ease and accuracy
- To begin to identify rhymes and rhyming sounds in familiar words, participate in rhyming games, and repeat rhyming songs and poems

Vocabulary

black	negro(a)
white	blanco(a)

DLM Materials

- *The Color Bear/El oso de colores* book and listening tape
- *Los niños alfabéticos*
- Oral Language Development Card 67
- *Teacher's Resource Anthology*
  "I Like White"/"Me gusta el blanco"
  "Six White Ducks"/"Los seis patos blancos"
  "The Sun and the Moon"/"El sol y la luna"

Materials to Gather

- basket of white items
- white chalk
- shaving cream
- contact-paper shapes
- index card

LITERACY

Focus

- Display the white items in your basket. Invite the children to name other white items. Ask: *Which animals are white?*
  ¿Qué animales son blancos?
  Are certain flowers white?
  ¿Algunas flores son blancas?
- Sing "Six White Ducks"/"Los seis patos blancos" or "Three White Mice"/"Los tres ratones blancos."
- Tell the children we will be learning about white today.

Develop

One Way to Develop the Lesson

- Show Oral Language Card 67. Use the suggestions on the back of the card to stimulate discussions about the color white. Ask the children to point out white things in the classroom. Explain that white is the absence of color.
- Encourage the children to think of words that rhyme with *white/blanco(a)*.

Another Way to Develop the Lesson

- Display the cover of *The Color Bear/El oso de colores*. Invite the children to recall what the book is about.
- Read the story. *What colors are on page three?*
  ¿Qué colores se ven en la página tres?
- Remind the children that white is the absence of color. Discuss the absence of color on pages 18 and 19.

Preparation

- Gather white items and place them in a basket.
- Cut shapes from solid-colored contact paper.

Practice

- Invite the children to add white to their color books.
- Place *The Color Bear/El oso de colores* book and tape in the Listening Center.
- Write *white* on a 4" × 6" index card with a black crayon or marker. Provide tracing paper, and encourage the children to trace the word with black markers or crayons.
- Place the contact-paper shapes on the top of a table. Cover the table with shaving cream, and invite the children to make designs in the shaving cream to uncover the colors underneath.
- Provide a chalkboard and chalk. Have the children draw or write on the chalkboard.

Second Language Learners

Trace items from yesterday's lesson onto white paper and cut them out. Teach the items' names in English and Spanish (scissors/tijeras). Display the cutouts and invite the children to use the new vocabulary to name them. Repeat vocabulary for reinforcement.

Anthology Support

"White Wings"
"Nubes de abril"
"April Clouds"
"Mary Had a Little Lamb"
"María tenía una corderita"
"Mister Moon"
"Señora Luna"

DAY 3

Letter Knowledge

English

- Invite the children to look for the letter *e* in magazines and newpapers.

Spanish

- Invite the children to find the letter *m* in magazines and newpapers.

Suggested Reading

The Snowy Day by Ezra Jack Keats
The Mixed-Up Chameleon by Eric Carle
El conejito marrón y las formas by Alan Baker
Grande o pequeño by Evelyne Mathiaud

Reflect/Assess

- *What do you think "white as snow" means? Why do people say this?*
  ¿Qué creen que significa "blanco como la nieve"? ¿Por qué la gente dice esto?
- *Name some of your favorite white things.*
  Nombren algunas de las cosas blancas que sean sus favoritas.

Literacy Circle

Storytime 1

- Read selections from *Los niños alfabéticos.*

Storytime 2

- Read the listening story "The Sun and the Moon"/"El Sol y la Luna." *What color is the moon?*
  ¿De qué color es la luna?

Content Connection

Physical Development

Objective
To begin to develop pincer control in picking up objects

Vocabulary
mix, knead, solid, liquid
mezclar, amasar, sólido, líquido

DLM Materials
Teacher's Resource Anthology
Gak

Materials to Gather
white paper

Activity 1

- Invite the children to help you mix up a batch of Gak. *What colors are the ingredients?*
  ¿De qué color son los ingredientes?
- *What color is Gak?*
  ¿De qué color es Gak?
- Encourage the children to shape and mold the Gak. *How is Gak different from play dough?*
  ¿En qué se diferencia Gak de la plastilina?

Activity 2

- Take the children outdoors for a cloud watch. *What shapes can you find? What colors are the clouds?*
  ¿Qué figuras pueden encontrar? ¿De qué colores son las nubes?
- Invite the children to make paper clouds. Show them how to tear sheets of plain white paper into different shapes. Try tearing the paper freely and then deciding what it looks like.

DAY 3

Objectives

- To describe similarities and differences between objects
- To sort objects into groups by an attribute and begin to explain how the grouping was done

Vocabulary

hexagon	hexágono
circle	círculo
triangle	triángulo
square	cuadrado
size	tamaño
large	grande
small	pequeño
thick	grueso
thin	delgado
color	color

DLM Materials

- *Math Resource Guide*
  Shape Step/Paso de figuras
  Memory Game: Geometry cards (Set A)
  Memory Game: Geometry version/Juego de memoria: versión geométrica
- *DLM Math* software
- *Making Music with Thomas Moore* CD
- *Teacher's Resource Anthology*
  Bunny Hop/Salto de conejo

Materials to Gather

- large white sheet
- ball
- construction-paper shapes (see Day1)

MATH

Focus

- Count from 1 to 15, pretending to march a step with each count. Count in groups of three today.
- Lay out the construction-paper shapes or attribute blocks and ask children to describe the shapes, encouraging them to give names, colors, and sizes. Conclude that the shapes have special attributes, such as shape, color, and size. It is important for children to understand that sorting can be done according to many different attributes, including size, shape, and color.

Develop

- Play Shape Step/Paso de figuras with the construction-paper shapes or attribute blocks. Name an attribute such as triangular or not triangular and have a small group of children step on appropriate shapes.
- Repeat with different groups of children and different attributes, such as size and color.

Practice

- Encourage the children to continue to play Shape Step/Paso de figuras.
- Invite the children to use the construction-paper shapes to make pictures on the floor.
- Suggest that children play Memory Game: Geometry version/Juego de memoria: versión geométrica individually or in pairs.
- Have the children work on Mystery Toys, Level 2 or Memory—Geometry, Level 1.

Reflect/Assess

- Show two different construction paper shapes. *How are these two shapes different? How are they the same?*
  ¿En qué se diferencian estas dos figuras? ¿En qué se parecen?
- *What toy did you make on the computer? What shapes were in the toy?*
  ¿Qué juguete hicieron en la computadora? ¿Qué figuras había en el juguete?

Music and Movement

- Play the "Bunny Hop" from the *Making Music with Thomas Moore* CD. Perform the Bunny Hop/Salto de conejo.
- Take a large white sheet outdoors and use it like a parachute. Invite the children to toss a ball into it, run under it, and play other parachute games. *What shape is the sheet?*
  ¿Qué forma tiene la hoja?

Content Connection

Fine Arts

Objectives

To use a variety of materials to create original work

To use different colors, surface textures, and shapes to create form and meaning

Materials to Gather

white felt shape cutouts, flannel boards, white tempera paint, shape sponges, black construction paper

Activity 1

- Cut out white felt shapes and encourage the children to use them to make designs on a black flannel board.

Activity 2

- Give the children shape sponges and have them use white tempera paint to make designs on black construction paper.

Suggested Reading

So Many Circles, So Many Squares by Tana Hoban

Reflect on the Day

- *What did you learn about colors and shapes? Which activity was your favorite?*
  ¿Qué aprendieron sobre los colores y las figuras? ¿Qué actividad fue su favorita?
- *Look for white shapes today when you go home. Tomorrow, I will ask you what you found.*
  Fíjense en figuras blancas cuando se vayan a su casa hoy. Mañana les preguntaré qué encontraron.

Home Connection

Remind families that you are collecting coat hanger tubes, oatmeal boxes, and coffee cans for an activity next Monday.

Begin the Day

- Sing "The Ants Go Marching"/"Las hormiguitas marchan." Discuss the size of ants.
- Invite the children to tell you about white shapes they found after school yesterday.
- Use the suggestions for Morning Circle offered in the front of this *Teacher's Edition.*

Objective

- To refine and extend understanding of known words

Vocabulary

big	grande
little	pequeño
medium size	tamaño mediano
large	grande
small	pequeño

DLM Materials

- Oral Language Development Cards 6 (elephant) and 30 (ant)
- Life Span sequence cards
- *Teacher's Resource Anthology*
  "The Ants Go Marching"/"Las hormiguitas marchan"
  "Three Bears Rap"/"El rap de los tres osos"
  "Ernestine's... Day"/"El... día de Ernestina"
  "The Three Billy Goats Gruff"/"Los tres chivitos Gruff"
  "Goldilocks and the Three Bears"/ "Goldilocks y los tres osos"
  sorting mats

Materials to Gather

- small, medium, and large items

LITERACY

Focus

- Display the things you have gathered in your basket. Discuss small, medium, and large sizes. Ask the children to point out small-, medium-, and large-sized things in the classroom.
- Sing or say "Three Bears Rap"/"El rap de los tres osos."
  Which bear is the largest?
  ¿Cuál oso es el más grande?
  Which bear is the smallest?
  ¿Cuál oso es el más pequeño?
- Tell the children that we will be discussing size today.

Develop

One Way to Develop the Lesson

- Ask the children if elephants are big or little.
  ¿Los elefantes son grandes o pequeños?
  Show them Oral Language Card 6 (elephants). Discuss the big elephant (mother) and the little elephant (baby) in the picture. Point out that even if something is large there may still be large and small variations of that thing. The mother and baby elephant are a good example of this.
- Show Oral Language Card 30 (ant). Ask the children what size ants are.
  ¿De qué tamaño son las hormigas?
- Discuss the size of ants compared to elephants.

Another Way to Develop the Lesson

- Tell the children that you are going to tell them a story about things that come in three sizes: small, medium, and large.
- Present the "Goldilocks and the Three Bears"/"Goldilocks y los tres osos" flannel board story.
- Discuss the sizes of the bears, bowls, chairs, and beds.

Practice

- Give the children the flannel board story and encourage them to sort the bowls, chairs, beds, and bears by size.
- Invite the children to sort the items in your basket into small, medium, and large categories. Encourage them to look for other things they can add to the basket. Provide small, medium, and large sorting mats.
- Encourage them to build a block tower that is bigger/taller than they are and another tower that is smaller/shorter than they are.
- Provide the Life Span sequence cards. Encourage the children to put the cards in the correct sequence from infancy to adulthood.
- Give the children leaves to sort into categories of large and small. Write *large* on one sheet of construction paper and *small* on a smaller sheet. Use them as sorting mats.

Preparation

- Gather pairs of things that come in small, medium, and large sizes.
- Prepare the flannel board stories, if not already prepared.
- Gather or prepare sheets of construction paper that are small, medium, and large to use as sorting mats.
- Prepare the Life Span sequence cards

Scaffolding Strategies

More Help Use only large and small sizes for comparison.

Extra Challenge Invite the children to find items in a variety of sizes. Encourage them to sort the items they find according to size.

Second Language Learners

Show three items in small, medium, and large. Help children identify each item's size. Explain that another way to say *little* is *small* and another word for *big* is *large.* Explain that the other item is not big or little, it is *middle-sized/Es mediano. Pequeño* and *chico* are Spanish words for small; *grande* describes large in Spanish.

DAY 4

Letter Knowledge

English

- Call attention to the *e* in *elephant* during the discussion about size and the music and movement activity.
- Have an *e* hunt in the classroom. How many items can the children find that start with *e*?

Spanish

- Call attention to the *m* in *medium-size.* Have an *m* hunt in the classroom. How many things can the children find that start with the letter *m*?

Suggested Reading

Is It Larger? Is It Smaller? by Tana Hoban
Nature Spy by Shelley Rotner
Formas y lo que forman
by Joan Wade Cole, Karen K. Welch

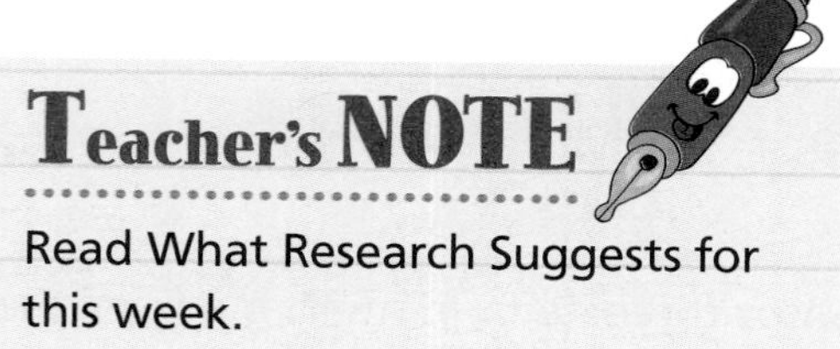

Teacher's NOTE

Read What Research Suggests for this week.

Anthology Support

"Sometimes"
"A veces"
"Soy alto, soy bajito"
"¡Qué alto!"
"Stand Up Tall"

Reflect/Assess

- *If I asked you to name something big at your houses, what would you name? What about something small?*
  Si les pido que nombren algo grande de sus casas, ¿qué nombrarían? ¿Y algo pequeño?
- *Are you big or little?*
  ¿Ustedes son grandes o pequeños?

Literacy Circle

Storytime 1

- Present the "Ernestine's . . . Day"/"El . . . día de Ernestina" flannel board story. *Is Ernestine the largest or smallest member of her family?*
  ¿Ernestina es el más grande o más pequeño de su familia?

Storytime 2

- Invite the children to act out the story of "The Three Billy Goats Gruff"/"Los tres chivitos Gruff." Discuss the sizes of the goats compared to one another and compared to the troll.

Content Connection

Math

Objectives
To participate in creating and using real and pictorial graphs
To begin to recognize, describe, and name shapes

Vocabulary
favorite, monochromatic
favorito(a), monocromático

Materials to Gather
construction-paper squares, construction-paper shapes, wallpaper shapes

Activity 1

- Invite the children to select their favorite colors. Provide construction-paper squares in red, yellow, orange, blue, green, purple, black, and white, and let the children choose the colored squares that represent their favorite colors and make a graph out of them.

Activity 2

- Provide construction-paper and wallpaper shapes cut in a variety of sizes. Encourage the children to make monochromatic collages using the shapes in their favorite colors.

DAY 4

Objective

- To sort objects into groups by an attribute and begin to explain how the grouping was done

Vocabulary

hexagon	hexágono
circle	círculo
triangle	triángulo
square	cuadrado
size	tamaño
large	grande
small	pequeño
thick	grueso
thin	delgado
color	color

DLM Materials

- *Math Resource Guide*
  Guess My Rule/Adivina mi regla
  Shape Step/Paso de figuras
  Memory Game: Geometry version/ Juego de memoria: versión geométrica
  Memory Game: Geometry cards (Set A)
- *DLM Math* software
- *Where Is Thumbkin?* CD
- *Teacher's Resource Anthology*
  "Ten Little Fingers"/"Diez deditos"
  I Spy/Yo espío

Materials to Gather

- attribute blocks or construction-paper shapes
- balls (3 sizes)

MATH

Focus

- Recite "Ten Little Fingers"/"Diez deditos" with the children. Encourage them to find ten other things to count.
- Play I Spy/Yo espío with the children using at least two attributes to describe each object. Remind the children that color, shape, and size are all attributes they can use.

Develop

- Play Guess My Rule/Adivina mi regla. Explain that you are going to sort the paper shapes and that all the shapes that are the same in some way will go together. Begin a pile for each different shape that is in the set. Continue sorting by shape until you have two or three of each shape in each pile. Pick up another piece and make gestures to ask the children in which pile the shape belongs. Place the shape in the appropriate pile. Repeat with the rest of the shapes. When all shapes are sorted, ask the children what rule you used for sorting. (In this case, you sorted by shape.) Repeat with a new rule, sorting by color or size.
- Play Shape Step/Paso de figuras with the paper shapes. Have small groups of children step on all the shapes that are small, red, rectangles, and so on. Encourage children to help each other find the appropriate shapes.

Practice

- Encourage the children to continue playing Guess My Rule/Adivina mi regla, choosing their own rules for sorting.
- Invite small groups of children to play Shape Step/Paso de figuras.
- Encourage children to play Memory Game: Geometry version/Juego de memoria: versión geométrica.
- Have children work on Mystery Toys, Level 2.

Reflect/Assess

- *How did you figure out what my rule was?*
  ¿Cómo supieron cuál era mi regla?

Physical Development

Objectives

To begin to manipulate play objects that have fine parts

To begin to throw or kick an object in a particular direction

Materials to Gather

square sheet of paper (one per child); posterboard circle, square, rectangle, and triangle

Activity 1

- Give each child a sheet of paper that is cut into a square. Have the children fold their squares in half. *What shape is it now?*
  ¿Qué forma tiene ahora?
- *Have them fold their papers in half again. Now what shape is it?*
  ¿Ahora qué forma tiene?

Activity 2

- Cut a circle, a square, a triangle, and a rectangle out of posterboard. Have the children experiment with rolling each of the shapes. *Which one rolls?*
  ¿Cuál rueda?

Music and Movement

- Play the game "One Elephant" from the *Where Is Thumbkin?* CD.
- Take small, medium, and large balls outdoors and play games using all three balls. *Which ball is the easiest to catch?*
  ¿Qué pelota fue la más fácil de atrapar?

Suggested Reading

So Many Circles, So Many Squares by Tana Hoban

Reflect on the Day

- *What did you learn about sizes and shapes? Which activity was your favorite?*
  ¿Qué aprendieron sobre los tamaños y las figuras? ¿Qué actividad fue su favorita?
- *Look for big and small things today when you go home. Tomorrow, I will ask you what you found.*
  Fíjense en cosas grandes y pequeñas cuando se vayan a su casa hoy. Mañana les preguntaré qué encontraron.

Home Connection

Every Thursday, send home with four children a take-home book pack. Provide an opportunity for each child to take a book home to share with his or her family. You will find the directions and a recording sheet in the *Home Connections Resource Guide*.

Begin the Day

- Recite "This Is the Circle That Is My Head" or "La cabeza." *Which body parts mentioned in the rhyme are circles?*

  ¿Cuáles partes del cuerpo que se mencionan en la rima son círculos?
- Use the suggestions for Morning Circle offered in the front of this *Teacher's Edition*.

Objective

- To show a steady increase in listening and speaking vocabulary

Vocabulary

circle	círculo
square	cuadrado
triangle	triángulo
rectangle	rectángulo

DLM Materials

- *Blue Cat/Gato azul*
- *Teacher's Resource Anthology*
  "This Is the Circle That Is My Head"
  "La cabeza"
  "Tillie Triangle"/"El Triángulo Tilín"
  "Freddie the Snake"/"Braulio, la culebra"
  play dough

Materials to Gather

- shape blocks
- surprise package
- construction-paper shapes

LITERACY

Focus

- Show the box you have wrapped. Ask the children if they can guess what might be inside. Pass the package around and let everyone shake it.
- Open the package. Take out the items one at a time. Invite the children to identify the shape of each item.
- If you used snacks in your package, invite the children to sample each shape.
- Tell the children that we will be discussing shapes today.

Develop

One Way to Develop the Lesson

- Tell the children that you are going to tell them a story about a shape called Tillie/Tilín. Explain that Tillie/Tilín is a triangle.
- Present the "Tillie Triangle"/"El Triángulo Tilín" chalk story.
- Ask the children to recall all the shapes that Tillie/Tilín tried to become.
- Retell the story and invite the children to make the shapes in the air with their hands as they are mentioned.

Another Way to Develop the Lesson

- Play Mystery Shape/Forma misteriosa. Place a shape block in a paper bag. Give the children clues until they guess which shape is in the bag. Continue the game using different shapes.

Practice

- Give the children play dough and encourage them to make shapes with it. Provide cookie cutters or bottle or box lids to make shape "cookies."
- In the Language Center, invite the children to draw Tillie/Tilín on the board or on chart paper.
- Cut circles, squares, triangles, and rectangles out of felt and invite the children to create pictures on the flannel board.
- Cut large shapes out of construction paper. Lay them on the floor. Give the children a beanbag. Encourage them to call out shapes and then try to toss the beanbags onto those shapes.
- Provide construction-paper shapes. Invite the children to pick their favorite shapes and write their names inside the shapes.

Preparation

- Review the "Tillie Triangle"/"El Triángulo Tilín" chalk story.
- Make the "Freddie the Snake"/"Braulio, la culebra" flannel board story.
- Gather shape blocks for Mystery Shape/Forma misteriosa.
- Wrap a surprise package. Put differently shaped items inside.
- Make play dough.

Scaffolding Strategies

More Help Invite the children to trace around each shape with their fingers.

Extra Challenge Invite the children to name some shapes that Tillie/Tilín didn't try to become.

Second Language Learners

Draw large chalk shapes outdoors on the sidewalk. Let children walk, hop, and slide around the shapes. After you return to your room, have them draw the shapes and help them name the shapes. Acknowledge their answers: *Yes, Yuki, that is a circle./Sí, Yuki, ése es un círculo.* Children may repeat your model or expand on it.

DAY 5

Letter Knowledge

English

- Invite the children to make the letter *e* with their bodies. Use the Think, Pair, Share game with this activity.
- Read "Eletelephony" from the *SRA Alphabet Book.*

Spanish

- Invite the children to make the letter *m* with their bodies. Use the Piensa, aparea, comparte game with this activity.
- Read "Mono" from *Los niños alfabéticos.*

Suggested Reading

Shapes, Shapes, Shapes by Tana Hoban
Who Said Red? by Mary Serfozo
¿De qué color es Piggy Wiggy? by Christyan and Diane Fox
Amigos by Alma Flor Ada

Anthology Support

"Window Watching"
"A Square Is a Square"
"Un cuadrado es un cuadrado"
"My Hat, It Has Three Corners"

Reflect/Assess

- *Which shapes do you like best? Why?*

  ¿Qué formas les gustan más? ¿Por qué?
- *What shape is a baseball? What shape is a baseball field? What shapes are bases?*

  ¿Qué forma tiene una pelota de béisbol? ¿Qué forma tiene un campo de béisbol? ¿Qué forma tienen las bases?

Literacy Circle

Storytime 1

- Reread *Blue Cat/Gato azul*. Review the colors in the story. Call attention to the shapes in the borders of the illustrations. Invite the children to name the shapes.

Storytime 2

- Present the "Freddie the Snake"/"Braulio, la culebra" flannel board story. Retell the story a second time and let the children make the shapes of the snake with pieces of yarn.
- *What do Freddie and Tillie have in common?*

  ¿Qué tienen en común Braulio y Tilín?

Content Connection

Science

Objective
To begin to perform simple investigations

Vocabulary
roll, curved lines, corners
rodar, líneas curvas, esquinas

Materials to Gather
posterboard shapes, empty toilet-paper tubes, plastic foam plates, blocks, dice, pennies, marbles, buttons

Activity 1

- Give the children posterboard circles, squares, rectangles, triangles, stars, and hearts. Invite them to experiment with the shapes to see which ones roll. Add empty toilet-paper tubes, plastic foam plates, and blocks to extend the investigation.

Activity 2

- Provide marbles, pennies, buttons, dice, and small blocks. Invite the children to experiment to see which items will roll the farthest.

DAY 5

MATH

Objectives

- To sort objects into groups by an attribute and begin to explain how the grouping was done
- To follow basic oral or pictorial cues for operating programs successfully

Vocabulary

size	tamaño
color	color

DLM Materials

- *Math Resource Guide*
  Guess My Rule/Adivina mi regla
  Shape Step/Paso de figuras
  Memory Game: Geometry version/ Juego de memoria: versión geométrica
  Memory Game: Geometry cards (Set A)
- *DLM Math* software
- *Teacher's Resource Anthology*
  The Statues of Marfil/Las estatuas de Marfil
  Circle 'Round the Zero/Círculo alrededor de cero

Materials to Gather

- set of construction-paper shapes
- objects to sort (jar lids, bottoms, plastic counters)

More Help Give the children 1 attribute by which you want them to sort.

Extra Challenge Ask the children to sort by 2 attributes at 1 time, such as big and green.

Focus

- Distribute the paper shapes to the children. If necessary, children can work in pairs. Ask them to sit down and listen carefully. Then call out directions such as *All triangles stand up/Que se paren todos los triángulos.* Continue using different attributes and actions. If the children are ready, you may wish to use two attributes, such as *All small circles clap your hands/Que aplaudan todos los círculos pequeños.*

Develop

- Play Guess My Rule/Adivina mi regla as you did yesterday. Now play a variation of Guess My Rule/Adivina mi regla using the objects you gathered. Spread out one group of objects, such as the buttons, and allow the children to examine them. Have them discuss what attributes they notice—color, size, what they are made of, how they feel, and so on. Then tell them you are going to sort the objects so that all the things that are the same in some way will be together. Sort into two sets using one of the attributes mentioned during the examination of the material, such as red buttons and not red buttons. After making the sets, ask children what rule they think you used. Accept any reasonable answers. Repeat using another attribute.

Practice

- Invite small groups of children to play Shape Step/Paso de figuras with the paper shapes.
- Remind children they can play Memory Game: Geometry version/Juego de memoria: versión geométrica individually or in pairs with the cards.
- Put out the various objects to be sorted. Challenge children to sort groups of objects any way they choose. Ask them to tell you their rule for sorting.
- Have the children work on Mystery Toys, Level 2.

Reflect/Assess

- *How did you figure out what my rule was?*
  ¿Cómo supieron cuál era mi regla?
- Computer Show: *How do you figure out what shapes to use?*
  ¿Cómo determinan qué formas o figuras deben usar?

Music and Movement

- Play The Statues of Marfil/Las estatuas de Marfil.
- Play Circle 'Round the Zero/Círculo alrededor del cero. Discuss the shape of the circle you make for the game and the shape of a zero.

Content Connection

Personal and Social Development

Objectives
To begin to develop friendships with others
To begin to share and cooperate with others in group activities

Materials to Gather
blocks, construction paper, empty pizza boxes

Activity 1

- Encourage the children to find a partner and play a stacking tower game. Have the partners each stack square blocks as high as they can without the blocks falling. The child who stacks the taller tower is the winner.

Activity 2

- Cut a strip of construction paper the length of one side of a pizza box. Invite the children to stack the pizza boxes until their height equals the construction-paper strip. Tape the stacked boxes together to make a cube. Encourage the children to measure every side with the construction-paper strip. Ask them if every side is the same.

Suggested Reading

So Many Circles, So Many Squares by Tana Hoban

Reflect on the Day

- *What have you learned about colors, shapes, and sizes this week?*
  ¿Qué aprendieron esta semana sobre los colores, las figuras y los tamaños?
- *If you could have a cup in any color or size, which color and size cup would you choose? Why?*
  Si pudieran tener una taza de cualquier color o tamaño, ¿qué color y tamaño escogerían? ¿Por qué?

Home Connection

Encourage the children to have their families help them find road signs shaped like triangles, circles, rectangles, diamonds, and squares.

Looking Ahead

Connecting to the Theme: Things That Go Together

Building on previous themes, this week's lessons strengthen children's ability to link items to one another based on how they function together. Through various activities, children will begin to examine familiar things and the way(s) they "go together."

	Objectives	DLM Materials	Materials to Gather
DAY 1	• To show a steady increase in listening and speaking vocabulary • To cooperate with others in a joint activity • To count by ones to 10 or higher • To start, use, and exit software programs • To identify common features of the local landscape	• *Wordsong/Canto de palabras* • Oral Language Cards 38–39 and 49–50 • *Teacher's Resource Anthology* • *Math Resource Guide* • *Animal Orchestra/La orquesta de los animales* • *Four Baby Bumblebees* CD • *Making Music with Thomas Moore* CD	• basket of things that go together • paper sacks • yarn • coat hanger tube • box or coffee cans • paint • attribute blocks or construction paper shapes
DAY 2	• To refine and extend understanding of known words • To understand the roles, responsibilities, and services provided by community workers • To recognize numerals • To begin to name "how many" are in groups of up to three (or more) objects without counting • To understand that letters are different from numbers	• Brushing Your Teeth sequence cards • *Guess Who?/Adivina quién . . .* • *Teacher's Resource Anthology* • *Animal Orchestra/La orquesta de los animales* • *Math Resource Guide* • *DLM Math* software • *Where Is Thumbkin?* CD • counters	• clothing item pairs • single clothing items • worker props • attribute blocks or construction paper shapes • sandpaper • number stencils • poster board
DAY 3	• To refine and extend understanding of known words • To cooperate with others in a joint activity • To match numerals to collections of items • To recognize numerals • To participate in creating simple data charts	• *Animals That Build Their Homes/Animales que construyen sus nidos* • *Ginger/Jengibre* • Oral Language Cards 6–9 • *Teacher's Resource Anthology* • *Animal Orchestra/La orquesta de los animales*	• tactile numeral cards
DAY 4	• To refine and extend understanding of known words • To sort objects into groups by an attribute and begin to explain how the grouping was done • To recognize numerals • To match numerals to collections of items • To participate in classroom music activities • To begin to sing a variety of simple songs	• *Teacher's Resource Anthology* • rhythm band instruments • *Math Resource Guide* • *DLM Math* software • *Where Is Thumbkin?* CD	• foods that go together • kitchen tools and foods that go together • cereal box puzzles • jam • bread • felt cakes and candles • coffee can • tactile numeral cards (1–5)
DAY 5	• To refine and extend understanding of known words • To match numerals to collections of items • To begin to use technical terminology, such as "mouse," keyboard," "printer," "CD-ROM"	• *Martí and the Mango/ Martí y el mango* • counters • *Math Resource Guide* • *DLM Math* software • magnetic letters	• name puzzles • name cards • felt letters • beanbag • tactile numeral cards (1–5)

Learning Centers

BLOCKS

Driving Cars and Playing with Animals

Objective
To begin to engage in dramatic play with others

Materials to Gather
milk carton garages, masking tape, street signs, berry baskets, cars, plastic animals

Develop
Prepare milk carton garages, street signs, and masking tape parking spaces for the children to use in dramatic play with their vehicles. Add berry baskets to use as cages for plastic animals.

Reflect/Assess
What do you need to look out for when you drive a car?
¿En qué tienen que fijarse cuando manejan un carro?
Did you keep the animals in their cages or let them out to play?
¿Dejaron los animales en sus jaulas o los dejaron salir a jugar?

SCIENCE

Read About Animals

Objective
To show an interest in investigating unfamiliar objects, organisms, and phenomena

DLM Materials
Animals That Build Their Homes/Animales que construyen sus nidos book and listening tape

Develop
Keep the *Animals That Build Their Homes/Animales que construyen sus nidos* book and listening tape in the center all week. Children will listen to the tape and examine the pictures over and over, learning something new each time.

Reflect/Assess
Which animals live in nests?
¿Qué animales viven en nidos?
Which animals help each other build?
¿Qué animales se ayudan entre sí para construir?

FINE MOTOR

Playing Games

Objective
To begin to manipulate play objects that have fine parts

Materials to Gather
assorted games

Develop
Fill the center with games that have component pieces—things that go together to make up the game. For example, most board games have dice or a spinner, markers, and sometimes cards. Call attention to the need for all the pieces to be present in order to play the games properly.

Reflect/Assess
Which game was your favorite?
¿Cuál fue su juego favorito?
Do you like games with dice or spinners better?
¿Les gustan más los juegos con dados o con agujas giratorias?

What Research Suggests

The ability to see patterns and build relationships from those patterns is the cornerstone of intelligence. Helping children recognize patterns and expand their understanding of relationships is one of the most valuable gifts we can offer them.

Begin the Day

- Say the "Inside Out"/"Adentro afuera" rhyme with the children. Call their attention to the fact that how we feel on the inside goes together with how we look on the outside.
- Use the suggestions for Morning Circle offered in the front of this *Teacher's Edition*.

Objective

- To listen with increasing attention

Vocabulary

match emparejan
go together concuerdan
relationships relaciones

DLM Materials

- *Wordsong/Canto de palabras*
- Oral Language Development Cards 38–39 and 49–50
- *Teacher's Resource Anthology*
  Things That Go Together Concentration game
  Things That Go Together card patterns
- Brushing Your Teeth Sequence Cards

Materials to Gather

- basket of things that go together

Preparation

- Fill a basket or box with items that go together, such as a pencil and pad, knife and fork, and key and lock.
- Prepare the Things That Go Together card patterns to make the Things That Go Together Concentration game.

LITERACY

Focus

- Sing "The Mulberry Bush"/"La mata de moras" with the children. Make up verses that show how things go together, for example, brush my teeth, comb my hair, wash my face, and so forth. Point out the items that go with each activity.
- Tell the children that all this week we will be talking about things that go together.

Develop

One Way to Develop the Lesson

- Show the children the basket of things you have collected. Encourage them to describe how the items go together. Ask for volunteers to find other examples in the classroom of things that go together.
- Play What's Missing?/¿Lo que falta? Lay three sets of items from your box on the floor in random order. Have the children look at the items then close their eyes. While their eyes are closed, remove an item from the group. Ask them to open their eyes and tell you which item is missing.

Another Way to Develop the Lesson

- Show the children Oral Language Cards 38–39 and 49–50. Ask them to identify things that go together in each photo.

Practice

- Encourage the children to match the items in the go-together box and to look for additional items for the box.
- Invite the children to draw a picture of things that go together.
- Provide garages constructed from milk cartons in the Blocks Center for children to match.
- Provide the Things That Go Together Concentration game.
- Place the Brushing Your Teeth Sequence Cards in a center for sequencing.

Scaffolding Strategies

More Help Invite the children to look at their hands. Discuss the relationship of the fingers to the hand. Explain that fingers and hands go together.
Extra Challenge Remove two items (instead of one) from the What's Missing?/¿Lo que falta? game.

Second Language Learners

Place items that go together in the Dramatic Play center. You might select theme items (comb, hair dryer, empty shampoo bottle) so children can play the corresponding role (hairdresser). Pretend to get a haircut. Ask questions with a choice: *Would you like long hair or short?*
¿Les gustaría el cabello largo o corto?
Note any second language use.

Anthology Support

"Pepita's Things"
"Las cosas de Pepita"
"Wheels on the Bus"
"Ruedas del bus"

DAY 1

Letter Knowledge

English

- Introduce the letter *f* using the story "Frank" from the *English Phonics Resource Guide.*

Spanish

- Introduce the letter *s* using the story of "Susi" in the *Spanish Phonics Resource Guide.*

Suggested Reading

Susie Moriar by Tracy Moncure
Mr. Tall and Mr. Small by Barbara Brenner
¿Cómo te vistes? by Dami and Alicia Casado
Si le das una galletita a un ratón by Laura Joffe Numeroff

Reflect/Assess

- *What are your two favorite things that go together?*
  Entre sus favoritas, ¿Cuáles son dos cosas que concuerdan?
- *Can you think of something that goes with your bed?*
  ¿Pueden pensar en algo que concuerde con su cama?

Literacy Circle

Storytime 1

- Read *Wordsong/Canto de palabras.*
- Read it a second time and invite the children to use the pictures as cues to read with you.

Storytime 2

- Reread *How Happy I Would Be!/Me gustaría tener . . . .*
- Have a basket of story props (watch, ring, gloves, eyeglasses, pen, pants, thread) available.
- Challenge the children to recall the items that go with each animal in the story.

Content Connection

Social Studies

Objective

To cooperate with others in a joint activity

Vocabulary

kite, string, drum, drumstick
cometa, cuerda, hilo, tambor, baqueta, palillo de tambor

Materials to Gather

paper sacks (one per child), yarn, coat-hanger tube, box or coffee can (one per child), crayons, paint

Activity 1

- Have the children make drums. Give each child a box, a coffee can, or an oatmeal box to decorate as a drum. Provide coat hanger tubes for drumsticks. Encourage them to paint or color their drumsticks.
- Remind the children of the relationship between the drum and the sticks.

Activity 2

- Have the children make paper-sack kites. Give each child a lunch sack to decorate with markers and crayons. Attach a piece of yarn for a string.
- Remind the children of the relationship between the kite and the string—you can't fly a kite without a string.

DAY 1

Objectives

- To count by ones to 10 or higher
- To start, use, and exit software programs

Vocabulary

number número
curved curvo

DLM Materials

- counters
- rhythm band instruments
- *Animal Orchestra/La orquesta de los animales*
- *Math Resource Guide*
  Counting Card Game/Juego de contar en tarjetas
  Counting cards (1–5)
  Shape Step/Paso de figuras
  Memory Game: Geometry version/ Juego de memoria: versión geométrica
  Memory Game: Geometry cards (Set A)
- *DLM Math* software
- *Four Baby Bumblebees* CD
- *Making Music with Thomas Moore* CD
- *Teacher's Resource Anthology*
  "Five Little Fingers"/"Los dedos de la mano"

Materials to Gather

- attribute blocks or construction-paper shapes

Preparation

- Photocopy several sets of Counting cards (1–5).

MATH

Focus

- Recite "Five Little Fingers"/"Los dedos de la mano" with the children.
- Show a page or two of *Animal Orchestra/La orquesta de los animales* and discuss how there are different numbers of animals. Tell children numbers have names, just as children do. Help children make a connection between how many animals are shown and the written numbers that represent that idea.
- Have children name the numerals 1 to 5 in the book without reading or counting the animals on each page. The word *numerals* refers to written numbers. *Number* actually refers to a set of something.

Develop

- Review the Counting Card Game/Juego de contar en tarjetas from Opposites, Day 1, but add a new twist. Emphasize that children can read the numeral and then count out the correct number of counters. They can then put the counters on the dots on the card to check their counting.
- Introduce and demonstrate the activity Party Time, Level 2. Have children provide the answers. In this level, children help get ready for a party again, but this time they have to know how many items, such as plates, are needed by counting the place settings at the table and clicking on the numeral. Show children that if they forget any numerals, they can hold the mouse over the number and the computer will read it. They can also count the dots below the numerals.

Practice

- Invite children to continue playing the Counting Card Game/ Juego de contar en tarjetas.
- Encourage children to explore the numerals in *Animal Orchestra/ La orquesta de los animales.*
- Invite children to continue any of the Practice activities from last week.
- Invite the children to work on Party Time, Level 2.

Reflect/Assess

- Show a numeral between 1 and 5. *How do you know how to read this numeral?*
  ¿Cómo saben cómo leer este número?

Content Connection

Social Studies

Objective
To identify common features of the local landscape

Activity 1
- Have the children describe where they use numerals in their lives, such as on television channels, house addresses, road signs, and so on.

Activity 2
- Go on a numeral hunt throughout the school or neighborhood. If you like, take photographs of the numerals and create a class book.

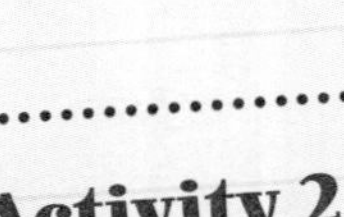

Music and Movement

- Play "Do-Re-Mi" from the *Four Baby Bumblebees* CD. Invite the children to sing along with the tape. Ask them which things in the song go together.
- Invite the children to play the rhythm band instruments to music from the *Making Music with Thomas Moore* CD. Discuss instruments that have two parts.

Suggested Reading

One Was Johnny: A Counting Book
by Maurice Sendak
Frog Counts to Ten
by John Liebler

Reflect on the Day

- *Which activity did you enjoy most today? Why?*
  ¿Cuál actividad disfrutaron más hoy? ¿Por qué?
- *Tonight I would like you to find some things during dinner that go together. I will ask you what you found tommorow.*
  Esta noche, durante la cena, me gustaría que buscaran algunas cosas que corresponden entre sí. Les preguntaré mañana lo que encontraron.

Begin the Day

- Do the "I Can Do It Myself"/"Lo puedo hacer yo solo" action rhyme with the children. Ask them which things go together when they get dressed.
- Ask the children about things that go together that they noticed last night at the dinner table.
- Use the suggestions for Morning Circle offered in the front of this *Teacher's Edition.*

Objective

- To refine and extend understanding of known words

Vocabulary

caps	gorras
mittens	mitones, guantes
shoes	zapatos
socks	medias, calcetines

DLM Materials

- Brushing Your Teeth Sequence Cards
- *Teacher's Resource Anthology* "Dress-Me-Bears for Fall"/"Vísteme para el otoño" flannel board story "Dress-Me-Bears for School"/"Vísteme para el escuela" flannel board story

Materials to Gather

- clothing item pairs (mittens, socks, and so on)
- single clothing items (hat, bracelet, and so on)
- pairs of socks

Preparation

- Prepare the "Dress-Me-Bears for Fall"/"Vísteme para el otoño" and "Dress-Me-Bears for School"/"Vísteme para la escuela" flannel board story if not already prepared.
- Gather items for the clothing and body part go-togethers.

LITERACY

Focus

- Sing "Head, Shoulders, Knees, and Toes"/"Cabeza, hombros, rodillas y dedos." Point out that the things named in the song all go together—they are body parts.
- Teach the children "Cap, Mittens, Shoes, and Socks"/"Gorra, mitones, zapatos y medias." Point out that the things named in the song all go together—they are clothes for our body parts.
- Tell the children that today we will be talking about clothing items that go together.

Develop

One Way to Develop the Lesson

- Show the children the clothing items you have selected to represent pairs, such as mittens, gloves, socks, and shoes. Discuss the paired relationship.
- Next show them the single clothing items you have selected, such as bracelets, rings, necklaces, bows, and ties. Let them tell the body part that goes with each item. Add some humor to the lesson by suggesting that clothes go in funny places, such as a sock on your ear. Explain that all these things are things that go together.

Another Way to Develop the Lesson

- Tell the children that you have a story about Rafita and Pepita and their fall clothes.
- Present the "Dress-Me-Bears for Fall"/"Vísteme para el otoño" flannel board story. Discuss the clothing items and the body part with which they go.

Practice

- Place the flannel board story in the Language Center and invite the children to retell the story or make up a new story.
- Place the clothing items you selected as pairs and the single clothing items in the Dramatic Play Center. Invite the children to try on the clothing items.
- Encourage the children to make jewelry out of scrap materials in the Art Center. They can use straws to make a necklace or yarn to make a bracelet.
- Give the children the Brushing Your Teeth Sequence Cards and invite them to place the cards in the correct sequence.
- Give the children pairs of socks to match.

Scaffolding Strategies

More Help Invite the children to try on the clothing items as you discuss the relationship between body parts and clothing.

Extra Challenge Encourage the children to think about how clothing changes with seasons and activities. For example, our winter hats are different from our summer hats; our hats for the beach are different from those we wear when playing baseball.

Second Language Learners

Tell the "Dress-Me-Bears for Fall"/"Vísteme para el otoño" flannel board story. First, pantomime the story. Children can also pantomime as you describe what they are doing. Then tell the story using the figures. Place the flannel board and its figures in a learning center. Invite the children to tell the story.

Anthology Support

"Helpful Friends"
"Amigos útiles"
"Three Little Kittens"
"Los tres gaticos"

DAY 2

Letter Knowledge

English

- Make the letter *f* in finger paint. Show the children how to make fingerprints using an inkpad. Encourage them to make fingerprints over a letter *f* that has been written on an index card.

Spanish

- Make the letter *s* in a sand tray. Encourage the children to find the letter *s* in magazines and newspapers.

Suggested Reading

Hello Feet, Hello Toes
by Ann Whitford Paul
Sylvester and the Magic Pebble
by William Steig
Silvestre y la piedrecita mágica
by William Steig

Teacher's NOTE

This lesson presents a good opportunity for discussing cultural differences in clothing.

Reflect/Assess

- *Which clothing items go with bedtime?*
  ¿Qué ropa concuerda con la hora de dormir?
- *What items go with bath time?*
  ¿Qué ropa concuerda con la hora de bañarse?

Literacy Circle

Storytime 1

- Present the "Dress-Me-Bears for School"/"Vísteme para la escuela" flannel board story.
- Invite the children to name the items that go together.

Storytime 2

- Present the "Dress-Me-Bears for Fall"/"Vísteme para el otoño" flannel board story.
- *What clothing items and body parts are mentioned in the story?*
  ¿Qué ropa y partes del cuerpo se mencionan en el cuento?

Content Connection

Social Studies

Objective
To understand the roles, responsibilities, and services provided by community workers

Vocabulary
police officer, firefighter, letter carrier, baker, doctor, pilot
policía, bombero, cartero(a), panadero(a), médico, doctor(a), piloto

DLM Materials
Guess Who?/Adivina quién . . .

Materials to Gather
worker props (optional)

Activity 1

- Discuss some of the helpers in the community, such as the firefighter, police officer, letter carrier, and baker. Show any photos that you have of community helpers.
- Ask the children about the uniforms these people wear. Discuss the go-together relationship of the workers and their uniforms. Explain that uniforms help us recognize people.

Activity 2

- Read the book *Guess Who?/Adivina quién . . .* to the children. Stop on all pages where clothing items are specific to the worker. Invite the children to describe the clothing that the workers are wearing.
- Place any community-helper uniforms that you have in the Dramatic Play Center for children to explore.

DAY 2

Objectives

- To recognize numerals
- To begin to name "how many" are in a group of up to three (or more) objects without counting

Vocabulary

number número

DLM Materials

- *Animal orchestra/La orquesta de los animales*
- *Math Resource Guide* Snapshots/Instantáneas
- See Day 1
- *DLM Math* software
- *Where Is Thumbkin?* CD
- *Teacher's Resource Anthology* "This Is the Way We Dress for Fall"/ "Así nos vestimos en otoño"

Materials to Gather

- attribute blocks or construction-paper shapes
- index cards
- sandpaper
- number stencils
- foam numerals (optional)
- posterboard

Preparation

- Make tactile numeral cards by using stencils to cut numerals out of sandpaper. Glue the same numeral on each side of an index card. Use stencils to make numeral cutouts from posterboard.

MATH

Focus

- Review how to play Snapshots/Instantáneas. (See Friends, Day 3.) Secretly put 2 counters in your hand. Hold out your closed hand, open it for 2 seconds, then close it. Have children tell you how many counters they saw. Repeat with other numbers, 1 to 5.

Develop

- Display tactile numeral cards from 1 to 5 in order. Allow time for the children to see and touch the numerals. Ask children to name the ones they know. Encourage them to tell you what they notice about how each numeral looks and what parts it has. To recognize numerals, children need to know what the parts are (a 3 is made with curved lines), how the parts fit together (1 curve is on top of the other), and left-right (the curves are open on the left). Use geometric terms like *vertical, horizontal,* and *slanted lines* to describe the parts of the numerals.
- Hold up tactile numeral cards and ask children to show that many counters.
- Review Party Time, Level 2.

Practice

- Invite small groups of children to play the Counting Card Game/ Juego de contar en tarjetas.
- Invite children to explore the numerals in *Animal Orchestra/La orquesta de los animales* and the tactile numeral cards, the foam numerals, or the numeral cutouts. Encourage children to tell about the parts they see or feel.
- Encourage the children to play any of the Practice activities from last week.
- Have the children work on Party Time, Level 2.

Reflect/Assess

- *Show me the 2. How do you know how to read this numeral?*
  Muéstrenme el 2. ¿Cómo saben cómo leer este número?

Content Connection

Literacy

Objective
To understand that letters are different from numbers

Activity 1

- Have the children describe where numerals are found in books, especially in page numbers. *Why are there numbers on the pages?*
  ¿Por qué hay números en las páginas?

Activity 2

- Discuss the use of numbers and letters in books. Have a volunteer explain their different functions.

Music and Movement

- Sing "Where Is Thumbkin?" from the *Where Is Thumbkin?* CD. Invite the children to do the hand motions with the song. Point out the relationship between the fingers and the hand.
-  Sing "This Is the Way We Dress for Fall"/"Así nos vestimos en otoño" with the children.

Suggested Reading

One Was Johnny: A Counting Book by Maurice Sendak
Frog Counts to Ten by John Liebler

Reflect on the Day

- *What other songs that we sing together have hand movements?*
  ¿Qué otras canciones que cantamos juntos tienen movimientos con las manos?
- *Tonight when you take your bath, pay attention to all the things that go with your bath. Tomorrow we will make a list.*
  Esta noche cuando se bañen, pongan atención a todas las cosas que tienen que ver con su baño. Mañana haremos una lista.

What Research Suggests

Representing the number in a collection of objects with spoken words, and then written symbols, are key steps toward abstract mathematical thinking.

Begin the Day

- Sing “Over in the Meadow”/“Sobre la pradera.” Point out the relationship of mothers to baby animals.
- Make a list of the things that children decided went with their baths last night. Teach the children “After My Bath”/“Después del baño.”
- Use the suggestions for Morning Circle offered in the front of this *Teacher's Edition.*

Objective

- To refine and extend understanding of known words

Vocabulary

mother	mamá, madre
baby	bebé
nest	nido
burrow	madriguera
hive	colmena

DLM Materials

- *Animals That Build Their Homes/ Animales que construyen sus nidos*
- *Ginger/Jengibre*
- Oral Language Development Cards 6–9
- *Teacher's Resource Anthology*
  Mother and Baby Animal card patterns
  Animal Homes card patterns
  “Ms. Bumblebee Gathers Honey”/ “La avispa Zumbi lleva miel” prop story

Materials to Gather

- tracing paper
- word cards

LITERACY

Focus

- Sing “Birdie, Birdie, Where Is Your Nest?”/“¿Pajarito, pajarito, donde está tu nido?” or teach the children “Mothers and Their Babies”/ “Mamás y sus bebés.”
- Discuss the relationships of animals to their homes and mother animals to their babies.
- Tell the children that today we will learn about animals that go together.

Develop

One Way to Develop the Lesson

- Show the children Oral Language Cards 6–9. Point out that the baby animals all have a mother to which they belong.
- Invite the children to name other mother animals and their babies. Explain that babies often have names that are different from the mother, such as *cat* and *kitten.*
- Show the children the Mother and Baby Animal card patterns. Invite them to help you make pairs of the animals.

Another Way to Develop the Lesson

- Show the cover of the book *Animals That Build Their Homes/Animales que construyen sus nidos*. Tell the children that this book is about animals and their homes. Explain that many animals have homes that are specific to them.
- Show them the pictures in the book. Do not read all of the text, just point out the animal and its home. Encourage the children to discuss what they know about the animals and their homes.

Practice

- Place the *Animals That Build Their Homes/Animales que construyen sus nidos* book and listening tape in the Listening Center for children to enjoy.
- Invite the children to match animals and their mothers using the Mother and Baby Animal Match game. Some children may prefer to play Concentration.
- Encourage the children to match animals to their homes using the Animals and Homes Match game.
- Have the children draw a picture of an animal and its home.
- Write *mama* and *baby/bebé* on index cards. Provide tracing paper and encourage the children to trace the words.

Preparation

- Prepare the Mother and Baby Animal Match game, using the Mother and Baby Animal card patterns and the Animal Homes Match game, using the Animal Homes card patterns if not already prepared.
- Prepare the "Ms. Bumblebee Gathers Honey"/"La avispa Zumbi lleva miel" prop story.
- Write *mama* and *baby/bebé* on index cards to make word cards.

Second Language Learners

As you play the Mother and Baby Animal Match game, chant: *(Chick), (Chick), where are you? Here I am, Mother (Hen); Peek-a-boo!* (perform actions). Substitute words in parentheses for other baby and mother animals depicted on the cards.

Anthology Support

"Five Dancing Dolphins"
"Cinco delfines bailarines"
"Los bebés de los animales"
"Five Little Speckled Frogs"
"Cinco ranitas manchadas"

DAY 3

Letter Knowledge

English

- Have the children locate the letter *f* in magazines and newspapers.

Spanish

- Have the children locate the letter *s* in magazines and newspapers.

Suggested Reading

Are You My Mother? by Philip D. Eastman
¿Eres tú mi mamá? by Philip D. Eastman
A Fish Out of Water by Helen Palmer
Arco iris de animales by Enrique Martinez

Reflect/Assess

- *What are some of the materials animals use to build their homes?*
  ¿Cuáles son algunos de los materiales que usan los animales para construir sus hogares?
- *Which animals have homes that are similar?*
  ¿Qué animales tienen hogares parecidos?

Literacy Circle

Storytime 1

- Present the "Ms. Bumblebee Gathers Honey"/"La avispa Zumbi lleva miel" prop story.
- Point out the relationship of the hive, the honey, and the flower to the bee.

Storytime 2

- Read *Ginger/Jengibre*.
- *What things go with each cat in the story?*
  ¿Qué cosas concuerdan con cada gato en el cuento?

Content Connection

Social Studies

Objective
To cooperate with others in a joint activity

Vocabulary
dog, bone, elephant, peanut
perro, hueso, elefante, cacahuate, maní

DLM Materials
- *Teacher's Resource Anthology*
  Dog and Bone card patterns
  Elephant and Peanut card patterns
  Dog and Bone/El perro y el hueso
  One Elephant/Un elefante

Activity 1

- Invite the children to play the Number Association game using the Dog and Bone card patterns. You can vary this game and review the lessons on color at the same time. Color the bones and collar tags on the dogs to match and invite the children to match colored bones to same-color dog collar tags.
- Invite the children to play the game Dog and Bone/El perro y el hueso.

Activity 2

- Encourage the children to match the correct number of peanuts to the number on the elephants' saddles.
- Invite the children to play One Elephant/Un elefante.

DAY 3

Objectives

- To match numerals to collections of items
- To recognize numerals

Vocabulary

number número

DLM Materials

- counters
- *Animal Orchestra/La orquesta de los animales*
- *Math Resource Guide*
  Listen and Copy/Escucha e imita
  Counting Card Game/Juego de contar en tarjetas
  Counting cards (1–5)
- *DLM Math* software
- *Teacher's Resource Anthology*
  "Over in the Meadow"/"Sobre la pradera"
  Who Took the Cookie from the Cookie Jar?/¿Quién se comió la galleta?
  "Where Is Thumbkin?"/"¿Dónde está Pulgarcito?"
  "Going on a Bear Hunt"/"Vamos a cazar un oso"

Materials to Gather

- tactile numeral cards

MATH

Focus

- Sing "Over in the Meadow"/"Sobre la pradera" with the children.

Develop

- Play Listen and Copy/Escucha e imita. Clap a certain number of times, 1–5, and have children clap the same number of times in the same way. You may choose to clap quickly, slowly, or with pauses in order to create patterns, such as clap, clap, pause, clap.
- Distribute the tactile numeral cards. Teach the children Who Took the Cookie from the Cookie Jar?/¿Quién se comió la galleta?, but use number names (1–5) in place of children's names. For example, you might say *Two took the cookie from the cookie jar/El dos tomó la galleta del galletero*. The child holding the given numeral responds when his or her numeral is called. Play the game again, giving the tactile numerals to different children.
- Allow the children to feel the numerals on the tactile numeral cards. Then have them make great big numerals in the air with their fingers. As the children make the numerals, describe them using the terms *slanted, horizontal,* and *vertical* as appropriate.

Practice

- Invite the children to make rubbings of the tactile numeral cards.
- Encourage children to play the Counting Card Game/Juego de contar en tarjetas.
- Allow children to continue to explore the numerals in *Animal Orchestra/La orquesta de los animales*.
- Have the children work on Party Time, Level 2.

Reflect/Assess

- Show the numeral 3. *How do you know how to read this numeral?* *¿Cómo saben cómo leer este número?*

Music and Movement

- Sing a variation of "Where Is Thumbkin?"/"¿Dónde está Pulgarcito?" called "Where Is Bear?"/"¿Dónde está Oso?" with the children.
- Do the action rhyme "Going on a Bear Hunt"/"Vamos a cazar un oso" with the children.

Content Connection

Science

Objective

To participate in creating and using simple data charts

Activity 1

- Ask the children their ages. Make a graph showing how many children are 3, how many are 4, and how many are 5.

Activity 2

- Ask the children how many siblings they have. Make a graph illustrating how many children have no siblings, one sibling, two siblings, and so on.
- Discuss the relationship between the children and their siblings.

Suggested Reading

Numbers by Henry Arthur Pluckrose

Puzzlers by Suse MacDonald

Reflect on the Day

- *Which animal's home do you like best? Why?* *¿Cuál hogar de animales les gusta más? ¿Por qué?*
- *In what ways are animal homes like our homes?* *¿En qué se parecen los hogares de los animales a los nuestros?*

Home Connection

Next Wednesday, you will be providing a junk table for the children to explore. Send a note home to families requesting contributions of items such as locks and keys, hinges, nuts and bolts, broken clocks, doorknobs, and so on.

Begin the Day

- Teach the children the "Ice Cream Chant"/"La canción del helado."
- *Who likes ice cream?*

  ¿A quién le gusta el helado?
- *Do you like ice cream on a cone or in a dish?*

  ¿Les gusta el helado en barquilla o en un plato?
- Use the suggestions for Morning Circle offered in the front of this *Teacher's Edition*.

Objective

- To refine and extend understanding of known words

Vocabulary

food comida, alimento
kitchen cocina
tools utensilios

DLM Materials

- *Teacher's Resource Anthology*
  "Smart Cookie's Best Friend, Gabby Graham"/"Gabby Graham, la mejor amiga de Smart Cookie" flannel board story
  "Miguel's Birthday"/"El cumpleaños de Miguel" flannel board story

Materials to Gather

- foods that go together
- kitchen tools and foods that go together
- cereal box puzzles
- jam
- bread
- plastic eggs
- egg carton
- funnels, measuring cups and spoons

Focus

- Teach the children "I Like Peanut Butter and Jelly"/"Me gusta mantequilla y jalea."
- Encourage the children to tell you about combinations of foods they like.
- Add new verses to the song to reflect the children's likes.
- Tell the children that today we will be learning about foods that go together.

Develop

One Way to Develop the Lesson

- Show the children the pairs of food items you have brought. Ask the children to help you pair the items.
- Invite the children to brainstorm a list of other foods that go together. Write their list on a piece of chart paper.

Another Way to Develop the Lesson

- Show the children the kitchen tools and related items you have brought to illustrate tools and foods that go together. Ask the children to help you pair the items.
- Invite the children to brainstorm a list of other kitchen tools that go with a specific food. Write their list on a piece of chart paper.

Practice

- Place the empty food containers in the Dramatic Play Center and invite the children to match the items or pair the items.
- Place the kitchen tools in the Science Center and invite the children to pair the items. If possible, allow the children to use the kitchen tools. For example, allow them to squeeze the juice from an orange with the juicer.
- Cut puzzles from cereal boxes and encourage the children to put the puzzles together.
- Serve bread and jam. Invite the children to spread their own jam on the bread.
- Let the children place plastic eggs into an egg carton.
- Provide funnels, measuring cups, and measuring spoons for children to explore in the Sand and Water Center.

Preparation

- Gather empty cartons and containers to illustrate foods that go together such as milk and cereal, peanut butter and jelly, and bread and butter.
- Gather kitchen tools that go together with certain foods, such as a juice squeezer and a fruit, potato masher and potato, and so forth.
- Prepare the flannel board stories.

Scaffolding Strategies

More Help Invite the children to hold the matching item in their hands. If possible, construct a peanut butter and jelly sandwich, allowing the children to help.

Extra Challenge Encourage the children to be specific about foods that go together by asking them to limit their thinking to a holiday or a specific meal, such as breakfast.

Second Language Learners

Place restaurant items that go together (menus with food photos and labels, napkins, and so on) in the Dramatic Play center. Pretend to be a server and take an order. Use appropriate greetings and vocabulary. Ask questions with a choice: *Would you like pizza or a hot dog?* *¿Te gustaría pizza o un hotdog?* Note any second language use.

DAY 4

Letter Knowledge

English

- Read "It's Fun to Be a Fire Dog" from the *SRA Alphabet Book.*

Spanish

- Read "El señor" from *Los niños alfabéticos.*

Suggested Reading

Green Eggs and Ham by Dr. Seuss
Bread and Jam for Frances by Russel Hoban
Si le das un panqueque a una cerdita by Laura Joffe Numeroff

Teacher's NOTE

This lesson offers the opportunity to expose the children to a variety of ethnic and cultural foods and eating utensils. For example, you might introduce a pair of chopsticks or a pestle and mortar.

Anthology Support

"Little Red Apple"
"Manzanita roja"
"The Runaway Cookie Parade"
"El desfile de la galleta fugitiva"
"Peanut Butter"
"Mantequilla de maní"

Reflect/Assess

- *What are your favorite paired foods?*
  ¿Cuáles pares de comida son sus favoritos?
- *What kitchen tool could go with mayonnaise?*
  ¿Cuál utensilio de cocina se usaría para la mayonesa?

Literacy Circle

Storytime 1

- Present the "Smart Cookie's Best Friend, Gabby Graham"/"Gabby Graham, la mejor amiga de Smart Cookie" flannel board story.
- Discuss the go-together relationship of friends.
- Use this opportunity to review the lessons on shape from last week.

Storytime 2

- Present the "Miguel's Birthday"/"El cumpleaños de Miguel" flannel board story.
- *What is the relationship between the cake and the candles?*
  ¿Cuál es la relación entre el pastel y las velas?

Content Connection

Math

Objective
To sort objects into groups by an attribute and begin to explain how the grouping was done

Vocabulary
cake, candles
pastel, torta, velas

Materials to Gather
felt cakes and candles

Activity 1

- Do the action rhyme "Let's Pretend to Bake a Cake"/"Pretendamos como que horneamos un pastel."
- Discuss the ingredients that go in the cake and the relationship of candles to birthday cakes.

Activity 2

- Prepare felt cakes and candles for the flannel board.
- Construct cakes with the correct number of candles for each child's next birthday.

DAY 4

Objectives

- To recognize numerals
- To match numerals to collections of items

Vocabulary

number número

DLM Materials

- Animal Orchestra/La orquesta de los animales
- *Math Resource Guide*
  Snapshots/Instantáneas
  Listen and Count/Escucha y cuenta
  Numeral cards (1 set of 1–5 for each child)
  Dot cards
  Memory Game: Numbers version/ Juego de memoria: versión números
  Numeral Jump/Saltar números
- See Day 1
- *DLM Math* software
- *Where Is Thumbkin?* CD
- *Teacher's Resource Anthology*
  Mother, May I?/Mamá, ¿puedo?
  Who Took the Cookie from the Cookie Jar?/¿Quién se comió la galleta?

Materials to Gather

- coffee can
- tactile numeral cards (1–5)

Scaffolding Strategies

More Help Play Memory Game: Numbers version with fewer cards.

Extra Challenge Children who are able may play Memory Game: Numbers version using sets of cards that include the numbers 1 to 10.

MATH

Focus

- Play Mother, May I?/Mamá, ¿puedo? with the children using numbers from 1 to 5.
- Play Snapshots/Instantáneas with 1 to 5 counters.

Develop

- Give each child a set of Numeral cards, 1–5. Play Listen and Count/ Escucha y cuenta. Have the children listen quietly as you slowly drop a number of marbles or counters into a coffee can. Have children hold up their Numeral cards to show how many items are in the can. Count to check, or ask a volunteer to count. After a while, you may wish to include pauses between drops, such as drop, drop, pause, drop. Start with 1 to 4 drops, then add 1 or 2 more.
- Introduce the Memory Game: Numbers version/Juego de memoria: versión números with matching Numeral and Dot cards. Arrange the cards with dots in one array and the cards with numerals in another one. (See Color, Shape, and Size 2, Day 2.)
- Play Numeral Jump/Saltar números. Tell the children you will show a tactile numeral card, and they should jump that many times. Repeat with several numerals.

Practice

- Encourage small groups or pairs of children to continue playing the Memory Game: Numbers version/Juego de memoria: versión números.
- Invite pairs or small groups of children to play Listen and Count/ Escucha y cuenta.
- Encourage the children to explore the numerals in *Animal Orchestra/ La orquesta de los animales.*
- Have the children work on Party Time, Level 2.

Reflect/Assess

- Show the numeral 4. *How do you know how to read this numeral?*

  ¿Cómo saben cómo leer este número?

Music and Movement

- Play Who Took the Cookie from the Cookie Jar?/¿Quién se comió la galleta? Discuss the relationship between cookies and cookie jars.
- Sing "Peanut Butter" from the *Where Is Thumbkin?* CD.

Content Connection

Fine Arts

Objectives

To participate in classroom music activities

To begin to sing a variety of simple songs

DLM Materials

- *Teacher's Resource Anthology*
  - "Five Little Ducks"/"Los cinco patitos"
  - "Six White Ducks"/"Los seis patos blancos"

Activity 1

- Sing "Five Little Ducks"/"Los cinco patitos." Discuss the use of numbers in the song. *How do the ducks go together?*

  ¿En qué corresponden los patos?

Activity 2

- Sing "Six White Ducks"/"Los seis patos blancos." Discuss the use of numbers in the song.

Suggested Reading

I Spy Two Eyes by Lucy Micklethwait

Reflect on the Day

- *Can you think of any other "go-togethers" that we didn't talk about today?*

  ¿Pueden pensar en otras "correspondencias" que no hayamos estudiado hoy?
- *What "go-together" do you think you may see on your dinner table tonight?*

  ¿Qué cosas que corresponden creen que verán esta noche al cenar?

Home Connection

- Ask children to find numerals at home and either tell about them or bring them in for sharing tomorrow.
- Send home a take-home book pack with four children. You will find the directions and a recording sheet for this activity in the *Home Connections Resource Guide*.

Begin the Day

- Sing "Bingo." Point out the letters in Bingo's name. Call attention to the letters that go together to spell Bingo's name.
- Use the suggestions for Morning Circle offered in the front of this *Teacher's Edition.*

Objective

- To refine and extend understanding of known words

Vocabulary

letters letras

DLM Materials

- *Martí and the Mango/Martí y el mango*

Materials to Gather

- magnetic letters
- name puzzles
- name cards
- felt letters

Preparation

- Make a name puzzle for each child by printing his or her first name on a 4" × 8" strip of tag board, then his or her last name on a matching strip of tag board. Then make puzzle cuts between each letter.
- Make felt alphabet letters.

LITERACY

Focus

- Make up a "Letter Cheer"/"Canción de las letras" for your school name or mascot. For example, if your school mascot is an eagle, your cheer would go like this. You say the first part, and the children do the echo.

Give me an E	(children echo E)
Give me an A	(children echo A)
Give me a G	(children echo G)
Give me an L	(children echo L)
Give me an E	(children echo E)
What's that spell?	(children shout *Eagles*)
Gooooo Eagles!	(everyone shouts)

Develop

One Way to Develop the Lesson

- Use the magnetic letters to spell Bingo's name. Next use the letters to spell your school name or mascot.
- Invite a couple of children to come forward and use the letters to spell their names. Emphasize that letters go together to spell names and words.
- Invite the children to put their names together with the name puzzles you made. Point out again that the letters in their names go together to make up their names.

Another Way to Develop the Lesson

- Teach the children the First and Last Name Cheer. Write the cheer on chart paper, leaving the first and last names blank.
- Go around the circle, allowing each child to fill in his or her name when the cheer is read. Point to the words as you read the cheer.
- Tell the children their first and last names go together to make up their full names. Their first and last names are things that go together.
- Give the children two name cards, one with their first names and one with their last names. Have the children put the two cards together to make their full names.

Practice

- Invite the children to work their name puzzles and the name puzzles of their friends.
- Encourage the children to draw a self-portrait. Have them use their name cards to copy their first and last names onto their portraits.
- Give the children the magnetic letters and encourage them to practice spelling their names, Bingo's name, or the name of their school.
- Make felt letters. Encourage the children to use the letters to spell their names on the flannel board.

Scaffolding Strategies

More Help Encourage the children to find the first letter of their names instead of spelling their entire names.

Extra Challenge Invite the children to spell names of members of their families during the practice session.

Second Language Learners

In some languages, last names precede the first (Chinese, for example). If Jiang's last name is Li, then her Chinese-speaking friends would call her Li Jiang, unless they used American language patterns.

Anthology Support

"The ABC Song"
"La canción del abecedario"
"Nursery Rhyme Rap"
"El rap infantil"

DAY 5

Letter Knowledge

English

- Brainstorm a list of words that start with the letter *f.* Remind the children that the words go together in a group because they all start with the same letter.

Spanish

- Brainstorm a list of words that start with the letter *s*. Remind the children that the words go together in a group because they all start with the same letter.

Suggested Reading

Chicka Chicka Boom Boom by John Archambault and Bill Martin Jr.
Onions and Garlic by Eric Kimmel
Si le das un panecillo a un alce by Laura Joffe Numeroff

Reflect/Assess

- *We put special letters together to spell your name. Who remembers what it is called if we put the letters of your first and last name together?*
  Unimos letras especiales para deletrear nombres. ¿Quién recuerda cómo llamamos al unir las letras del nombre y del apellido?
- *Are any of the letters in your first and last name the same letters?*
  ¿Algunas de las letras de sus nombres y apellidos son iguales?

Literacy Circle

Storytime 1

- Read *Martí and the Mango/Martí y el mango* to the children.
- Point out the alliteration in the story and that the first letter of each animal's name matches the description that the animal gives to Martí for a clue. Words that begin with the same first letter go together because they begin with the same sound.

Storytime 2

- Reread *Wordsong/Canto de palabras* or read the listening story *Pepita's Things/Las cosas de Pepita.*

Content Connection

Physical Development

Objective

To begin to throw or kick an object in a particular direction

Materials to Gather

magnetic or felt letters, beanbag

Vocabulary

letters
letras

Activity 1

- Hide magnetic letters or felt letters indoors or outdoors.
- Have a Letter Hunt where the children try to find the letters they need to spell their names. The first child to find all the necessary letters wins the game.

Activity 2

- Place felt letters on the floor in random order. Have the children take turns tossing a beanbag onto the letter that is the same as the first letter of their names.

DAY 5

Objectives

- To match numerals to collections of items
- To begin to use technical terminology, such as "mouse," "keyboard," "printer," "CD-ROM"

Vocabulary

number número

DLM Materials

- counters
- *Math Resource Guide*
  Listen and Copy/Escucha e imita
  Counting cards (1–5)
  Numeral cards (1 set of 1–5 for each child
  Dot cards
  Memory Game: Numbers version/ Juego de memoria: versión números
  Numeral Jump/Saltar números
  How Many Now?/¿Cuántos hay ahora?
  Cookie Game 1/Juego de la galleta 1 with activity sheet
  Numeral cube
- *DLM Math* software
- *Teacher's Resource Anthology*
  play dough

Materials to Gather

- tactile numeral cards (1–5)
- jump-rope rhymes

Preparation

- Make one copy of the Cookie Game 1 activity sheet for each child.
- Make a Numeral cube with the numerals 1, 2, 3, 4, 5, and 6 on the faces.

MATH

Focus

- Play Listen and Copy/Escucha e imita. Clap any number of times between 1 and 5, inserting pauses occasionally, such as clap, pause, clap, clap, pause; clap, pause, clap; clap, pause; and so on.
- Play Numeral Jump/Saltar números. Tell children you will show a numeral, and they should jump that many times. Repeat with several numerals, changing the action that children perform.
- Ask the children to describe numerals they noticed at home last night.

Develop

- Play How Many Now?/¿Cuántos hay ahora? Give each child a set of 1–5 Counting cards. Show a number of counters (between 1 and 4) and count them with the children. Have the children hold up their Counting cards to show how many there are. Then add 1 counter. Ask children to show the appropriate card. Count to check. Continue, adding or taking away 1 counter each time.
- Reintroduce Cookie Game 1/Juego de la galleta 1 (see Friends, Day 4) with a twist. Children will use a Numeral cube instead of a Dot cube.

Practice

- Cover the tactile numeral cards with clear plastic and challenge the children to make the numbers out of play dough snakes by laying the snakes over the sand numbers.
- Invite the children to play the Memory Game: Numbers version/ Juego de memoria: versión números with matching Numeral and Dot cards.
- Encourage children to play Cookie Game 1/Juego de la galleta 1 with a friend.
- Have the children work on Party Time, Level 2.

Reflect/Assess

- Show the numeral 5. *How do you know how to read this numeral?*
  ¿Cómo saben cómo leer este número?
- *On Party Time, how did you figure out how to get the right number for the party?*
  En La hora de la fiesta, ¿cómo determinaron cómo obtener el número correcto para la fiesta?

Music and Movement

- Play Things That Go Together Musical Chairs. Place one of a pair of go-together items in each chair. When the music stops, have the children find the person who has the match to their item. For example, if I have a shoe, I look for someone with a sock.
- Teach the children jump-rope rhymes that spell words and invite them to jump over a rope to the rhythm of the rhyme.

Suggested Reading

Count! by Denise Fleming
Counting by Karen Bryant-Mole

Content Connection

Social Studies

Objective
To cooperate with others in a joint activity

DLM Materials
Teacher's Resource Anthology
Ants on a Log

Activity 1

- **Allergy Warning** Post simple numeral-word-picture recipes for Ants on a Log for the children to follow: 1 celery stick, 2 spoons peanut butter, 5 raisins. Count the ants and eat!

Activity 2

- Write the numerals 1, 2, and 3 on index cards and lay them on the floor. Have the children call out a numeral and then toss a beanbag to hit that numeral.

Reflect on the Day

- *What other kinds of games could you play with go-together items?*
  ¿Qué otros tipos de juegos podrían jugar con objetos que corresponden?
- *How are things that go together like opposites?*
  ¿En qué se parecen las cosas que van junitas con los opuestos?

Looking Ahead

Connecting to the Theme: Under Construction

Sentences are constructed, items of clothing are constructed, pieces of art are constructed, and so on. Knowing that things are built by combining smaller parts in a certain order, children will begin to understand spatial order. Children's vocabulary should also expand as they learn specialized spatial words.

	Objectives	DLM Materials	Materials to Gather
DAY 1	• To link new learning experiences and vocabulary to what is already known about a topic • To begin to develop pincer control in picking up objects	• Rafita and Pepita • *Teacher's Resource Anthology*	• shape blocks • paper bag • construction paper shapes • felt shapes • shape puzzles • masking tape • shape lacing cards • yarn
DAY 2	• To link new learning experiences and vocabulary to what is already known about a topic • To use a variety of materials to create original work	• Rafita and Pepita • *Sing a Song of Opposites/Canta una canción de opuestos* • *The Itsy Bitsy Spider/La araña pequeñita*	• beanbag • box • plastic foam tray • lace • ribbon • blocks • cups • funnels • finger paint
DAY 3	• To refine and extend understanding of known words • To use simple measuring devices to learn about objects	• Oral Language Cards 33, 42–43, 47–48 • Building Blocks Sequence Cards • *Teacher's Resource Anthology*	• tools • tool puzzles • bulletin board paper • small cars • tempera paint • sand tray • broken toys • bucket • hinges • keys and locks • kitchen gadgets • nuts and bolts • pulley • rope • tubing
DAY 4	• To refine and extend understanding of known words • To begin to engage in dramatic play with others	• *A Birthday Basket for Tía/Una canasta de cumpleaños para Tía* • Birthday Cake Sequence Cards • *The Tortilla Factory/La tortillería* • *Animal Orchestra/La orquesta de los animales*	• orange construction paper • peanut butter • graham crackers • dried flowers • lace • paper plates • rickrack • tissue paper • yarn
DAY 5	• To refine and extend understanding of known words • To begin to perform simple investigations	• *Animals That Build Their Homes/Animales que construyen sus nidos* • *Teacher's Resource Anthology*	• clay • bubble wrap • tempera paint • magnetic letters • chenille wires • powder/flour • tweezers • twigs

(See individual lesson pages for complete lists of materials.)

Learning Centers

CONSTRUCTION

Creative Building and Collage

Objective
To use a variety of materials to create original work

Materials to Gather
construction materials

Develop
Create an active Construction Center. Stock the center with boxes and empty paper towel/toilet paper/wrapping paper tubes. Add egg crates, unused plastic foam trays, orange juice cans, paper plates, and oatmeal containers. Make glue, paste, rickrack, wallpaper samples, tissue paper, magazines, beads, sequins, play dough, and goop available. Encourage the children to build sculptures and make collages.

Reflect/Assess
Which activity did you enjoy most, building a sculpture or making a collage?
¿Qué actividad disfrutaron más, hacer una escultura o hacer un collage?
Which materials did you like using?
¿Qué materiales les gustó usar?

BLOCKS

Our Own Neighborhood

Objective
To group organisms and objects as living or nonliving and begin to identify things people have built

Materials to Gather
brown and green paint, cars, milk cartons or other boxes, plastic toy people, signs, small boxes for homes and buildings, strips of paper for roadways, trucks

Develop
Fill the center with building materials. Prepare ground covers by painting quarter sections of old white sheets brown and green to resemble Earth. Make buildings out of large paper bags and draw storefronts with signs, windows, and doors on them. Have materials on hand for making homes by covering boxes or milk cartons.

Reflect/Assess
Did you choose to build a house, a store, or something else? Why?
¿Eligieron construir una casa, una tienda o algo más? ¿Por qué?

WRITING

Construction Book

Objective
To begin to dictate words, phrases, and sentences to an adult recording on paper

Materials to Gather
crayons, paper, plastic bag book

Develop
Encourage the children to create a class book. Have them draw pictures of what they are learning about construction. Ask them to dictate sentences describing their drawings. At the end of the week, place their drawings in a plastic bag book in the Library Center.

Reflect/Assess
How did you decide what to draw?
¿Cómo decidieron qué pintar?

What Research Suggests

The human brain is under construction. It begins to form on the twenty-fifth day of pregnancy and continues to evolve throughout a person's lifetime. The foundation is wired during the first twelve years of life. During this time, connections are made for everything from vision to fine motor skills to rational thought. During puberty, the brain will prune away all unused circuitry.

Begin the Day

- Sing "Three Straight Sides"/"Tres lados rectos."
- Use the suggestions for Morning Circle offered in the front of this *Teacher's Edition.*

Objective

- To link learning experiences and vocabulary to what is already known about a topic

Vocabulary

circle	círculo
rectangle	rectángulo
square	cuadrado
triangle	triángulo

DLM Materials

- Rafita and Pepita
- *Teacher's Resource Anthology*
  "Freddie the Snake"/"Braulio, la culebra" flannel board story
  "Three Straight Sides"/"Tres lados rectos"
  "Tillie Triangle"/"El Triángulo Tilín"

Materials to Gather

- shape blocks
- paper bag
- construction paper shapes
- felt shapes
- shape puzzles

Preparation

- Make the "Freddie the Snake"/"Braulio, la culebra" flannel board story, if not already made.
- Gather shape blocks for the Mystery game/Juego misterioso.

Literacy

Focus

- Play Mystery Shape/Juego misterioso. Place a shape block in a paper bag. Use Rafita and Pepita to give the children clues about which shape is in the bag. Provide clues until the children guess the shape. Continue playing, using different shapes.
- Tell the children that this week we will be discussing things that we construct. Today we will be reviewing shapes.

Develop

One Way to Develop the Lesson

- Invite the children to make shapes using their bodies. Play the Think, Pair, Share/Piensa, aparea, comparte game. Give the children a shape and a moment to think about it. Have the children select partners with whom to share their ideas. After the pairs have had time to discuss their ideas, encourage them to share with the rest of the class.

Another Way to Develop the Lesson

- Go on a shape search. Take a walk through the school and outdoors. Look for shapes in windows, doors, walls, floors, tiles, and so on. Keep a clip chart with you to list shapes that the children find.

Practice

- Hand out play dough, and encourage the children to make shapes with it. Provide cookie cutters or bottle and box lids to make shapes.
- Cut out felt circles, squares, triangles, and diamonds. Invite the children to create pictures on the flannel board.
- Cut large shapes out of construction paper. Place them on the floor. Give the children a beanbag. Have them call out shapes and try to toss the beanbag onto those shapes.
- Provide shape templates for the children to trace.
- Give the children shape puzzles to work.
- Draw a shape on a piece of paper, and encourage the children to make something out of the shape.

Scaffolding Strategies

More Help Encourage the children to trace each of the shape blocks with their fingers.

Extra Challenge Invite the children to give clues about the shape in the bag.

Second Language Learners

Prior to your shape search, make shapes with straws and strings and talk about them. Reinforce important vocabulary: *I am making a square with my sticks. It has four sides.* Point and count. Ask children to say as much as they can about the shape they make. Expand on their ideas.

Anthology Support

"Window Watching"
"A Square Is a Square"
"Un cuadrado es un cuadrado"
"Circle 'Round the Zero"
"Círculo alrededor de cero"

DAY 1

Letter Knowledge

English

- Introduce the letter *h* with the story "Hasani" in the *English Phonics Resource Guide*.
-  Invite the children to construct letter pretzels in the form of the letter *h*.

Spanish

- Introduce the letter *p* with the story "Pepita" in the *Spanish Phonics Resource Guide*.
- Invite the children to construct letter pretzels in the form of the letter *p*.

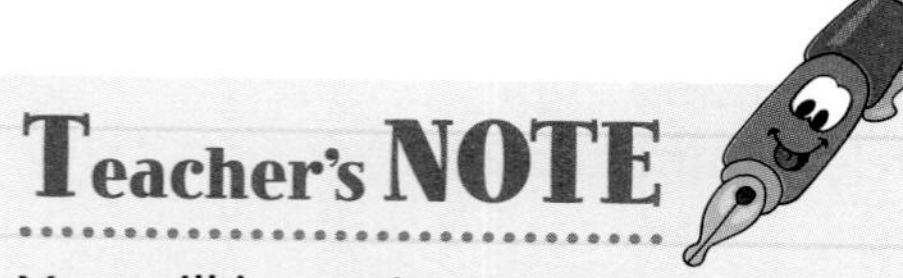

Suggested Reading

Is It Round? Is It Square? by Tana Hoban
The Grandpa Days by Joan Blos
La casa que Jack construyó by Elizabeth Falconer

Teacher's NOTE

You will be reviewing shapes today as an introduction to construction.

Reflect/Assess

- *What shapes did you notice during our tour of the school? Which shapes might you be able to use for your buildings?*

  ¿Qué figuras vieron durante nuestro paseo por la escuela? ¿Qué figuras serían capaces de usar para sus diseños?
- *Why are shapes important when we build things?*

  ¿Por qué son importantes las figuras cuando construímos algo?

Literacy Circle

Storytime 1

- Present the "Freddie the Snake"/"Braulio, la culebra" flannel board story. Give the children pieces of yarn. Using the yarn, have them make the shapes that Freddie/Braulio changes into in the story.

Storytime 2

- Present the "Tillie Triangle"/"El Triángulo Tilín" chalk story.

Content Connection

Physical Development

Objectives

To begin to share and cooperate with others in group activities

To begin to develop pincer control in picking up objects

Vocabulary

circle, rectangle, square, triangle

círculo, rectángulo, cuadrado, triángulo

Materials to Gather

masking tape, shape lacing cards, yarn

Activity 1

- Hand out shape lacing cards, and invite the children to lace various shapes.

Activity 2

- Tape small dots of masking tape (about 6 inches apart) on the floor, making the outlines of a circle (hula-hoop size), a 2-by-2-foot square, a triangle with a 2-foot base, and a 1-by-3-foot rectangle. Give the children 8-foot pieces of yarn. Ask them to work with partners to connect the dots with yarn.

DAY 1

Objectives

- To begin to recognize, describe, and name shapes
- To start, use, and exit software programs

Vocabulary

circular	circular
rectangular	rectangular
triangular	triangular
cylinder	cilindro

DLM Materials

- *Math Resource Guide*
  Memory Game: Geometry version/ Juego de memoria: versión geométrica
  Memory Game: Geometry cards (Sets A and D)
- *DLM Math* software
- *Teacher's Resource Anthology*
  "A Square Is a Square"/"Un cuadrado es un cuadrado"
  Hopscotch/Rayuela
  Square Dance/Baile de figuras

Materials to Gather

- building blocks or several sets of 3-dimensional shapes (cylinders, cones, balls)

Preparation

- Prepare Memory Game: Geometry cards (Sets A and D).

MATH

Focus

- Recite "A Square Is a Square"/"Un cuadrado es un cuadrado" with the children.

Develop

- Give each child a small set of building blocks. Ask the children to describe the blocks. Help them clarify their language. The goal is for children to explore and describe 3-dimensional shapes in their own words, but it is often appropriate to help them clarify their thinking. For example, when they call a block a rectangle, you might confirm that they are correct, it is a rectangular block, and the faces are all rectangles.
- Using the blocks, build something as the children watch. Express your thoughts as you are building. For example, *I think I will put this big block on the bottom. Then I will put this triangular block on top*, and so on.

  Creo que voy a poner este bloque grande en la parte de abajo. Luego pondré este bloque triangular arriba y así sucesivamente.

  Challenge them to copy your structure with their blocks.
- Introduce the computer activity Memory—Geometry, Level 2. Children match similar shapes that are different sizes, such as a large square with a small square. Have children point out matching shapes.

Practice

- Invite the children to play freely with the building blocks. Suggest using the blocks for construction. Talk with them about why they used certain shaped blocks in their building.
- Encourage pairs or small groups of children to play the Memory Game: Geometry version/Juego de memoria: versión geométrica.
- Have the children work on Memory—Geometry, Level 2.

Reflect/Assess

- *Why were some pieces helpful in making your buildings?*
  ¿Por qué algunas piezas fueron útiles al hacer sus edificios?

Content Connection

Physical Development/Science

Objectives
To explore moving in space
To use patterns to predict what happens next

Materials to Gather
paintbrushes, paint

Activity 1

- Invite the children to get into groups of 3 and stand between a light source and the wall to create 3 shadows on the wall. Have them count the shadows. Show them how to move closer to the light source to make the shadows bigger.

Activity 2

- Invite the children to create patterns by painting 3 wide lines using a wide paintbrush, then 2 narrow lines using a thin paintbrush. Repeat the pattern. Discuss the role numbers play when making patterns.

Music and Movement

- Have the children play Hopscotch/Rayuela. Make a masking tape grid indoors or a chalk grid outdoors. Call attention to the shape of the grid. Use a circular chip or coin for the marker.
- Teach the children a simple Square Dance/Baile de figuras. Call attention to the fact that they are standing in a square. Point out that the dance is constructed by connecting various steps.

Suggested Reading

Changes, Changes by Pat Hutchins
Shape Space by Cathryn Falwell

Reflect on the Day

- *What is something new you learned about shapes?*
  ¿Qué cosa nueva aprendieron sobre las formas/figuras?
- *When you go home today, look for shapes in your houses. Tomorrow we will talk about any shapes that you found.*
  Cuando se vayan a la casa hoy, fíjense en las formas o figuras en sus casas. Mañana hablaremos sobre cualquier forma o figura que hayan encontrado.

Home Connection

Let families know that children will be learning about growing things next week. The class will discuss how people grow. Ask families to send baby photos and current photos of their children. Photos are needed by this Friday in order to get them copied in time.

Begin the Day

- Perform the action story "Going on a Bear Hunt"/"Vamos a cazar un oso." Use Rafita and Pepita to assist you. Discuss the spatial vocabulary from the story.
- Ask about the shapes that the children found at home last night.
- Use the suggestions for Morning Circle offered in the front of this *Teacher's Edition*.

Objective

- To link new learning experiences and vocabulary to what is already known about a topic

Vocabulary

bottom	parte inferior
down	abajo
in	dentro
inside	dentro de
middle	medio
near	cerca
off	fuera de
on	sobre
out	afuera
outside	exterior
over	sobre
top	parte superior
under	debajo
up	arriba

DLM Materials

- Rafita and Pepita
- *Sing a Song of Opposites/Canta una canción de opuestos*
- *The Itsy Bitsy Spider/La araña pequeñita*

Materials to Gather

- beanbag
- box
- plastic foam tray
- lace
- ribbon
- blocks
- cups
- funnels

Focus

- Set up an obstacle course in the classroom or outside. As the children move through the course, ask them to describe their movements. Encourage answers such as *over, under,* and *around*.
- Tell the children that today we will be talking about words that tell us where something is.

Develop

One Way to Develop the Lesson

- Invite two volunteers to sit back-to-back with six to eight different-shaped blocks in front of them. Give directions that let the volunteers know what to do with the blocks. For example, place a square block on top of a rectangular block; place an arched block beside a square block. Continue until you have given directions that utilize all the blocks.
- Have the children compare what they built. Children will enjoy analyzing how it is possible that two of them could produce different constructions while following the same instructions.

Another Way to Develop the Lesson

- Play I Spy/Yo espío. Give clues that require the children to use their knowledge of spatial vocabulary. For example, the child could say: *I spy something red on top of the desk. I spy something round near the door. I spy something long on the middle shelf.*

  Veo algo rojo sobre la mesa. Veo algo redondo cerca de la puerta. Veo algo largo en el estante del medio.

Practice

- Invite the children to weave lace and ribbon using the plastic foam looms.
- Provide a box and a beanbag. Invite the children to toss the beanbag into the box, beside the box, over the box, and near the box.
- Provide cups and funnels at the water play table for exploring *in* and *out*.
- Create a masking tape track. Invite the children to walk on the line with beanbags on their heads, under their arms, and in their hands.
- Use an empty area of the floor to let the children work on puzzles.

Preparation

- Prepare an obstacle course.
- Make weaving trays by running yarn around unused foam trays to create looms.

Scaffolding Strategies

More Help Create simple one-attribute and one-spatial direction clues for the I Spy/Yo espío.

Extra Challenge Invite the children to be the callers in I Spy/Yo espío.

Second Language Learners

Play the beanbag game before you play I Spy/Yo espío. Review children's spatial vocabulary by asking them to toss the beanbag into, beside, over, and near the box. If they miss, tell them where the beanbag fell: *It is not in the box. It is beside the box.* Stress key vocabulary.

Anthology Support

"Little Red Apple"
"Manzanita roja"
"Open, Shut Them"
"Ábranlas, ciérrenlas"

DAY 2

Letter Knowledge

English

- Have the children form the letter *h* with play dough.

Spanish

- Have the children form the letter *p* with play dough.

Suggested Reading

Look Up, Look Down by Tana Hoban
Over, Under and Through by Tana Hoban
Soy un pájaro by J. L. Garcia Sanchez
Machines at Work by Byron Barton

Reflect/Assess

- *Why is it important to understand directions?*
  ¿Por qué es importante entender las instrucciones?
- *Where can you find the following things: an airplane, a car, a giraffe, a clown?*
  ¿Dónde pueden encontrar las siguientes cosas: un avión, un carro, una jirafa, un payaso?

Literacy Circle

Storytime 1

- Read *Sing a Song of Opposites/Canta una canción de opuestos*. Discuss the spatial vocabulary in the story.

Storytime 2

- Read *The Itsy Bitsy Spider/La araña pequeñita*. Discuss the spatial vocabulary in the first part of the book. Review the theme of the book as it applies to things people make and build. Use the example of the man and the birdhouse.

Content Connection

Fine Arts

Objective
To use a variety of materials to create original work

Vocabulary
bottom, left, middle, right, top
parte inferior; izquierdo(a); medio, mitad; derecho(a); parte superior

Materials to Gather
finger paint, paper

Activity 1

- Have the children fold their papers in three sections. Instruct them to draw three different pictures (one in the top section, another in the middle, and a third in the bottom section).

Activity 2

- Invite the children to fold pieces of paper in half. Have them place their right palms in finger paint. Encourage children to make right hand prints on the right sides of their paper. Repeat on the left side with left hands.

Objectives

- To begin to use words that indicate where things are in space
- To begin to recognize when a shape's position or orientation has changed

Vocabulary

circular	circular
cylinder	cilindro
ball	pelota
cone	cono
block	bloque

DLM Materials

- *Math Resource Guide*
  Getting into Shape/Tomar forma
  Memory Game: Geometry version/ Juego de memoria: versión geométrica
  Memory Game: Geometry cards (Sets A and D)
- *DLM Math* software
- *Four Baby Bumblebees* CD
- *Teacher's Resource Anthology*
  bubble soap

Materials to Gather

- building blocks or several sets of 3-dimensional shapes (cylinders, cones, balls)
- oatmeal carton

MATH

Focus

- Show the children several cylinders. Discuss their attributes and what the children can do with them.
- Cylinders are made of circular faces (the bases or ends) and a curved surface (the side). Cones also have a circular face and a curved surface. Spheres have only a curved surface.

Develop

- Give each child a small group of 3-dimensional shapes. Ask children to tell you which blocks roll and which don't roll and why. As children respond, help them clarify their language and their thinking.
- Play Getting into Shape/Tomar forma. Show the oatmeal carton. Trace around the ends with your finger and then around the side with your hand. Invite the children to do the same. Encourage them to express how the shape feels. Ask children to stand up and pretend they are inside the oatmeal carton. As you give the following directions, model the behaviors. *Touch the insides. Touch the top of the cylinder. Trace around the top with your hands. What shape is that? Trace around the bottom with your foot. Now move all around inside the cylinder.*
  Toquen la parte de adentro. Toquen la parte de arriba del cilindro. Delineen la parte de arriba con sus manos. ¿Qué figura es ésa? Delineen la parte de abajo con un pie. Ahora sientan toda la parte de adentro del cilindro.

Practice

- Invite the children to play freely with the building blocks. Challenge them to sort blocks into those that roll and those that do not roll.
- Encourage pairs or small groups of children to play the Memory Game: Geometry version/Juego de memoria: versión geométrica.
- Children can work on Memory—Geometry, Level 2.

Reflect/Assess

- *What did you feel inside your pretend cylinder? How did the top feel?*
  ¿Qué sintieron adentro del cilindro imaginario? ¿Cómo se sintió la parte de arriba?
- *How many circle faces did your cylinder have?*
  ¿Cuántas caras circulares tenía el cilindro?

Music and Movement

- Perform "Looby Loo" from the *Four Baby Bumblebees* CD. Discuss the spatial vocabulary.
- Give the children bubble soap and wands. Have them blow bubbles. Discuss with them what the bubbles do.

Content Connection

Social Studies/Science

Objectives
To identify common features of local landscapes
To begin to perform simple investigations

Materials to Gather
books with cylinder shapes, coffee cans, blocks of different weights

Activity 1

- Explain that cans are a shape called *cylinders*. Ask what else is in the shape of a cylinder, such as cans (silos, tanker trucks, building blocks). Look through books to find pictures of them.

Activity 2

- Place blocks of different weights inside coffee cans. Encourage the children to roll the cans to determine what difference the weight makes.

Suggested Reading

Cubes, Cones, Cylinders & Spheres by Tana Hoban
Shape Space by Cathryn Falwell

Reflect on the Day

- *Where is your bed where you live?*
  ¿Dónde tienen su cama donde viven?
- *What do you need to know in order to be able to tell someone where you live?*
  ¿Qué tienen que saber para poder decirle a alguien dónde viven?

Home Connection

Suggest that the children work with their families to create simple maps of their routes from home to school.

Begin the Day

- Sing "Wheels on the Bus"/"Ruedas del bus." Ask: *On what do buses travel?*

  ¿Por dónde circulan los autobuses?
- Use the suggestions for Morning Circle in the front of this *Teacher's Edition.*

Objective

- To refine and extend understanding of known words

Vocabulary

architects	arquitectos(as)
bulldozers	topadora
construction	construcción
construction workers	trabajadores de la construcción
highways	autopistas
roads	caminos
skyscrapers	rascacielos
tractors	tractores

DLM Materials

- *SRA Photo Library* software
- Oral Language Development Cards 33, 42, 43, 47, 48
- Building Blocks Sequence Cards
- *Teacher's Resource Anthology*
  "The Three Little Pigs"/"Los tres cerditos" flannel board story
  "This Is the House That Jack Built"/"Ésta es la casa que Juan construyó" flannel board story
  Tool Match card patterns

Materials to Gather

- tools
- tool puzzles
- bulletin board paper
- small cars
- tempera paint
- sand tray

LITERACY

Focus

- Sing "Johnny Works with One Hammer"/"Juan trabaja con un martillo."
- Tell the children that they will be learning about the construction of roads, highways, buildings, and homes today. Describe construction as building or putting something together.

Develop

One Way to Develop the Lesson

- Display Oral Language Cards 42–43 and 47–48. Discuss the differences between these vehicles. Ask: *Why can't buses and cars drive on sidewalks?*

  ¿Por qué los autobuses y los carros no pueden circular por las aceras?
- Discuss road construction (most children have seen this). Talk about bulldozers, tractors, dump trucks, and other equipment. Discuss what it takes to make roads for vehicles.

Another Way to Develop the Lesson

- Display Oral Language Card 33. Discuss the construction of buildings and homes. Ask: *What does it take to build a home? Who are the people who work on buildings? How are tall buildings different from homes?*

  ¿Qué hay que hacer para construir una casa? ¿Quiénes son las personas que trabajan en las construcciones? ¿En qué se diferencian los edificios altos de las casas?
- Discuss tools used for construction. Show typical tools such as a hammer, a saw, a screwdriver, and so on. Be sure to keep any real tools out of reach of the children. If you don't have real tools, show cards from the Tool Match game. Ask: *Have you ever seen these tools used? Who was using them? What were they doing?*

  ¿Alguna vez han visto cómo se usan estas herramientas? ¿Quién las usaba? ¿Qué hacían?

Practice

- Encourage the children to build highways and roads in the Blocks Center. Color bulletin board paper gray and place it on the floor to create a highway. Give the children yellow markers and white crayons to draw a dotted line down the middle of the road.
- Invite the children to sequence the Building Blocks Sequence Cards.
- Provide tempera paint and small cars. Invite the children to roll cars through the paint and then across the paper to create a track.
- Give the children the Tool Match game. Have them match the cards or play a game of Tool Concentration.
- Invite the children to work on tool puzzles.
- Write *tool* on an index card and have the children copy the word in a sand tray using their fingers.
- Have the children find the items in the Equipment category of the *SRA Photo Library* software that are used for building. Have them use the photos to fill in this sentence. I took my ___________ to tighten the screws. Then I used my ___________ to make a hole and my ___________ to tighten the nut on the bolt I put through the hole.

Preparation

- Prepare flannel board stories.
- Gather construction tools.
- Prepare the Tool Match game using the tool match card patterns.
- Photocopy another set of tool patterns. Laminate the copies, and cut them into puzzle pieces.
- Have the children explore the Structures on the *SRA Photo Library* software. Ask them to identify a structure they would like to see.

Scaffolding Strategies

More Help Take the children outdoors to look at nearby roads and sidewalks.

Extra Challenge Invite the children to look at a road map. Point out the roads. Call attention to roads that are local and to roads that are highways.

Second Language Learners

Play Make Yours Like Mine using color and shape blocks. Two children sit back to back. Each has a shoe box lid and a sack of color and shape blocks (the sacks hold identical block sets). One child describes where to put the blocks. The other child follows the directions. Note their language and check if their designs are the same.

Letter Knowledge

English

- Have the children locate the letter *h* in magazines and newspapers.

Spanish

- Have the children locate the letter *p* in magazines and newspapers.

Suggested Reading

Construction Zone by Tana Hoban
Soy una roca by J. L. Garcia Sanchez
Truck by Donald Crews

Anthology Support

"El cochecito"
"Go In and Out the Windows"
"Entra y sale por la ventana"

Reflect/Assess

- *How are highways and sidewalks different? How are they alike?*
  ¿En qué se diferencian las autopistas y las aceras? ¿En qué se parecen?
- *Which tools and materials do you think people used to build this school?*
  ¿Qué herramientas y materiales creen que usaron las personas que construyeron esta escuela?

Literacy Circle

Storytime 1

- Present "The Three Little Pigs"/"Los tres cerditos" flannel board story. Discuss the materials that each pig uses to build his home.

Storytime 2

- Present the "This Is the House That Jack Built"/"Ésta es la casa que Juan construyó" flannel board story. Encourage the children to clap out a few lines of the story to pick up the rhythm.

Content Connection

Science

Objective
To use simple measuring devices to learn about objects and organisms

Materials to Gather
broken toys, bucket, hinges, keys and locks, kitchen gadgets, nuts and bolts, pulley, rope, tubing

Activity 1

- Create a safe junk table. Allow the children to explore the items. If possible, provide plastic tools (screwdrivers, wrenches, and so on) for them to use on the junk.

Activity 2

- Construct a pulley in the classroom. If it is sturdy enough, hang it from the ceiling. Run a rope through the pulley, knot one end of the rope, and tie a pail to the other end. Invite the children to experiment with lifting various items (blocks) using the pulley.

DAY 3

Objective

- To begin to recognize, describe, and name shapes

Vocabulary

circular	circular
cylinder	cilindro
ball	pelota
block	bloque

DLM Materials

- *Math Resource Guide* Getting into Shape/Tomar forma
- See Day 1
- *DLM Math* software
- *Four Baby Bumblebees* CD
- *Teacher's Resource Anthology* Red Light! Green Light!/¡Luz roja! ¡Luz verde!

Materials to Gather

- an assortment of balls
- See Day 1

More Help Give the children many opportunities to manipulate a variety of cylindrical and spherical objects.

Extra Challenge Ask the children to express how the cylinders and the spheres are the same and how they are different.

MATH

Focus

- Distribute an assortment of balls. Ask the children to describe the attributes of the balls. Encourage them to express what they can do with the balls as well as how they look.

Develop

- Play Getting into Shape/Tomar forma with a large beach ball. Ask the children to sit in a circle. Show the ball to the children and feel all around the outside of it. Mention that you don't feel any corners on this shape. Roll the ball back and forth across the circle and encourage the children to feel it. Take the ball away and ask the children to pretend they are holding it. Invite them to move their hands all around it to show its shape and size. Roll it to each other. Then ask them to pretend they are inside the ball. *Feel all around the inside of your ball, or sphere. Go all around the inside with your fingertips. Can you touch the inside with other parts of your body?*

  Toquen toda la parte de adentro de su pelota o esfera. Toquen toda la parte de adentro con las puntas de sus dedos. ¿Pueden tocar la parte de adentro con otras partes de su cuerpo?
- You may wish to suggest that the children close their eyes as they pretend to be inside the 3-dimensional shape.

Practice

- Invite the children to play freely with the building blocks.
- Encourage children to play Memory Game: Geometry version/Juego de memoria: versión geométrica with the cards.
- Have the children work on Memory—Geometry, Level 2.

Reflect/Assess

- *Describe the shape of your ball.*
  Describan la forma de su pelota.
- *What can your ball do?*
  ¿Qué puede hacer la pelota?

Music and Movement

- Play "Who's Afraid of the Big Bad Wolf?" from the *Four Baby Bumblebees* CD.
- Play Red Light! Green Light!/¡Luz roja! ¡Luz verde!

Content Connection

Fine Arts

Objectives
To use different colors, surface textures, and shapes to create form and meaning
To use a variety of materials to create original work

Materials to Gather
large box, round containers, wallpaper scraps, glue

Activity 1

- Invite the children to draw and make designs on the faces of a large box.

Activity 2

- Invite the children to decorate a round container, such as an oatmeal box or potato chip can, with wallpaper scraps.

Suggested Reading

Cubes, Cones, Cylinders & Spheres by Tana Hoban

Reflect on the Day

- *What are all of the things we talked about that can be constructed?*
  ¿Cuáles son todas las cosas de las que hablamos y que se pueden construir?
- *What do you enjoy about constructing something?*
  ¿Qué les gusta al construir algo?

Home Connection

On Thursday of next week, the class will make tortillas. Send a note home asking for family volunteers to help with the cooking.

Begin the Day

- Sing "Peanut Butter"/"Mantequilla de maní." Discuss how sandwiches are constructed.
- Use the suggestions for Morning Circle offered in the front of this *Teacher's Edition*.

Objective

- To refine and extend understanding of known words

Vocabulary

construct construir
construction construcción

DLM Materials

- *A Birthday Basket for Tía/Una canasta de cumpleaños para Tía*
- Birthday Cake Sequence Cards
- *The Tortilla Factory/La tortillería* book and listening tape
- *Animal Orchestra/La orquesta de los animales*

Materials to Gather

- orange construction paper
- peanut butter
- graham crackers
- felt cake and candles

Preparation

- Gather the felt cake and candles from last week's lesson.
- Gather graham crackers and peanut butter.
- Cut large sheets of orange construction paper into diamond shapes.

LITERACY

Focus

- Invite the children to make up a song. Suggest a simple tune like "Mary Had a Little Lamb"/"María tenía una corderita" or "Itsy Bitsy Spider"/"La araña pequeñita." Give them a topic such as playing ball or painting at the easel.
- Explain that they have just constructed a song.

Develop

One Way to Develop the Lesson

- Review construction. Ask the children to name things discussed in yesterday's lesson. Remind them that *construction* means "putting things together." Explain that they "constructed" a song this morning. Invite them to help you make a list of things that can be constructed (for example, books, costumes, meals, music, gifts, homes, and so on). Make sure your list has only one item per line, has well-spaced lowercase letters, and uses picture symbols as well as words.
- Reread the book *A Birthday Basket for Tía/Una canasta de cumpleaños para Tía*. Because the book is long, you may want to read it in two parts. Ask the children what Cecilia is constructing in the story. *¿Qué construye Cecilia en el cuento?*
- Ask the children about things they have made. Discuss something you have made. Remind them about making kites and drums last week.

Another Way to Develop the Lesson

- Read *The Tortilla Factory/La tortillería*. Ask what is constructed in the story.
- Discuss the steps it takes for seeds to be made into tortillas. Talk about the workers who plant the seeds and the workers who make the tortillas. Discuss what these workers are called.
- Ask the children to describe their own experiences with cooking. *Have you ever made something to eat? If so, how did you do it?* *¿Alguna vez han hecho algo para comer? Si es así, ¿cómo lo hicieron?*

Practice

- **(Allergy Warning)** Invite the children to construct a snack of graham crackers and peanut butter.
- Prepare the flannel board cake and candles from last week's lesson. Invite the children to pretend to be bakers designing birthday cakes. You could add stars, hearts, and flowers as decorations.
- Invite the children to make "Under Construction" signs for the Blocks Center. Cut large sheets of orange construction paper into diamond shapes. Write the words *Under Construction* on one as a pattern.
- Place *The Tortilla Factory/La tortillería* book and tape in the Listening Center.
- Place the Birthday Cake Sequence Cards in the Language Center. Have children sequence the cards.

Scaffolding Strategies

More Help Encourage the children to think about getting dressed this morning. Each item they put on was a step in constructing their outfits.

Extra Challenge Encourage the children to think about how putting a sentence together is constructing a sentence.

Second Language Learners

Make a recipe poster using labels for graham cracker snacks. Describe the snack's preparation and tape the directions. Place graham crackers, an empty peanut butter jar, and plastic knives in the Listening Center. Have children pretend to make the snack as they listen to the tape.

Anthology Support

"Pat-a-Cake"
"Humpty Dumpty Sat on a Wall"
"Humpty Dumpty se sentó en la pared"
"Let's Pretend to Bake a Cake"
"Pretendamos como que horneamos un pastel"

DAY 4

Letter Knowledge

English

- Read "I'll walk halfway to your house" from the *SRA Alphabet Book.*

Spanish

- Read "El pato" from *Los niños alfabéticos.*

Suggested Reading

Jennie's Hat by Ezra Jack Keats
El pintorcito de Sabana Grande by Patricia Maloney Markun
Architecture: Shapes by Michael Crosbie and Steve Rosenthal

Teacher's NOTE

Point out the many times a day that the children construct things (for example, by painting in the Art Center or building in the Blocks Center).

Reflect/Assess

- *Who can tell me about something that they constructed?*
  ¿Quién me puede hablar sobre algo que construyeron?
- *Does anyone you know have a job that involves construction?*
  ¿Alguna persona que conocen tiene un trabajo que tenga que ver con la construcción?

Literacy Circle

Storytime 1

- Read the last half of *A Birthday Basket for Tía/Una canasta de cumpleaños para Tía*. Help the children name all of the items that Cecilia included.
  Nombren todos los objetos que Cecilia incluyó.

Storytime 2

- Read *Animal Orchestra/La orquesta de los animales*. Discuss the music and how the orchestra will construct it together.

Content Connection

Fine Arts

Objective
To begin to engage in dramatic play with others

Vocabulary
artisans, construct, designers, milliners
artesanos, construir, diseñadores, sombrerero

Materials to Gather
dried flowers, lace, paper plates, rickrack, tissue paper, yarn

Activity 1

- Invite the children to make hats. Cut the center out of 8-inch paper plates. Carefully staple 12-inch pieces of yarn to each side of the plates. Have the children decorate their hats with tissue paper, dried flowers, or whatever materials are available. Tell them that they are pretending to be milliners.

Activity 2

- Provide dress-up clothes and accessories in the Dramatic Play Center. Let the children pretend to be fashion designers.

DAY 4

Objective

- To begin to recognize, describe, and name shapes

Vocabulary

circular	circular
rectangular	rectangular
triangular	triangular
cylinder	cilindro
ball	pelota
cone	cono
box	caja
block	bloque

DLM Materials

- *Math Resource Guide*
  Getting into Shape/Tomar Forma
  Memory Game: Geometry version/ Juego de memoria: versión geométrica
  Memory Game: Geometry cards (Sets A and D)
- *DLM Math* software
- *Where Is Thumbkin?* CD
- *Teacher's Resource Anthology*
  "Hi, My name is Joe!"/"¡Hola, me llamo Joe!"

Materials to Gather

- building blocks or several sets of 3-dimensional shapes (cylinders, cones, balls)
- large appliance box
- rectangular box

MATH

Focus

- Give each child a small set of 3-dimensional shapes. Ask them which blocks stack well, which can be stacked on, which are good only on the top of a stack, which won't stack at all, and which roll. As children respond, help them clarify their language and their thinking.
- Just as lines can be parallel, the faces of a 3-dimensional shape can be parallel. The parallel faces of cylinders (the 2 circular bases) make them good for stacking. Rectangular blocks (prisms) have several parallel faces, so they stack in several ways.

Develop

- Play Getting into Shape/Tomar Forma with a rectangular box. Pass it around and allow the children to examine it. Then ask children to pretend they are inside the box. *Touch the insides. Choose one face and feel every bit of it. What shape is it? Feel the top and the bottom. Move your hands to a corner of the box. How does that feel?* Have them move their hands and feet to a corner.
  Toquen la parte de adentro. Escojan una cara y tóquenla toda. ¿Qué forma tiene? Toquen la parte de arriba y la de abajo. Muevan sus manos a una esquina de la caja. ¿Cómo se siente? Muevan sus manos y pies a una esquina.
- Invite children to investigate the large appliance box, inside and out. Encourage them to describe all their experiences.

Practice

- Encourage children to play freely with the building blocks. Challenge them to use the blocks in new ways. Have children express their ideas.
- Invite children to play Memory Game: Geometry version/Juego de memoria: versión geometríca with the cards.
- Encourage the children to work on any of last week's Practice activities.
- Have the children work on Memory—Geometry, Level 2.

Reflect/Assess

- *Which blocks stack the best when you build? Why?*
  ¿Qué bloques se apilan mejor cuando construyen? ¿Por qué?
- *What did you feel inside your pretend box? How did the top feel?*
  ¿Qué sintieron al tocar la parte de adentro de la caja imaginaria? ¿Cómo se sintió la parte de arriba?

Music and Movement

- Sing "Peanut Butter" from the *Where Is Thumbkin?* CD.
- Perform the "Hi, My Name Is Joe!"/"¡Hola, me llamo Joe!" action chant. Discuss factories and what happens in them.

Content Connection

Social Studies

Objectives

To identify common features of local landscapes

To begin to use words to indicate relative location

DLM Materials

SRA Photo Library software

Activity 1

- Show the children the structures on the *SRA Photo Library* software.
- Have the children find 3-dimensional shapes in these constructions. Have the children look for *stacking* in any of the constructions.

Activity 2

- During clean-up time, have the children pay attention to how materials are stacked. Ask: *Which shapes of toys stack best?*
  ¿Qué formas de juguetas se apilan mejor?

Suggested Reading

Building a House
by Byron Barton
Bridges Connect
by Less Sullivan Hill
Up Goes the Skyscraper!
by Gail Gibbons
I Spy Two Eyes: Numbers in Art devised and selected by Lucy Micklethwait

What Research Suggests

Children name most 3-dimensional shapes like a block, as 2-dimensional shapes. They can learn to distinguish the two and start to use 3-dimensional and 2-dimensional names appropriately.

Reflect on the Day

- *What did you learn about construction?*
  ¿Qué aprendieron sobre la constucción?
- *Which activity was your favorite?*
  ¿Qué activadad fue su favorita?

Home Connection

Send take-home book packs home with four children. The directions and a recording sheet for this are in the *Home Connections Resource Guide*. Remind families that you need baby and current photos by tomorrow.

Begin the Day

- Sing "The Ants Go Marching"/"Las hormiguitas marchan." Discuss how ants build their homes underground.
- Use the suggestions for Morning Circle offered in the front of this *Teacher's Edition.*

Objective

- To refine and extend understanding of known words

Vocabulary

burrows	madrigueras
caves	cuevas
dam	cabaña
hills	colinas
hives	colmenas
nest	nidos
web	red

DLM Materials

- *Animals That Build Their Homes/ Animales que construyen sus nidos* book and listening tape
- *Teacher's Resource Anthology* Animal Homes card patterns

Materials to Gather

- clay
- bubble wrap
- tempera paint
- magnetic letters

Preparation

- Make the Animal Homes Match game, if not already made, using the Animal Homes card patterns.

Literacy

Focus

- Help the children recall all the things that can be constructed. Make a list on chart paper.
- Tell them that animals construct things. Explain that they will learn about how animals build their homes.

Develop

One Way to Develop the Lesson

- Show the cover of *Animals That Build Their Homes/Animales que construyen sus nidos*. Ask the children to name the animals on the cover.
- Read the book to page 17. If the text seems long, you may paraphrase. Pause as each animal is mentioned. Discuss the name of the animal's home and how the animal builds its home. Review some tools animals use to build, such as beaks, teeth spinners, pinchers, and legs.

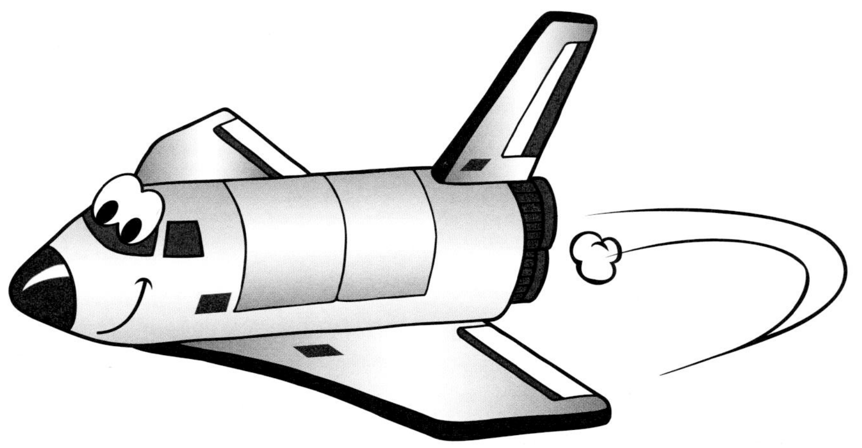

Another Way to Develop the Lesson

- Read the rest of *Animals That Build Their Homes/Animales que construyen sus nidos*. Again, paraphrase if necessary. Pause for discussion after each animal is introduced.

Practice

- Place *Animals That Build Their Homes/Animales que construyen sus nidos* book and listening tape in the Listening Center.
- Give the children the Animal Homes Match game. Invite them to match the cards or to play a game of Concentration.
- Give the children clay, and invite them to shape a wasp's nest.
- Provide bubble wrap. Have the children dip it in paint and press it onto paper to create honeycomb prints.
- Write the word *animals/animales* on an index card. Encourage the children to copy it using magnetic letters.

Scaffolding Strategies

More Help Take the children outdoors to find animal homes. Be sure to discuss the dangers of getting too close to an anthill or a bee's nest.

Extra Challenge Help children brainstorm a list of animals for which people provide homes (cats, birds, or dogs). Discuss where else they would live if they did not live with people.

Second Language Learners

Play Go Home, Go Home, Ant Go Home/ A tu casa, a tu casa, Hormiga, a tu casa. Use a plastic ant or a small photo of an ant. Lay animal home cards on the floor. Cover them, place an ant under an animal home, and then remove the cover. Children chant: *Go home, go home, ant go home.* Have them guess where the ant is: *Is it in the nest?* Flip the cards as the children guess. Repeat until they find the ant.

Anthology Support

"Birdie, Birdie, Where Is Your Nest?"
"¿Pajarito, pajarito, dónde está tu nido?"
"There Was a Little Turtle"
"Había una tortuguita"
"Over in the Meadow"
"Sobre la pradera"

DAY 5

Letter Knowledge

English

- Invite the children to make the letter *h* in sand trays. Provide sandpaper letters for the children to trace and rub.

Spanish

- Invite the children to make the letter *p* in sand trays. Provide sandpaper letters for the children to trace and rub.

Suggested Reading

Animal Homes by Illa Podendorf
Knee High Norman by Laurence Anholt
La casa en el aire by Edna Torres
La canción del lagarto by George Shannon

Reflect/Assess

- *How is a bird's nest like a beaver's dam?*
  ¿En qué se parecen un nido de aves y una cabaña de castores?
- *Which of the animal homes do you find most interesting?*
  ¿Cuál de las casas de animales encuentran más interesante?

Literacy Circle

Storytime 1

- Present the "Animal Homes"/"Hogares de animales" flannel board story.

Storytime 2

- Present the "Ms. Bumblebee Gathers Honey"/"La avispa Zumbi lleva miel" prop story.

Content Connection

Science

Objective
To begin to perform simple investigations

Vocabulary
beak, pollen
pico, polen

Materials to Gather
chenille wires, powder/flour, tweezers, twigs

Activity 1

- Invite the children to use tweezers to represent bird beaks. Provide small twigs. Encourage them to build a nest.

Activity 2

- Bend several chenille wires in half. Invite the children to use the chenille wires to pick up powder/flour. Have them brush the chenille wire ends together to disperse the powder/flour. Explain that this process is similar to the technique bees use to gather pollen.

DAY 5

Objectives

- To begin to recognize, describe, and name shapes
- To follow basic oral and pictorial cues for operating programs successfully

Vocabulary

circular	circular
rectangular	rectangular
triangular	triangular
cylinder	cilindro
ball	pelota
cone	cono
box	caja
block	bloque
touch	tocar

DLM Materials

- *Math Resource Guide*
  Mystery Box
  Memory Game: Geometry version/ Juego de memoria: versión geométrica
  Memory Game: Geometry cards (Sets A and D)
- *DLM Math* software
- *Where Is Thumbkin?* CD
- *Teacher's Resource Anthology*
  I Spy/Yo espío
  "Going on a Bear Hunt"/"Vamos a cazar un oso"

Materials to Gather

- familiar objects for Mystery Box
- 2 identical sets of building blocks or 3-dimensional shapes (cylinders, cones, balls)

MATH

Focus

- Play I Spy/Yo espío using geometric terms to describe objects.

Develop

- Secretly hide a familiar object in the Mystery Box. Have a child feel the object and try to identify it before pulling it out to check.
- Show 1 of the 2 identical sets of solids. Pass the shapes around. Explain that you have to feel the whole shape to know what it is, not just 1 part. Secretly put 1 solid from 1 of the sets into the Mystery Box. Have the children feel the shape and identify which of the displayed shapes they are feeling. Repeat.
- All objects have 3 dimensions. Help children see that we are looking at faces of the objects (e.g., the top of a drum is a circle). Similarly, a child may confuse a ball (sphere) with a circle, in which case a "slice" of the sphere is a circle.
- Complete a task from Memory—Geometry, Level 2, with the children. As you identify each shape on the computer, ask the children if they can find a face on a block that is the same shape.

Practice

- Encourage children to continue to work with the Mystery Box, using the identical sets of 3-dimensional shapes.
- Invite the children to play freely with the building blocks.
- Invite children to play Memory Game: Geometry version/Juego de memoria: versión geométrica.
- Have the children work on Memory—Geometry, Level 2.

Reflect/Assess

- *How did you know what shape you felt in the Mystery Box?*
  ¿Cómo supieron qué forma sintieron en la Caja misteriosa?
- *What part did you feel?*
  ¿Qué parte tocaron?

Music and Movement

- Perform the "Going on a Bear Hunt"/"Vamos a cazar un oso" action rhyme. Discuss the cave where the bear lives.
- Play "One Elephant" from the *Where Is Thumbkin?* CD. Ask: *Where is the spider? What would happen to the spider's home if an elephant played on it?*
  ¿Dónde está la araña? ¿Qué le pasaría al hogar de la araña si un elefante jugara en ella?

Content Connection

Science

Objective
To identify similarities and differences among objects and organisms

DLM Materials
Teacher's Resource Anthology gelatin jigglers

Materials to Gather
spatula, cookie cutters, plastic knives

Activity 1

- Encourage the children to sort the shapes of the food containers during lunch time or snack time.

Activity 2

- Make gelatin jigglers.
- Prepare gelatin mix using half of the water the directions call for. Pour into a shallow pan and refrigerate. When the gelatin is set, invite the children to cut it into shapes using plastic knives or cookie cutters. To remove the shapes, dip the bottom of the pan in warm water. Slide a spatula under the shape and lift it out. Let children eat the gelatin shapes.

Suggested Reading

Alexander and the Terrible, Horrible, No Good, Very Bad Day by Judith Viorst

Reflect on the Day

- *What did you learn about construction this week?*
  ¿Qué aprendieron esta semana sobre la construcción?
- *If you look for animal homes after school, where will you look?*
  Si buscan hogares de animales después de clases, ¿dónde buscarían?

PLANNER

Looking Ahead

Connecting to the Theme: Growing Things

As young children may not have the vocabulary to communicate with others about the world around them, observation is a key skill in how they learn. The knowledge of how and why things grow should be integrated with that observation. The lessons in this theme will allow the children the opportunity to ponder how they have grown and changed over time.

	Objectives	DLM Materials	Materials to Gather
DAY 1	• To begin to engage in conversation and follow conversational rules • To become aware of routine healthy behaviors • To begin to participate in group games involving movement	• *The Itsy Bitsy Spider/La araña pequeñita* • *Teacher's Resource Anthology* • *Making Music with Thomas Moore CD*	• "me" puzzles • baby and current photos of children • scale • measuring tape • previous weight and height records
DAY 2	• To ask questions and make comments related to the current topic of discussion • To use simple measuring devices to learn about objects and organisms	• Rafita and Pepita • *Sara Sidney: The Most Beautiful Iguana in the World/Sara Sidney: la iguana más bella del mundo* • Oral Language Cards 9, 13, 14, 17, 21 • *Teacher's Resource Anthology*	• play dough • yarn • hand template • masking tape
DAY 3	• To understand that different text forms are used for different functions • To use one or more senses to observe and learn about objects, events, and organisms • To describe observations	• *Fall/El otoño* • Seed to Flower Sequence Cards • Oral Language Cards 55, 56 • Rafita and Pepita • *Teacher's Resource Anthology*	• easel paper • tempera paint • paintbrushes • lima beans • self-sealing plastic bags • paper towels • nature books • paper sacks • outdoor treasures • crayons or chalk
DAY 4	• To listen for different purposes • To recognize changes in the environment over time • To show an interest in investigating unfamiliar objects, organisms, and phenomena	• From Field to Table Sequence Cards • Building Blocks Sequence Cards • *The Tortilla Factory/La tortillería* • *The Little Red Hen/La gallinita roja* • *Teacher's Resource Anthology*	• mortar and pestle • various grains • plastic lids • potting soil and seeds • tweezers • straws • bowls • play dough • cooking utensils • tortilla ingredients
DAY 5	• To begin to understand cause-and-effect relationships • To begin to engage in dramatic play with others • To begin to share and cooperate with others in group activities	• Building Blocks Sequence Cards • *Martí and the Mango/Martí y el mango* • *Animals That Build Their Homes/Animales que construyen sus nidos*	• blocks • play dough • puzzles • bulletin board paper • tempera paint • dress-up clothes • accessories

(See individual lesson pages for complete lists of materials.)

Learning Centers

SCIENCE

Living Things

Objective
To use one or more senses to observe and learn about objects, events, and organisms

Materials to Gather
photographs, plants, fungi, moss, insects, pet (optional), magnifying lenses, watering can

Develop
Fill the center with examples of living things. Use both concrete items (such as insects, pets, fungi, plants, and so on) and photographs. Provide magnifying lenses. Provide watering cans. Create a care schedule, if you do not already have one. Encourage the children to share the responsibility of caring for the plants and/or animals.

Reflect/Assess
Which living thing is your favorite? Why?
¿Cuál ser vivo es su favorito? ¿Por qué?

DISCOVERY

Baking

Objective
To begin to engage in dramatic play with others

Materials to Gather
bakery props

Develop
Make the center into a bakery. Fill it with pots, pans, aprons, and baker hats. Add felt cookies and various cooking utensils. Be sure to include play dough, plastic cookie cutters, and a rolling pin.

Reflect/Assess
What are some foods a baker makes?
¿Cuáles son algunos de los alimentos que prepara un pastelero?
What types of tools does a baker use?
¿Qué tipos de instrumentos usa un pastelero?

DRAMATIC PLAY

Caring for Babies

Objective
To begin to create or re-create stories, moods, or experiences through dramatic representations

Materials to Gather
baby dolls, bath props, empty food containers, bottles, baby toys, rocking chair, doll bed

Develop
Encourage the children to take care of babies this week. Provide baby dolls, empty baby food containers, bottles, diapers, diaper bags, bathing props, and baby toys. Have the children role-play the things they need to do to keep their babies healthy, happy, and growing.

Reflect/Assess
How can you show love to a baby?
¿Cómo pueden demostrar amor a un bebé?
Is taking care of a baby hard work?
¿Cuidar a un bebé es un trabajo duro?

What Research Suggests

All living things need water and oxygen. The human brain needs both water and oxygen to function at its maximum capacity. Make sure children are drinking water roughly every ninety minutes throughout the day to hydrate the brain properly. Plants supply oxygen to the air. Research indicates that plants in the environment raise mental productivity by ten percent. One plant can affect 100 square feet of space. Take breathing breaks during the day.

Begin the Day

- Recite "When I Was One"/"Cuando yo tenía un año." Talk about how the children have grown since age one.
- Use a suggestion for Morning Circle offered in the front of this *Teacher's Edition.*

Objective

- To begin to engage in conversation and follow conversational rules

Vocabulary

baby	bebé, nené
little	pequeño, chiquito
big	grande
grow	crecer

Materials

DLM Materials

- *The Itsy Bitsy Spider/La araña pequeñita*
- Life Span Sequence Cards
- *Teacher's Resource Anthology*
  "Ernestine's. . . Day"/"El. . .día de Ernestina" flannel board story
  "I Can, You Can!"/"¡Yo puedo, tú puedes!" flannel board story
  "When I Was One"/"Cuando yo tenía un año"

Materials to Gather

- "me" puzzles
- baby and current photos of the children
- scale
- measuring tape
- previous weight and height records

LITERACY

Focus

- Change the words of "If You're Happy and You Know It"/"Si estás contento" to "If You're Growing and You Know It." Use the following actions: stand up tall, wink your eye, and tug your ear.
- Explain that the children will be learning about growing things, including themselves, this week.

Develop

One Way to Develop the Lesson

- Display baby photos and current photos of the children. Talk about their physical changes. Discuss what the children can do now that they could not do when they were babies.
- Invite them to demonstrate differences in the ways they can do things and the ways they did the same things as babies. For example, discuss walking. Have a volunteer demonstrate how he or she got around before he or she could walk. Other behavioral changes might include talking, picking up a ball, waving goodbye, or eating.

Another Way to Develop the Lesson

- Present the "Ernestine's . . . Day"/"El . . . día de Ernestina" flannel board story. Talk about Ernestine's size. *When Ernestine grows up, will she still be the littlest member of her family?*

  Cuando Ernestina crezca, ¿ella todavía será la más pequeña de su familia?
- Compare the members of Ernestine's family and sequence them by size on the flannel board.
- Invite the children to discuss their positions in their families. *Will your size relationship to your family members change as you grow?*

  ¿La relación entre su tamaño y el tamaño de sus familiares cambiará a medida que crezcan?

Practice

- Give the children the "Ernestine's . . . Day"/"El . . . día de Ernestina" flannel board story. Encourage them to retell the story or create a new one.
- Place the Life Span Sequence Cards in the Language Center and have the children sequence the cards from infancy to adulthood.
- Provide "me" puzzles for the children to put together.
- Place photocopies of the baby and current photographs in a center. Challenge the children to match baby photos with their current counterparts.
- Weigh and measure the children, and record the results. Compare the weights and measurements to those you took at the beginning of the school year. Have there been any changes? Review your findings with the children.

Preparation

- Photocopy current photos of the children, laminate them, and cut them into puzzle pieces called "me" puzzles.
- Make the "I Can, You Can!"/"¡Yo puedo, tú puedes!" flannel board story.

Scaffolding Strategies

More Help Make suggestions concerning the children's early behaviors. Ask leading questions such as: *When you were little, did you walk or did you crawl?* *Cuando eran pequeños, ¿caminaban o gateaban?*

Extra Challenge Encourage the children to list things they will improve upon as they grow.

Second Language Learners

Display children's baby photos. Practice using past tense. You might have them guess who is in a photo. Continue with other photos and patterned language. Children may join in or spontaneously use the past tense. If they use verbs incorrectly, repeat their response in the correct form using a conversational tone.

DAY 1

Letter Knowledge

English

- Discuss the letter *i* with the story "Ima" from the *English Phonics Resource Guide.*

Spanish

- Read the story "Tito" from the *Spanish Phonics Resource Guide.*

Suggested Reading

When I Get Bigger by Mercer Mayer
The Reason for a Flower by Ruth Heller
El motivo de una flor by Ruth Heller
El árbol de Rita by Rosa Flores

Anthology Support

"All by Myself"
"These Are Things I Like to Do"
"Éstas son las cosas que me gusta hacer"
"Birthday Candles"

Reflect/Assess

- *How do you think you have changed since you were a baby?*
  ¿Cómo han cambiado desde que eran bebés?
- *How will you continue to change as you grow?*
  ¿Cómo seguirán cambiando a medida que crezcan?

Literacy Circle

Storytime 1

- Present the "I Can, You Can!"/"¡Yo puedo, tú puedes!" flannel board story. Invite the children to discuss things they can do better now than when they were babies.

Storytime 2

- Read *The Itsy Bitsy Spider/La araña pequeñita.* Invite the children to discuss the things mentioned in the book they can do well and those that need improvement. Explain that practice usually helps our abilities.

Content Connection

Health and Safety

Objectives

To become aware of routine healthy behaviors

To begin to participate in group games involving movement

Vocabulary

diet, exercise, brain

dieta, ejercicio, cerebro

DLM Materials

Making Music with Thomas Moore CD

Activity 1

- Discuss the things that help people grow and stay healthy, such as eating a balanced diet, resting, and exercising.
- Explain that the children's brains are still developing and that they need plenty of water, healthful food, and exercise. This helps oxygen get to their brains. Encourage them to brainstorm how they can get plenty of water.

Activity 2

- Perform exercises to an instrumental selection from the *Making Music with Thomas Moore* CD.

DAY 1

Objectives

- To match numerals to collections of items
- To start, use, and exit software programs

Vocabulary

number número
six seis

DLM Materials

- counters
- *Math Resource Guide*
  How Many Now?/¿Cuántos hay ahora?
  Mystery Box
  Numeral cards (1–6)
  Dot cards (1–6)
  Memory Game: Numbers version/ Juego de memoria: versión números
  Cookie Game 1/Juego de la galleta 1 with activity sheet
  Numeral cube (1–6)
- *DLM Math* software

Materials to Gather

- tactile numeral cards (1–6)
- rectangular box
- 2 identical sets of three-dimensional shapes (cylinders, cones, balls)
- masking tape

Preparation

- Make a Numeral cube showing 1 through 6.
- Make copies of the Cookie Game 1 activity sheet.

MATH

Focus

- Show the children a rectangular block and ask them to help you count the 6 faces (top, bottom, and 4 sides). Then show the children a box and ask how many faces they think are on a box. Count and check.

Develop

- Show the 6 tactile numeral card. Talk about the parts: a 6 is a line and a circle, with the circle at the bottom of the line and to the right of the line. Have the children practice drawing a 6 in the air. Representing collections with written symbols is a key step toward abstract mathematical thinking.
- Give each child a set of Numeral cards. Play How Many Now?/ ¿Cuántos hay ahora? (See Things That Go Together, Day 5 to review How Many Now?)
- Introduce and demonstrate the activity Double Trouble, Level 4. The children must tell how many chips Mrs. Double hides under a napkin. Allow the children to tell you how to answer.

Practice

- Encourage the children to take turns hiding a three-dimensional shape in the Mystery Box and having another child identify it by showing the matching shape.
- Invite the children to play Memory Game: Numbers version/Juego de memoria: versión números using the Numeral and Dot cards.
- Invite the children to play Cookie Game 1/Juego de la galleta 1 using the 1–6 Numeral cube. You may wish to laminate the worksheets.
- Have the children work on Double Trouble, Level 4.

Reflect/Assess

- Show the numeral 6. *How do you know what this numeral is?*
  ¿Cómo saben qué número es éste?
- *Where have you seen a 6 at home?*
  ¿Dónde han visto un 6 en su casa?

Music and Movement

- Invite the children to have a baby crawl relay race/carrera de bebés gateando (a relay race with both teams crawling like babies).
- Make a start line on the floor with masking tape. Invite the children to see if they can jump distances equal to their heights.

Content Connection

Physical Development

Objective
To become more able to move from one place to another in different ways

Materials to Gather
balls

Activity 1

- Encourage the children to see how far they travel when they take 6 baby steps, skip 6 times, and jump 6 times. They can use beanbags to mark their starting and stopping places.

Activity 2

- Give the children balls and ask them to bounce the balls 6 times.

Suggested Reading

This Is the Sunflower
by Lola M. Schaefer

Reflect on the Day

- *What was your favorite activity?*
  ¿Cuál fue su actividad favorita?
- *When you go home, ask your family members about how you have grown. Ask what your first word was. Ask when you took your first step and to whom.*
  Cuando se vayan a la casa, pregúntenle a sus familiares cómo han crecido. Pregunten cuál fue la primera palabra que dijeron. Pregunten cuándo dieron sus primeros pasos y con quién.

Home Connection

Suggest that families help the children notice and read numerals throughout the day.

Begin the Day

- Sing "Over in the Meadow"/"Sobre la pradera."
- Use a suggestion for Morning Circle offered in the front of this *Teacher's Edition.*

Objective

- To ask questions and make comments related to the current topic of discussion

Vocabulary

living — vivo
nonliving — no vivo
iguana — iguana

DLM Materials

- *Sara Sidney: The Most Beautiful Iguana in the World/Sara Sidney: la iguana más bella del mundo* book and listening tape
- Rafita and Pepita
- Oral Language Development Cards 9, 13, 14, 17, 21
- Mother and Baby Animal Match game
- *Teacher's Resource Anthology*
  "Peanut, the Teeniest, Tiniest Pup on the Planet"/"Maní, el perrito más pequeñito del planeta" flannel board story
  "The Lion's Haircut"/"El corte de pelo del león" prop story
  "Over in the Meadow"/"Sobre la pradera"
  living and nonliving things card patterns
  mother and baby animal card patterns

Materials to Gather

- play dough
- yarn

LITERACY

Focus

- Tell the children that today they will learn about living and nonliving things.
- Use Rafita and Pepita to discuss animal growth. Point out that animals grow like people. Animals get bigger and better at doing things over time. They need proper diets, exercise, and rest to grow and stay healthy. Point out that all living things grow.
- Define living things as things that can move, breathe, and grow. Nonliving things do not move on their own, nor do they breathe. However, some can grow. Display the Living and Nonliving game cards, and let the children help you sort them. Encourage them to look around the room for examples of living and nonliving things.

Develop

One Way to Develop the Lesson

- Show Oral Language Cards 9, 13, 14, and 17. Discuss the sizes of the animals on the cards. Point out that the small animals are babies. They will grow up to be close to the same size as the corresponding adult animals.
- Encourage the children to help you create a list of names for baby and adult animals (for example, cow/calf, horse/colt, cat/kitten, dog/puppy, hen/chick, duck/duckling, and goat/kid). *Can you think of animals that have the same names as babies and adults?*

  ¿Pueden pensar en animales que tengan los mismos nombres que algunos bebés y adultos?

Another Way to Develop the Lesson

- Show Oral Language Card 21. Ask the children what they remember about the story of Sara Sidney.
- Tell them that Sara Sidney grew to be a large iguana, but when her owner first got her she was only 6 inches long. Show a piece of yarn that is 6 inches long. When Sara Sidney was one year old, she was 14 inches long. Lay a 14-inch piece of yarn next to the 6-inch piece of yarn. When Sara Sidney was two, she was 27 inches long. Continue laying out pieces of yarn. When Sara Sidney was three, she was 42 inches long, and when she was five, she was her full 52 inches. Sara Sidney grew because she was fed properly and enjoyed plenty of exercise.
- Read *Sara Sidney: The Most Beautiful Iguana in the World/Sara Sidney: la iguana más bella del mundo.*

Practice

- Place the *Sara Sidney* book and listening tape in the Listening Center. Invite the children to listen to the story again.
- Supply the Mother and Baby Animal cards, and encourage the children to match the pairs.
- Have the children draw pictures of mother and baby animals.
- Provide play dough. Encourage the children to roll snakes. Show them how to make their snakes grow by rolling them again and applying a bit of pressure.
- Give the children the Living and Nonliving cards to sort.

Preparation

- Make the "Peanut, the Teeniest, Tiniest Pup on the Planet"/"Maní, el perrito más pequeñito del planeta" flannel board story.
- Make the "The Lion's Haircut"/ "El corte de pelo del león" prop story.
- Photocopy the living and nonliving things card patterns; color, laminate, and cut them apart.
- Photocopy, color, laminate, and cut apart the mother and baby animal card patterns.

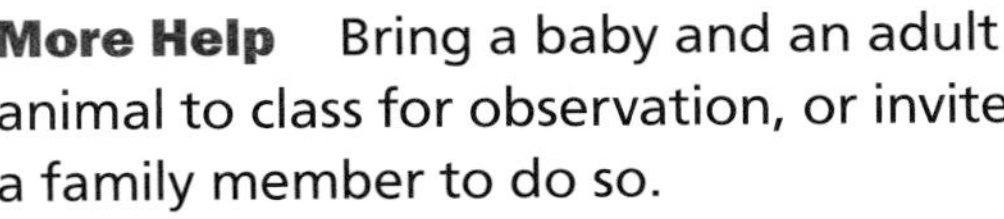

Scaffolding Strategies

More Help Bring a baby and an adult animal to class for observation, or invite a family member to do so.

Extra Challenge Write animal names on a chart. Have the children copy the names.

Second Language Learners

As you show the Mother and Baby Animal cards, do a call and response activity. Teach the baby's line (what the children will say) *Here I am, Mother (Duck); Peek-a-boo!* You say the mother's part first *(Duckling), (Duckling), where are you?* Repeat for other animals.

DAY 2

Letter Knowledge

English

- Read "Lizard Longing" from the *SRA Alphabet Book.*

Spanish

- Read "Tomás, el toro" from *Los niños alfabéticos.*

Suggested Reading

Fish Out of Water by Helen Palmer
My Father's Hands by Joanne Ryder
El árbol by Gallimard Jeunesse and Pascale de Bourgoing

Anthology Support

"Mary Had a Little Lamb"
"María tenía una corderita"
"Five Little Ducks"
"Los cinco patitos"

Reflect/Assess

- *Name some things that are alike concerning how animal and humans grow.*
  Nombren algunas cosas que sean iguales sobre el crecimiento de animales y seres humanos.
- *What do animals need in order to grow and stay healthy?*
  ¿Qué necesitan los animales para crecer y mantenerse saludables?

Literacy Circle

Storytime 1

- Present the flannel board story "Peanut, the Teeniest, Tiniest Pup on the Planet"/"Maní, el perrito más pequeñito del planeta."

Storytime 2

- Present "The Lion's Haircut"/"El corte de pelo del león" prop story. *What changed about the lion as he grew?*
  ¿Qué le cambió al león a medida que crecía?

Content Connection

Science

Objective
To use simple measuring devices to learn about objects and organisms

Vocabulary
length, height, hands, nonstandard unit of measurement, measure
largo, longitud; altura, estatura (for people); manos; unidad de medida no estándar; medir

Materials to Gather
hand template, masking tape, yarn

Activity 1

- Pass out pieces of yarn representing Sara Sidney's growth. Have the children sequence the yarn pieces from shortest to longest.
- Cut a piece of yarn (in a different color) to match each child's height. Encourage the children to match their yarn to the yarn pieces that represent Sara Sidney's lengths. *Which piece of yarn is the closest match to yours?*
  ¿Qué pedazo de cuerda es el más parecido al de ustedes?
- Label each child's yarn by attaching a piece of masking tape to the end. You will need these again on Thursday.

Activity 2

- Explain that when horses are measured, their heights are recorded in hands. This is a nonstandard unit of measurement.
- Give the children a measuring hand to use, and challenge them to figure out their heights in "hands." They can work with partners, or they can lay their yarn on the floor to see how many hands it takes to measure the yarn.

DAY 2

Objectives

- To match numerals to collections of items
- To recognize numerals

Vocabulary

number número
seven siete

DLM Materials

- counters
- *Math Resource Guide*
  How Many Now?/¿Cuántos hay ahora?
  Mystery Box
  Numeral cards (1–7)
  Dot cards (1–7)
  Memory Game: Numbers version/ Juego de memoria: versión números
  Places Scenes (farm background)
- *DLM Math* software
- *Teacher's Resource Anthology*
  "Ten Little Fingers"/"Diez deditos"
  Who Took the Cookie from the Cookie Jar?/¿Quién se comió la galleta?
  Duck, Duck, Goose/Pato, pato, ganso

Materials to Gather

- 2 identical sets of three-dimensional shapes (cylinders, cones, balls)

Preparation

- Make photocopies of Places Scenes.

MATH

Focus

- Say "Ten Little Fingers"/"Diez deditos" up to verse 7. Repeat the finger play, holding up Numeral cards for each verse.
- Play How Many Now?/¿Cuántos hay ahora? (see Things That Go Together, Day 5) with 1 to 6 counters.

Develop

- Tell the children that the numeral 7 is made with a horizontal line at the top and a slanted line at the right.
- Play Who Took the Cookie from the Cookie Jar?/¿Quién se comió la galleta? with the Numeral cards 1 to 7.
- Give each child a Places Scenes background and a set of Numeral cards. Have the children choose a Numeral card, put it on the sheet, and put that many counters on the sheet. If you wish, have the children do this in small groups. Freely prompt the children who need help recognizing or remembering their numerals.
- Reintroduce the activity Double Trouble, Level 4, from Day 1.

Practice

- Have the children place counters on the Places Scenes background. Challenge them to put a different Numeral card and the appropriate number of counters on each one. You may wish to laminate several sets of these so they can be used over and over.
- Continue to have a small group play How Many Now?/¿Cuántos hay ahora? with an adult.
- Encourage the children to work with the Mystery Box and three-dimensional geometric shapes. (See Day 1.)
- Invite the children to play Memory Game: Numbers version/Juego de memoria: versión números.
- Have the children work on Double Trouble, Level 4.

Reflect/Assess

- Show the numeral 7. *How do you know how to read this numeral?*
  ¿Cómo creen que deben leer este número?
- *Where have you seen a 7 at home?*
  ¿Dónde han visto un 7 en su casa?

Music and Movement

- Play Duckling, Duckling, Duck/Patito, patito, pato like you would Duck, Duck, Goose/Pato, pato, ganso.
- Invite the children to move like animals. Ask them if older animals move in ways that are different from younger animals. You might remind them about the wobbly legs of newborn calves, ponies, deer, and giraffes.

Content Connection

Science

Objective
To describe observations

Materials to Gather
balls

Activity 1

- Draw simple flowers with petals ranging from 1 to 6. Ask the children to count the petals.

Activity 2

- Encourage the children to draw flowers with petals. Have them tell you how many petals their flowers have.

Suggested Reading

This Is the Sunflower by Lola M. Schaefer

Reflect on the Day

- *What do you think it would be like if animals never grew up?*
  ¿Cómo sería si los animales no crecieran?
- *What was your favorite story?*
  ¿Cuál fue su cuento favorito?

What Research Suggests

Children remember and understand written numerals better when they know what the parts are and how they fit together.

Begin the Day

- Introduce "Shade Trees"/"Árboles que dan sombra."
- Use a suggestion for Morning Circle offered in the front of this *Teacher's Edition.*

Objective

- To understand that different text forms are used for different functions

Vocabulary

seeds	semillas
plants	plantas
living	vivo
nonliving	no vivo

DLM Materials

- *Fall/El otoño*
- Oral Language Development Cards 55 and 56
- Seed to Flower Sequence Cards
- *Teacher's Resource Anthology*
  "Jack and the Beanstalk"/"Jaime y los frijoles mágicos" flannel board story
  "The Fall of the Last Leaf"/"La caída de la última hoja" action story
  "Shade Trees"/"Árboles que dan sombra"
  "The Little Seeds"/"Partes de las plantas"

Materials to Gather

- easel paper
- tempera paint
- paintbrushes
- lima beans
- self-sealing plastic bags
- paper towels
- nature books

LITERACY

Focus

- Sing "The Little Seeds"/"Partes de las plantas".
- Tell the children that they will be learning about plants and trees as living things. Ask a volunteer to remind the class what a living thing is.

Develop

One Way to Develop the Lesson

- Show Oral Language Cards 55 and 56. Encourage the children to point out plants, flowers, and trees in the pictures. Use other suggestions on the backs of the cards to stimulate discussion about plants, flowers, and trees.
- Make a list of the ways that trees help people, such as providing lumber, shade, and fruit. Look around the room for items made of wood.
- Make a list of the ways people use flowers. Flowers add beauty to homes and gardens; people can send them as messages of cheer and love; some are the bases of perfumes and fragrances; and, in some cases, they are food.
- Show some seeds. Explain that most plants start out as seeds. Sing "The Little Seeds"/"Partes de las plantas" again.

Another Way to Develop the Lesson

- Tell the children that you are going to tell a make-believe story about something that grew from seeds.
- Present the "Jack and the Beanstalk"/"Jaime y los frijoles mágicos" flannel board story.
- Ask the children to help you separate the factual information from the make-believe information in the story.

Practice

- Place the "Jack and the Beanstalk"/"Jaime y los frijoles mágicos" flannel board story in the Language Center. Invite the children to retell the story or make up a new one.
- Provide easel paper, paints, and paintbrushes. Suggest that the children paint trees.
- Fill the Library Center with nature books about flowers and trees. Allow the children to explore them.
- Have the children draw pictures of things they like to do under the shade of trees. Have them dictate sentences describing their pictures. Collect the pictures and place them in a plastic bag book, making a Fun in the Shade book.
- Give the children the Seed to Flower Sequence Cards to place in order.
- Invite the children to start bean sprouts. Give each child a self-sealing plastic bag, a wet paper towel, and a lima bean. Show them how to place the beans and towels in the bags and seal them. Help the children write their names on their bags and tape their bags to the window. Tell them that in a few days their beans will begin to sprout.

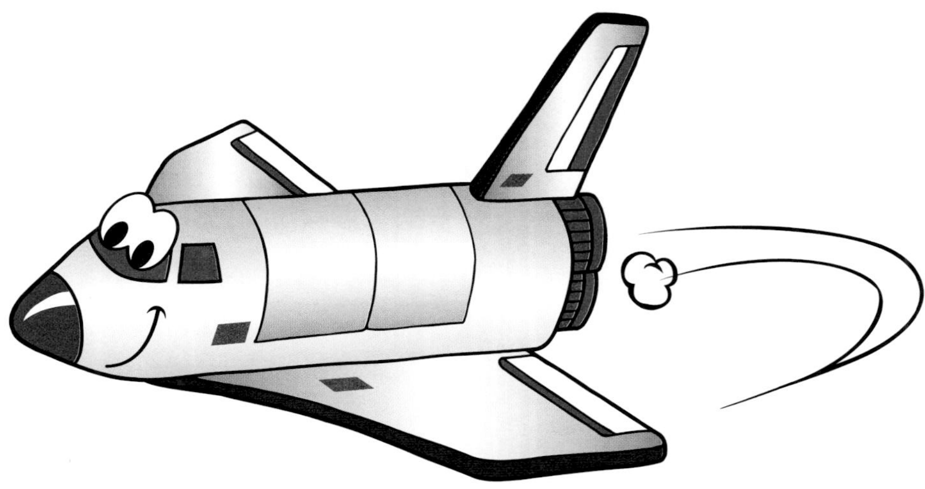

Preparation

- Make the "Jack and the Beanstalk"/"Jaime y los frijoles mágicos" flannel board story.

Scaffolding Strategies

More Help Ask the children direct questions about make-believe things mentioned in the story. *Have you ever seen a giant?*
¿Alguna vez han visto a un gigante?

Extra Challenge Discuss other stories the children know that are about giants.

Second Language Learners

Tell the "Jack and the Beanstalk"/"Jaime y los frijoles mágicos" flannel board story. First, pantomime the story. Children may pantomime also as you describe their actions using story language. Then tell the story using the figures. Place the flannel board and figures in a center for the children to retell the story.

Anthology Support

"Johnny Appleseed"
"Juan Semillita"
"Under the Spreading Chestnut Tree"

DAY 3

Letter Knowledge

English

- Write the letter *i* on an index card. Encourage the children to glue seeds over the letter *i.*

Spanish

- Write the letter *t* on an index card. Encourage the children to glue seeds over the letter *t.*

Suggested Reading

Planting a Rainbow by Lois Elhert
Flower Garden by Eve Bunting
The Carrot Seed by Ruth Kraus
La semilla de zanahoria by Ruth Kraus

Reflect/Assess

- *What do you like best about trees?*
  ¿Qué es lo que más les gusta de los árboles?
- *What would you do if you planted some seeds and they grew into beanstalks like Jack's?*
  ¿Qué harían si plantaran unas semillas y crecieran como las de Jaime?

Literacy Circle

Storytime 1

- Read *Fall/El otoño* to the children.

Storytime 2

- Invite the children to participate in the action story "The Fall of the Last Leaf"/"La caída de la última hoja."

Content Connection

Science

Objectives
To use one or more senses to observe and learn about objects, events, and organisms
To describe observations

Vocabulary
trees, fungi, moss, seeds, living, nonliving
árboles, hongos, moho, semillas, vivo, no vivo

DLM Materials
Rafita and Pepita

Materials to Gather
paper sack for collecting outdoor treasures, crayons or chalk

Activity 1
- Take a nature walk. Invite Rafita and Pepita to go along. Encourage the children to touch the bark of trees and to touch and crunch the leaves. *Which things are still living?*
  ¿Cuáles cosas están vivas todavía?
  Which things are not living?
  ¿Cuáles cosas están muertas?
  Can the children put their arms around the trunk of a tree? If not, how many of their friends do they need to help them completely surround the tree?
- Encourage them to bring leaves and pieces of bark back to the classroom to place in the Science Center.

Activity 2
- Encourage the children to make leaf and bark rubbings with the collection they brought back from their nature walk.

DAY 3

MATH

Objectives

- To match numerals to collections of items
- To recognize numerals

Vocabulary

number	número
seven	siete

DLM Materials

- counters
- *Math Resource Guide* Places Scenes (farm background)
- See Day 1
- *DLM Math* software
- *Teacher's Resource Anthology* "The Green Grass Grew All Around" Who Took the Cookie from the Cookie Jar?/¿Quién se comió la galleta?

Materials to Gather

- tactile numeral cards (1–7)
- connecting cubes

More Help Use fewer Numeral cards at one time for children who need more help.

Extra Challenge Have children use Numeral cards up to 10 or beyond.

Focus

- Play Who Took the Cookie from the Cookie Jar?/¿Quién se comió la galleta? with Numeral cards 1 through 7.

Develop

- Give each child a set of Numeral cards containing 1 through 7. Play How Many Now?/¿Cuántos hay ahora?
- Secretly hide 2 connecting cubes in the Mystery Box. Have a child place a hand in the box and tell how many cubes there are. Encourage the children to tell how they figured out how many cubes they were feeling. Repeat with 1–3 cubes (or more, if children are able).

Practice

- Invite the children to continue the Mystery Box activity in small groups.
- Encourage the children to work with the Places Scenes.
- Challenge the children to play How Many Now?/¿Cuántos hay ahora? in pairs or small groups.
- Invite the children to play Memory Game: Number version/Juego de memoria: versión números.
- Have the children work on Double Trouble, Level 4.

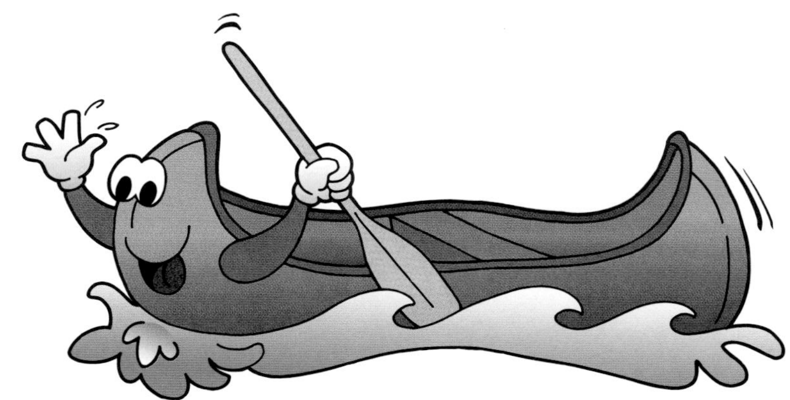

Reflect/Assess

- Show the numeral 7. *How do you know how to read this numeral?*
  ¿Cómo creen que deben leer este número?

Music and Movement

- Sing "The Green Grass Grew All Around."
- Encourage the children to pretend to be trees. Have them stand tall and spread their arms to the sky. Suggest that they blow with the wind. Have them drop their leaves and droop because they are thirsty.

Suggested Reading

Look Whooo's Counting by Suse MacDonald

Content Connection

Fine Arts

Objective

To use different colors, surface textures, and shapes to create form and meaning

Materials to Gather

tempera paint, paper

Activity 1

- At the art easel, challenge students to paint horizontal and slanted lines to make the numeral 7.

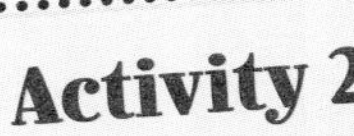

Activity 2

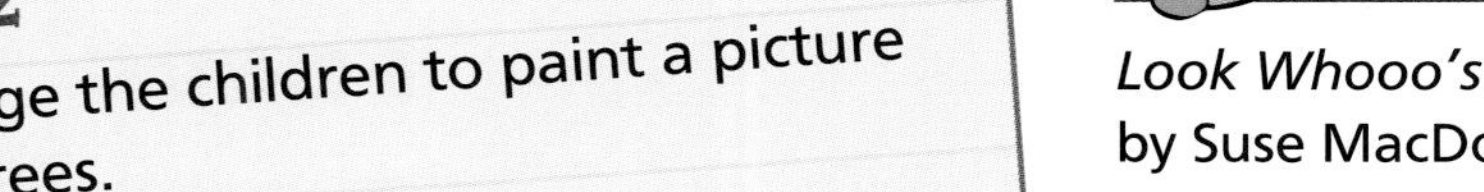

- Encourage the children to paint a picture with 7 trees.

Reflect on the Day

- *Did you know that some trees are so large that you could carve out the trunks and drive cars through them? What is the largest tree you have seen?*

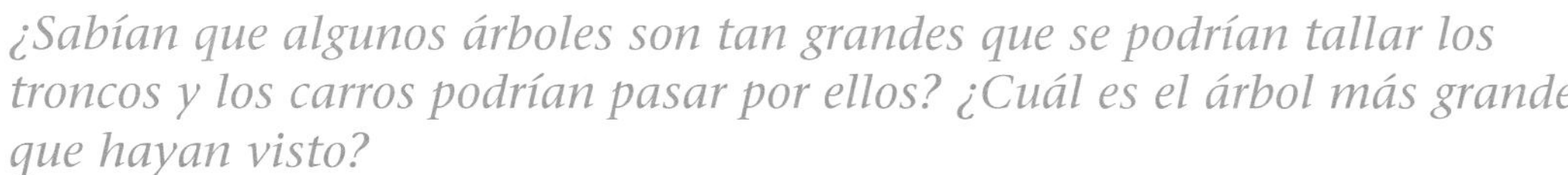

  ¿Sabían que algunos árboles son tan grandes que se podrían tallar los troncos y los carros podrían pasar por ellos? ¿Cuál es el árbol más grande que hayan visto?
- *Why are trees and flowers living things?*
  ¿Por qué los árboles y las flores son seres vivos?

Begin the Day

- Introduce "Johnny Appleseed"/"Juan Semillita." Tell the children who Johnny Appleseed was, and explain the words in the song.
- Use a suggestion for Morning Circle offered in the front of this *Teacher's Edition.*

Objective

- To listen for different purposes

Vocabulary

tortilla	tortilla
shop	tienda
plant	planta
harvest	cosecha
dry	seco
grind	moler

DLM Materials

- *The Tortilla Factory/La tortillería* book and listening tape
- *The Little Red Hen/La gallinita roja*
- *Teacher's Resource Anthology* "Let's Pretend to Make Tortillas"/ "Pretendamos que estamos haciendo tortillas" action story "Johnny Appleseed"/"Juan Semillita" play dough
- From Field to Table Sequence Cards

Materials to Gather

- mortar and pestle
- grains (corn, wheat, barley, rice)
- plastic lids
- yellow and white construction paper
- cooking utensils
- tortilla ingredients

LITERACY

Focus

- Present "Una tortilla, dos tortillas"/"One Tortilla, Two Tortilla" in both English and Spanish.
- Tell the children that tortillas are Mexican bread. Explain that tortillas are usually made from corn in the same way that some bread is made from wheat.

Develop

One Way to Develop the Lesson

- Display the cover of the book *The Tortilla Factory/La tortillería.* Read the title of the book, and ask the children what they think the book might discuss. Ask them why they think the cover of the book shows farmland if the story is about making tortillas.
- Read the book.
- Discuss the planting and harvesting of corn. Ask: *How do crop growers take care of the corn while it is growing?*

  ¿Cómo los agricultores cuidan del maíz a medida que crece?

  Why do pickers leave the corn to dry in the sun?

  ¿Por qué los colectores dejan que el maíz se seque bajo el sol?
- Show a pestle and mortar. Explain that large machines grind the corn in the tortilla shop, but if people want to grind it by hand, they use a pestle and mortar. Demonstrate how it works by grinding some wheat or corn.

Another Way to Develop the Lesson

- Tell the children that they are going to make flour and/or corn tortillas.
- Introduce the special guest who will be helping your class. Remind the children to use their best manners when asking questions and helping.
- Make tortillas. Have a copy of the recipe on a chart so the children can see that it is something to be read and used.
- You may want to invite another class to sample the tortillas after they are made.

Practice

- Place *The Tortilla Factory/La tortillería* book and listening tape in the Listening Center. Invite the children to listen to the story again.
- Place the mortar and pestle in the Science Center. Provide grains for the children to grind.
- Provide play dough and a rolling pin. Encourage the children to pretend to make tortillas.
- Give the children yellow and white construction paper and plastic lids. Encourage them to trace the lids to make corn and flour tortillas. Have them cut out their tortillas and write their names on them.
- Allow the children to place the From Field to Table Sequence Cards in order.

Preparation

- Write the recipe for tortillas on a piece of chart paper.
- Gather ingredients for tortillas.
- Gather grains for grinding.
- Make play dough.
- Photocopy, color, laminate, and cut out the Sequence Cards.

Second Language Learners

Make a recipe poster for tortillas. While modeling each step for making tortillas, record descriptions on audiotape. If possible, photograph the process step by step. Place photos, tape, tape player, and recipe poster in a center for children to pretend making tortillas.

Anthology Support

"Muffin Man"
"My Mother Is a Baker"
"Mi mamá es una pastelera"
"Oats, Peas, Beans"

DAY 4

Letter Knowledge

English

- Invite the children to make the letter *i* with their bodies. Use the Think, Pair, Share/Piensa, aparea, comparte game with this activity.

Spanish

- Call attention to the *t* in the tortilla activities today.
- Invite the children to make the letter *t* with their bodies. Use the Think, Pair, Share/Piensa, aparea, comparte game with this activity.

Suggested Reading

Bread, Bread, Bread by Ann Morris
Patatas y tomates by Joyce Dunbar
A sembrar sopa de verduras by Lois Ehlert
Algo está creciendo by Walter Krudrop

Reflect/Assess

- *In the story, why did the corn grow so well?*
  En el cuento, ¿por qué el maíz creció tan bien?
- *Do you eat more tortillas or bread at your house?*
  ¿Ustedes comen más tortillas o más pan en sus casas?

Literacy Circle

Storytime 1

- Read *The Little Red Hen/La gallinita roja*. Ask the children how this story is like *The Tortilla Factory/La tortillería*.
  ¿En qué se parece este cuento a The Tortilla Factory/La tortillería?

Storytime 2

- Invite the children to participate in the action story "Let's Pretend to Make Tortillas"/"Pretendamos que estamos haciendo tortillas."

Content Connection

Science

Objectives
To recognize changes in the environment over time
To show an interest in investigating unfamiliar objects, organisms, and phenomena

Vocabulary
seeds, transfer
semillas, transferir

Materials to Gather
seeds, potting soil, magnifying lenses, tweezers, straws, two bowls or dishes

Activity 1
- Show a variety of seeds. Encourage the children to look at the seeds using magnifying lenses.
- Invite them to plant flower seeds on the playground, if an area is available, or in a planter for your classroom windowsill.
- Discuss the use of flowers to beautify our surroundings.

Activity 2
- Discuss the fact that seeds are often carried from one spot to another by the wind and/or animals.
- Demonstrate how the wind carries seeds. Place seeds on a table and encourage the children to blow the seeds across the table using straws.
- Demonstrate how birds pick up and move seeds, providing tweezers to use as beaks. Encourage the children to transfer the seeds from one dish to another using the tweezers.

DAY 4

Objectives

- To count by ones to 10 or higher
- To recognize numerals

Vocabulary

number número
eight ocho

DLM Materials

- counters
- *Math Resource Guide*
  Numeral Jump/Saltar números
  Cookie Game 1/Juego de la galleta 1 with activity sheet
  Numeral cube (3–8)
  Mystery Box
  Numeral cards (1–8)
  Dot cards (1–8)
  Memory Game: Numbers version/ Juego de memoria: versión números
- *DLM Math* software
- *Four Baby Bumblebees* CD
- *Diez deditos* CD
- *Teacher's Resource Anthology*
  "Ten Little Fingers"/"Diez deditos"
  Drop the Handkerchief/Suelta el pañuelo

Materials to Gather

- tactile numeral cards
- connecting cubes

Preparation

- Make a new Numeral cube that shows 3, 4, 5, 6, 7, and 8 on the faces.

MATH

Focus

- Reintroduce "Ten Little Fingers"/"Diez deditos" through verse 8. Teach verse 8. Repeat it, holding up the tactile numeral cards for each verse.

Develop

- Show the children the numeral 8. Ask them what parts they see in this numeral, and ask them how the parts fit together.
- Explain that an 8 is 2 circles, 1 right on top of the other.
- Play Numeral Jump/Saltar números. Tell the children that you will show a tactile numeral card and that they should jump that many times. Repeat with several numerals. For variety, you could give the children different actions to perform also, such as patting their tummies, turning around, clapping their hands, and so on.
- Reintroduce Cookie Game 1/Juego de la galleta 1. Have the children use the Numeral cube that shows 3 to 8.

Practice

- Encourage the children to continue to play Cookie Game 1/Juego de la galleta 1 using a Numeral cube with numerals 3 to 8.
- Invite the children to do the Mystery Box activity with up to 8 cubes.
- Invite the children to play Memory Game: Numbers version/Juego de memoria: versión números with the cards. Adjust the number of cards for individual differences in ability.
- Have the children work on Double Trouble, Level 4.

Reflect/Assess

- Show the numeral 8. *How do you know how to read this numeral?*
  ¿Cómo creen que deben leer este número?
- *Where have you seen an 8 at home?*
  ¿Dónde han visto un 8 en su casa?

Music and Movement

- Play Drop the Tortilla/Suelta la tortilla as you would Drop the Handkerchief/Suelta el pañuelo. Use one of the tortillas made from construction paper.
- Sing "Oats, Peas, Beans and Barley Grow" from the *Four Baby Bumblebees* CD, or play "Tortillas" from the *Diez deditos* CD.

Content Connection

Fine Arts

Objectives

To use different colors, surface textures, and shapes to create form and meaning

To begin to respond to music of various tempos through movement

Activity 1

- At the art easel, challenge students to make the numeral 8.
- Discuss the 2 circles and how 1 is on top of the other.

Activity 2

- Invite the children to take their shoes off and sock skate on an uncarpeted area of the room. Teach them how to make figure 8's. Play some skating music.

Suggested Reading

Each Orange Had Eight Slices: A Counting Book by Paul Giganti

Reflect on the Day

- *What was your favorite activity?*
  ¿Cuál fue su actividad favorita?
- *What are tortillas made of?*
  ¿De qué se hacen las tortillas?

Home Connection

Send home take-home book packs with four children. You will find the directions and a record sheet for this activity in the *Home Connections Resource Guide*.

Begin the Day

- Sing "Farmer in the Dell"/"El granjero en la cañada." Point out that the farmer's group grows as new friends are asked to join.
- Use a suggestion for Morning Circle offered in the front of this *Teacher's Edition.*

Objective

- To begin to understand cause-and-effect relationships

Vocabulary

living vivo
nonliving no vivo

DLM Materials

- *Martí and the Mango/Martí y el mango*
- *Animals That Build Their Homes/Animales que construyen sus nidos*
- *Teacher's Resource Anthology*
  "Farmer in the Dell"/"El granjero en la cañada"
  "My Mother Is a Baker"/"Mi mamá es una pastelera"
- Building Blocks Sequence Cards

Materials to Gather

- play dough
- puzzles
- blocks

LITERACY

Focus

- Tell the children that they will continue to learn about growing things today.
- Remind the children that living things move, breathe, and grow. Remind them that nonliving things do not move on their own, nor do they breathe, but they can grow.

Develop

One Way to Develop the Lesson

- Give every child a block. Make a small tower out of blocks. Invite the children to add their blocks to the tower one at a time. *What happens to the tower as blocks are added?*

  ¿Qué le sucede a la torre a medida que se agregan los bloques?
- Help the children think of things they can make bigger by adding to them (such as a sandwich, a pot of soup, a picture, a story, or a group of children). Make a list of examples. Point out that the length of the list grows longer as new thoughts are added.

Another Way to Develop the Lesson

- Introduce the song "My Mother Is a Baker"/"Mi mamá es una pastelera." Point out how the song grows each time the singer adds another person and verse to the song.
- Invite the children to add a verse to the song. You may want to teach four or five verses and then ask them to create their verse, allowing for more ideas.

Practice

- Invite the children to work on puzzles. Point out that the pictures grow as puzzle pieces are added.
- Provide play dough. Encourage the children to make objects with the play dough, and then have them add more play dough to see their creations grow.
- Have each child build a structure in the Blocks Center. Then have the children find ways to connect their structures to make one large structure.
- Hand out the Building Blocks Sequence Cards. Encourage the children to sequence the cards to show the structure growing.

Scaffolding Strategies

More Help Invite the children to form a human chain. Start with two children standing arm in arm. Ask a third child to join the group. Keep adding children so that they can visually see the chain getting longer.

Extra Challenge Encourage the children to consider the reverse concept of today's lesson. *Does something get smaller when you take part of it away?* *Cuando le quitan una parte a un objeto, ¿se hace más pequeño?*

Second Language Learners

Talk about the lima beans that were planted on Day 3 of this week. Help the children describe what happened to their beans. They may use vocabulary from their first language. Acknowledge their ideas and expand on what they said. If a bean has not sprouted, provide another.

Anthology Support

"Calliope Song"
"The More We Get Together"
"Mientras más estemos juntos"

DAY 5

Letter Knowledge

English

- Invite the children to make the letter *i* in sand trays.

Spanish

- Invite the children to make the letter *t* in sand trays.

Suggested Reading

The Best Mouse Cookie by Laura Joffe Numeroff

Oliver's Vegetables by Vivian French

Éste es el árbol: La historia del baobab by Miriam Moss and Adrienne Kennaway

Reflect/Assess

- *Name something that kept growing. Why did it keep growing?*
  Nombren algo que siguió creciendo. ¿Por qué siguió creciendo?
- *How are nonliving and living things alike? How are they different?*
  ¿En qué se parecen los seres vivos y los no vivos? ¿En qué se diferencian?

Literacy Circle

Storytime 1

- Read *Martí and the Mango/Martí y el mango*. Point out that the amount of Martí's information grows each time he gets a new clue.

Storytime 2

- Look at the pictures in *Animals That Build Their Homes/Animales que construyen sus nidos*. Call attention to the animal homes and how they grow.

Content Connection

Fine Arts

Objectives
To begin to engage in dramatic play with others
To begin to share and cooperate with others in group activities

Vocabulary
mural, accessories
mural, accesorios

Materials to Gather
bulletin board paper, tempera paint, dress-up clothes, accessories

Activity 1

- Invite the children to paint a mural. Point out that the painting grows as each child adds his or her part to the picture.

Activity 2

- Provide dress-up clothes and accessories. Invite the children to create an outfit and add to it with accessories.

DAY 5

Objectives

- To match numerals to collections of items
- To begin to recognize numerals

Vocabulary

number	número
eight	ocho

DLM Materials

- counters
- *Math Resource Guide*
  Numeral Jump/Saltar números
  Cookie Game 1/Juego de la galleta 1 with activity sheet
  Mystery Box
  Numeral cube (3–8)
  Numeral cards (1–8)
  Dot cards (1–8)
  Memory Game: Numbers version/ Juego de memoria: versión números
- *DLM Math* software
- *Where Is Thumbkin?* CD
- *Making Music with Thomas Moore* CD
- *Teacher's Resource Anthology*
  One Elephant/Un elefante

Materials to Gather

- tactile numeral cards
- connecting cubes

MATH

Focus

- Play Numeral Jump/Saltar números by showing a tactile numeral card and having the children jump that many times. Repeat with several numerals, changing the action the children perform.

Develop

- Secretly hide 3 connecting cubes in the Mystery Box. Have a child place a hand in the box and tell how many cubes there are. Put 1 more cube in the box. Ask the child how many there are now. Then have the child check by feeling the stack. Repeat.
- Complete a task from Double Trouble, Level 4, with the children. Have them tell how they knew how many were under the napkin.

Practice

- Challenge the children to continue to use the Mystery Box, adding cubes 1 or 2 at a time.
- Invite the children to play Memory Game: Numbers version/Juego de memoria: versión números.
- Encourage the children to play Cookie Game 1/Juego de la galleta 1 with a friend, using a Numeral cube with numerals 3 to 8.
- Have the children work on Double Trouble, Level 4.

Reflect/Assess

- *How did you know how many cubes there were in the Mystery Box?*
  ¿Cómo sabían cuántos cubos había en la Caja Misteriosa?
- *In Double Trouble, how did you figure out how many were hidden under the napkin?*
  En Double Trouble, ¿cómo determinaron cuántos había escondidos debajo de la servilleta?

Music and Movement

- Play One Elephant/Un elefante. Point out that the group of elephants grows as new elephants join the line.
- Listen to "De colores" on the *Making Music with Thomas Moore* CD. Call attention to the fact that the music grows in volume and richness as each new instrument joins in.

Suggested Reading

Each Orange Had Eight Slices: A Counting Book by Paul Giganti

Content Connection

Fine Arts

Objective
To use a variety of materials to create original work

Materials to Gather
finger paint, blocks

Activity 1
- Challenge the children to build a road shaped like the numeral 8 with the blocks in the Blocks Center.

Activity 2
- Pour finger paint directly on a tabletop and have the children make the numeral 8 in the paint.

Reflect on the Day

- *What living things did we talk about this week?*
  ¿De qué seres vivos hablamos esta semana?
- *How are living things like the under-construction things we discussed last week?*
  ¿En qué se parecen los seres vivos y los objetos en construcción que estudiamos la semana pasada?

Looking Ahead

Connecting to the Theme: Food and Nutrition

Building on last week's theme of **Growing Things,** children begin to learn how people use food to grow. It is important for them to be exposed to the types of food and drinks that are healthful. The lessons will introduce and discuss the various food groups. The children will also participate in a class project as they help create a food pyramid.

	Objectives	DLM Materials	Materials to Gather
DAY 1	• To understand that print carries a message by recognizing labels, signs, and other print forms in the environment • To begin to predict what will happen next in a story • To match numerals to collections of items • To start, use, and exit software	• Oral Language Development Card 71 • *The Tortilla Factory/La tortillería* • *The Little Red Hen/La gallinita roja* • The Little Red Hen sequence cards • *Teacher's Resource Anthology* • *DLM Math* software • *Four Baby Bumblebees* CD • *Diez deditos* CD	• baking tins • cookie sheets • breadboards • rolling pins • newspapers • alphabet cereal • magazines • cereal boxes • muffin tin • food packages • bread and jam or tortillas and butter • cereal, pasta, and bread samples • four boxes of graduated sizes
DAY 2	• To understand that print carries a message by recognizing labels, signs, and other print forms in the environment • To begin to perform simple investigations • To match numerals to collections of items • To begin to recognize numerals • To use a variety of materials to create original work	• *Los niños alfabéticos* • *SRA Alphabet Book* • *Martí and the Mango/Martí y el mango* • Oral Language Cards 68 & 69 • *Teacher's Resource Anthology* • *Math Resource Guide* • *Where Is Thumbkin?* CD • *Esta es mi tierra* CD	• fruit and vegetables • four boxes from Day 1 • unshelled peas • magazines • coffee filters • eyedroppers • tactile numeral cards (1-10) • muffin tins • clay
DAY 3	• To understand that print carries a message by recognizing labels, signs, and other print forms in the environment • To prepare simple healthy snacks • To count by ones to 10 or higher • To begin to recognize numerals 1 to 10 • To become more able to move from one space to another in different ways	• Oral Language Development Card 70 • *Fish Wish/Deseos de un pez* • *Teacher's Resource Anthology* • dinosaur counters • Rafita and Pepita puppets • *Math Resource Guide* • *DLM Math* software • *Where Is Thumbkin?* CD • *Diez deditos* CD	• four-box food pyramid • nuts • coat hanger tube • yarn • magnet • magazines • fast-food packaging • peanuts (shelled and unshelled) • oil • crackers • tactile numeral cards • muffin tin
DAY 4	• To understand that print carries a message by recognizing labels, signs, and other print forms in the environment • To use different colors, surface textures, and shapes to create form and meaning • To match numerals to collections of items • To begin to recognize numerals 1 to 10	• Oral Language Development Card 72 • *The Farm/La granja* • *Teacher's Resource Anthology* • dinosaur counters • Rafita and Pepita puppets • *Math Resource Guide* • *DLM Math* software	• food pyramid • dairy products • magazines • milk cartons • buttermilk • plastic knives • cookie cutters • cheese slices • crackers • small containers • vegetables • leaves • seeds • paint
DAY 5	• To understand that print carries a message by recognizing labels, signs, and other print forms in the environment • To begin to be responsible for individual behavior and actions • To match numerals to collections of items • To use a variety of software packages with audio, video, and graphics to enhance learning experiences	• Oral Language Cards 68–72 • *SRA Alphabet Book* • *Los niños alfabéticos* • *Teacher's Resource Anthology* • dinosaur counters • *Math Resource Guide* • *DLM Math* software • *Four Baby Bumblebees* CD	• examples of healthful and unhealthful food • food pyramid • fast-food packaging • plastic food • play money • muffin tins • lemon drops • gumdrops

(See individual lesson pages for complete lists of materials.)

Learning Centers

DRAMATIC PLAY

Grocery Store

Objective
To begin to engage in dramatic play with others

Materials to Gather
grocery props, cash register, signs, play money

Develop
Turn the center into a grocery store. Stock it with empty food cans, boxes, crates, and cartons. Make signs for produce, meats, dairy, and so on. Add baskets and a cash register. Encourage the children to role-play being the grocery manager, the butcher, the produce manager, stockers, and shoppers. Encourage them to make grocery lists. Provide clipboards, paper pads, and pencils.

Reflect/Assess
Which role did you like playing?
¿Qué parte les gustó más actuar?

SCIENCE

Experimenting with Weight

Objective
To use simple measuring devices to learn about objects and organisms

Materials to Gather
plastic fruits and vegetables, grains

Develop
Provide scales and grains and real or plastic fruit and vegetables to weigh. Encourage the children to use the appropriate vocabulary. Encourage them to look for items that are equal in weight.

Reflect/Assess
What is the heaviest thing you weighed?
¿Cuál es la cosa más pesada que han levantado?

DISCOVERY CENTER

Sense of Taste

Objective
To express interest and self-direction in learning

Materials to Gather
food items, recording chart

Develop
Set up a tasting station. Each day, use food items from the food group that is being explored. Encourage the children to taste the food(s). Provide a recording chart with two columns: one for *I like this* (smiling face) and another for *I do not care for this* (frowning face). Encourage the children to record their reactions to what they have tasted.

Reflect/Assess
Which food did you like the most?
¿Qué comida les gustó más?
Which food did you like the least?
¿Qué comida no les gustó?

What Research Suggests

The brain needs proper nutrition both to build connections and to function appropriately. Protein is brain food. Eggs, fish, nuts, and cheeses are high in protein. The natural sugars found in most fruits and in carrots stimulate and aid memory. Research indicates that Americans eat too few fruits, vegetables, and complex carbohydrates. Children in particular do not get sufficient amounts of complex carbohydrates. Apples are a good source of complex carbohydrates.

Begin the Day

- Say "Una tortilla, dos tortillas"/"One Tortilla, Two Tortillas." Remind the children that a tortilla is a type of bread.
- Use one of the suggestions for Morning Circle offered in the front of this *Teacher's Edition.*

Objectives

- To understand that print carries a message by recognizing labels, signs, and other print forms in the environment
- To begin to predict what will happen next in a story

Vocabulary

bread	pan
rice	arroz

DLM Materials

- Oral Language Development Card 71
- *The SRA Alphabet Book*
- *The Tortilla Factory/La tortillería*
- *The Little Red Hen/La gallinita roja*
- The Little Red Hen sequence cards
- *Teacher's Resource Anthology*
  "Una tortilla, dos tortillas"/"One Tortilla, Two Tortillas"
  "Pat-A-Cake"
  "Let's Pretend to Make Tortillas"/"Pretendamos que estamos haciendo tortillas"

Materials to Gather

- four boxes of graduated sizes
- baking tins, cookie sheets
- breadboards, rolling pins
- magazines
- cereal boxes
- bread and jam or tortillas and butter
- food packages
- cereal, pasta, and bread samples
- alphabet cereal

LITERACY

Focus

- Say "Pat-A-Cake." Have the children mark the cakes with the initials of their first names. Then say the rhyme again and have them mark the cakes with the letter focus of the week: English *j* and Spanish *l*.
- Tell the children that the cakes in the rhyme are like pancakes; they are a type of bread. Point out that they will learn about food and nutrition this week, and today the focus will be on bread, cereal, and pasta.

Develop

One Way to Develop the Lesson

- Show the four boxes of graduated sizes. Tell the children that people need to eat a variety of foods each day. *We put foods into four groups. This box on the bottom, the biggest, is for the bread, cereal, and pasta group. We need to eat a lot of foods from this group; that is why it is the biggest box.*

  Dividimos los alimentos en cuatro grupos. Esta caja en la parte de abajo, la caja más grande, es para el grupo del pan, el cereal y la pasta. Tenemos que comer bastante de este grupo, por eso es la caja más grande.
- Ask the children which cereals and breads they like to eat.
- Show Oral Language Card 71 (breads, cereals, and grains). Use the questions on the back of the card to stimulate discussion.
- Read "Crusty Corn Bread" in the *SRA Alphabet Book.*

Another Way to Develop the Lesson

- Show the cover of *The Little Red Hen/La gallinita roja. Who remembers what this story is about?* Remind the children that the hen is baking bread.
  ¿Quién recuerda de qué trata este cuento?
- Read the story and discuss the steps the hen used to bake her bread.

Practice

- Place *The Little Red Hen/La gallinita roja* book and listening tape in the Listening Center and invite the children to listen to the story.
- Give the children play dough, baking tins, cookie sheets, bread-boards, and rolling pins and let them pretend to make breads.
- Encourage the children to cut out pictures from magazines to make bread, cereal, and pasta collages.
- Cut cereal-box fronts into puzzles. Encourage the children to put them back together.
- Give the children The Little Red Hen/La gallinita roja Sequence Cards and have them use the cards to sequence the events in the story.
- Serve bread and jam or tortillas and butter.

Preparation

- Gather pastas, breads, and cereals.
- Prepare the From Field to Table Sequence Cards.
- Gather bread and jam or tortillas and butter.

Second Language Learners

Last week the children had the chance to make tortillas and review the process in the listening center. Put a blank tape in the recorder and tell children they will make a tape for a stuffed animal, so it can learn to make tortillas, too. Review the tape and note the strategies children use. Do they use some of the home language to describe tortilla making? Are their grammatical constructions somewhat like those of children their age or slightly younger?

Anthology Support

"On Top of Spaghetti"
"Muffin Man"
"Hot-Cross Buns!"
"Arroz con leche"
"Rice with Milk"

Technology Support

Have the children find examples of the foods that are discussed each day on the *SRA Photo Library* software in the Food category. Encourage them to select a favorite food from each category and describe what they like about that food.

DAY 1

Letter Knowledge

English

- Introduce the letter *j* using the story "Jacy" from the *English Phonics Resource Guide.* Encourage the children to look for the letter *j* in the alphabet cereal.

Spanish

- Introduce the letter *l* using the story "Lluvia" in the *Spanish Phonics Resource Guide.*

Suggested Reading

Tingo Tango Mango Tree by Marcia Vaughan

Pachanga deliciosa by Pat Mora

Delicious Hullaballoo by Pat Mora

Teacher's NOTE

Over the next four days, you will build a food pyramid. Prepare boxes to represent the four basic food groups and the food pyramid. On the largest box, write *Bread, Cereals, and Pasta.* Label the next box *Fruits and Vegetables,* the next *Meats,* and the smallest one *Dairy.* Glue one or two pictures of appropriate foods on each box. You might prefer to use actual food or food packages to build the food pyramid. If so, use open boxes and stack the food and/or food packages in the boxes.

Reflect/Assess

- *Do you think the Little Red Hen did the right thing when she decided not to share her bread? Why?*

  ¿Creen que la gallinita roja hizo lo correcto cuando decidió no compartir su pan? ¿Por qué?

- *What kinds of pasta do you like best?*

  ¿Qué tipos de pasta les gusta más?

Literacy Circle

Storytime 1

- Invite the children to participate in the action story "Let's Pretend to Make Tortillas"/"Pretendamos que estamos haciendo tortillas."

Storytime 2

- Read *The Tortilla Factory/La tortillería.*

Content Connection

Science

Objective
To investigate unfamiliar objects, organisms, and phenomena

Vocabulary
first, next, last, harvest, mill, yeast
primero; siguiente, próximo; último; cosecha; molino; levadura

DLM Materials
- From Field to Table Sequence Cards
- *Teacher's Resource Anthology* letter pretzels

Activity 1

- Discuss where bread comes from. Use the From Field to Table Sequence Cards to show the steps grain goes through before people place it on their tables. Place the sequence cards in the Science Center and invite the children to put them in order.

Activity 2

- Have the children make letter pretzels. Some children may want to make the letters of their names.

DAY 1

Objectives

- To match numerals to collections of items
- To start, use, and exit software

Vocabulary

number — número
nine — nueve

DLM Materials

- dinosaur counters
- *Math Resource Guide*
  Numeral cards (1–9)
  Dot cards (1–9)
  Memory Game: Numbers version/ Juego de memoria: versión números
  Places Scenes (dinosaur background)
- *DLM Math* software
- *Four Baby Bumblebees* CD
- *Diez deditos* CD
- *Teacher's Resource Anthology*
  Who Took the Cookie from the Cookie Jar?/¿Quién se comió la galleta?

Materials to Gather

- tactile numeral cards (1–9)
- muffin tin
- foam or paper numerals
- pretzels

MATH

Focus

- Play Who Took the Cookie from the Cookie Jar?/¿Quién se comió la galleta? with the numerals 1 to 9.

Develop

- Explain that a 9 is a small circle and a vertical line with the circle at the top and to the left side of the vertical line.
- Give the children foam or paper numerals. Show the children the muffin tin. Ask them to put all of the numeral 1s in the first cup, numeral 2s in the second cup, and so on. Representing collections with written symbols is important in developing abstract mathematical thinking. These activities also develop children's ability to identify and correct counting errors, which helps them develop reliable skills.
- Introduce and demonstrate Dinosaur Shop, Level 1. The children's first job in the shop is to label boxes with numerals telling how many things are inside.

Practice

- Challenge the children to continue sorting numerals. Encourage the children to sort in order 1 to 9 or, if you prefer, label each muffin cup with a numeral. Provide a display of counting numerals for checking.
- Encourage the children to play Memory Game: Numbers version/ Juego de memoria: versión números with the cards. This game is a good opportunity to assess the children's ability to read numerals.
- The children may work on Dinosaur Shop, Level 1. A benefit of the computer is that it creates a motivating scene that gives a meaningful context for learning.
- Have the children place counters on the Places Scenes background (see Growing Things, Day 2).

Reflect/Assess

- Show the numeral 9. *How do you know what this numeral is?*
  ¿Cómo saben qué número es éste?
- *Where have you seen the numeral 9 used at home or in other places?*
  ¿Dónde han visto que se usa el número 9 en su casa o en otros lugares?

Music and Movement

- Sing "Oats, Peas, Beans and Barley Grow" from the *Four Baby Bumblebees* CD or "Tortillas" from the *Diez deditos* CD.
- Play Pass the Pretzel/Pasa el pretzel. Form 2 teams for a relay race. Have each team place a pretzel on the ends of their fingers. Pass the pretzel from the index finger of 1 child to the index finger of another child.

Content Connection

Physical Devlopment

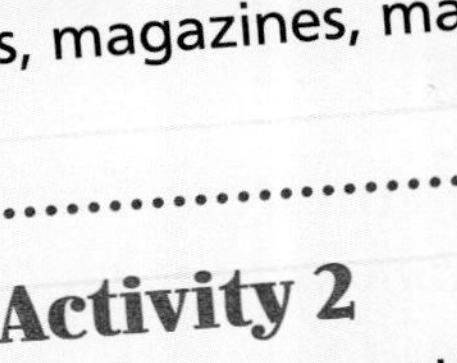

Objectives
To explore moving in space
To begin to use scissors

Materials to Gather
newspapers, magazines, masking tape

Activity 1
- Make a numeral 9 with masking tape on the floor. Encourage the children to walk the tape with a beanbag on their heads.

Activity 2
- Encourage the children to find and cut out 9s from newspapers and magazines.

Reflect on the Day

- *Which activity was your favorite today?*
  ¿Cuál fue su actividad favorita de hoy?
- *What kind of cereal did you eat for breakfast today?*
  ¿Qué tipo de cereal comieron hoy en el desayuno?

Suggested Reading

Count-a-saurus by Nancy Blumenthal
My Visit to the Dinosaurs by Aliki

Begin the Day

- Sing "Apples and Bananas" or chant "Mango"/"Mango."
- Use one of the suggestions for Morning Circle offered in the front of this *Teacher's Edition.*

Objective

- To understand that print carries a message by recognizing labels, signs, and other print forms in the environment

Vocabulary

avocado	aguacate
coconut	coco
guava	guayaba
kiwi	kiwi
mango	mango

DLM Materials

- *Los niños alfabéticos*
- *SRA Alphabet Book*
- *Martí and the Mango/Martí y el mango*
- Oral Language Development Cards 68 & 69
- *Teacher's Resource Anthology*
  "Apples and Bananas"
  fruit and vegetable patterns
  "The Great Big Turnip"/"El nabo gigante"
  "A Special Surprise"/"Una sorpresa especial"

Materials to Gather

- fruits and vegetables
- four boxes from Day 1
- chart paper
- unshelled peas
- magazines
- easel paper
- red tempera paint

LITERACY

Focus

- Ask the children about the foods they had for dinner last night. *Did anyone eat bread, cereal, or pasta?*
  ¿Alguien comió pan, cereal o pasta?
- Ask: *Who remembers what we talked about yesterday? Who wants to guess which foods go into/on the next box?*
  ¿Quién recuerda de qué hablamos ayer? ¿Quién quiere adivinar cuáles alimentos van en la siguiente caja?

Develop

One Way to Develop the Lesson

- Show the fruits and vegetables. Ask the children what kinds of food they think will go in the box. Have them identify the fruit and vegetables you're holding.
- Display Oral Language Cards 68 and 69. Use the suggestions on the backs of the cards to stimulate discussion. Remind the children that their bodies need both fruits and vegetables every day to stay healthy.
- Read "La piña" in the *Los niños alfabéticos* or "An Anteater" from the *SRA Alphabet Book.* Ask the children to locate and name the fruit in the illustrations.

Another Way to Develop the Lesson

- Show the cover of *Martí and the Mango/Martí y el mango*. Invite a volunteer to tell the class what he or she remembers about the story.
- Point out that Martí uses a notebook to write down the clues he discovers about mangos. Tell the children that you are going to write down the clues in the story just like Martí did. Use a piece of chart paper to record the clues. Encourage the children to help you figure out what to write.
- Read *Martí and the Mango/Martí y el mango*. Stop just before the end of the story and review all the clues. Encourage the children to tell you what a mango looks like. Then read the conclusion of the story. Help the children review the clues and evaluate their conclusions.

Practice

- Place the *Martí and the Mango/Martí y el mango* book and listening tape in the Listening Center. Invite the children to listen to the story again.
- Give the children the Fruit and Vegetable Concentration game. They can also sort the cards from the game into fruit and vegetable categories.
- **(Allergy Warning)** If fruits are available, dice and slice them and serve them for snack.
- Provide peas for the children to shell.
- Encourage the children to cut pictures of fruits and vegetables out of magazines to make a fruit and vegetable collage.
- Cut apple shapes out of easel paper and provide red tempera paint to paint them.

Preparation

- Gather fruits and vegetables.
- Prepare the flannel board story.
- Make the Fruit and Vegetable Concentration game by making two photocopies of all the fruit and vegetable patterns. Cut them out and laminate them.

Scaffolding Strategies

More Help Provide each of the fruits and vegetables mentioned in the story and let the children examine them as you read the story.

Extra Challenge After you have read the story, teach the children to play Twenty Questions. The child who is *IT* should think of a fruit or vegetable. To identify the fruit or vegetable, the other children may ask up to twenty questions that can be answered by *yes* or *no*.

Second Language Learners

(Allergy Warning) Bring all the fruits and vegetables mentioned in *Martí and the Mango/Martí y el mango.* Ask children to describe the inside and outside of each. Provide a taste of each. Accept all responses. Repeat or restate what children said, and add to what they say.

DAY 2

Letter Knowledge

English

- Read the *j* selection "Jack, Jack" from the *English Phonics Resource Guide*. Discuss juices that are made from fruit.

Spanish

- Read the *l* selection "Lali y Lola" from *Los niños alfabéticos.*

Suggested Reading

We Love Fruit! by Allan Fowler
¡Nos gustan las frutas! by Allan Fowler
Vegetable Soup by Ann Morris
Sopa de vegetales by Ann Morris
Caldo, Caldo, Caldo by Diane Gonzales Bertrand

Teacher's NOTE

A vegetable is the edible product of a plant, with a stem that is softer than the stem of a shrub or tree. Most vegetables are annuals. A fruit is an edible, seed-bearing food that has fleshy tissue and grows on a perennial (a plant that grows more than two years without being replanted).

Anthology Support

"Johnny Appleseed"
"Juan Semillita"
"Naranja dulce"
"Sweet Orange"

Reflect/Assess

- *What is your favorite fruit?*
  ¿Cuál es tu fruta favorita?
- *Which vegetables do you like best?*
  ¿Qué vegetales les gusta más?

Literacy Circle

Storytime 1

- Present "The Great Big Turnip"/"El nabo gigante" flannel board story.

Storytime 2

- Present the "A Special Surprise"/"Una sorpresa especial" chalk and prop story.

Content Connection

Science

Objective
To begin to perform simple investigations

Vocabulary
vegetables, dyes
vegetales, hortalizas, verduras; tintes

Materials to Gather
vegetables and fruit, coffee filters, eyedroppers, paintbrushes

Activity 1

- Invite the children to make vegetable dye from vegetable juice (beets, broccoli, blueberries, and so on). Use the water that remains after vegetables are cooked to make dye. Call attention to the changes that occur in the textures of vegetables as they are cooked.
- Provide eyedroppers and encourage the children to drop the dye onto coffee filters. *Is it easy to predict the dye color the vegetable will produce?*
  ¿Es fácil predecir el color del tinte que producirá la verdura?

Activity 2

- Provide vegetable dye and brushes and encourage the children to paint pictures. *How are the dyes different from paint?*
  ¿En qué se diferencian los tintes de la pintura?

DAY 2

Objectives

- To match numerals to collections of items
- To begin to recognize numerals

Vocabulary

number número
ten diez

DLM Materials

- dinosaur counters
- *Math Resource Guide*
  Numeral Jump/Saltar números
  Numeral cards (1–10)
- *DLM Math* software
- *Where Is Thumbkin?* CD
- *Esta es mi tierra* CD
- *Teacher's Resource Anthology*
  Fruit Salad Game/Juego de la ensalada de frutas
  Who Took the Cookie from the Cookie Jar?/¿Quién se comió la galleta?

Materials to Gather

- tactile numeral cards (1–10)
- muffin tins

More Help Freely prompt the children to recognize and remember numerals 1 to 10.

Extra Challenge Expose the children to multiples of 10, such as 100 and 1,000.

MATH

Focus

- Play Who Took the Cookie from the Cookie Jar?/¿Quién se comió la galleta? with the 1–9 tactile numeral cards.
- Play Numeral Jump/Saltar números (see Growing Things, Day 4). After doing 9, tell the children that they will do 9 and 1 more. Ask if anyone knows how many that is.

Develop

- Explain that 10 is a 1 next to a 0. Tell the children that the 1 means "one group of 10," and the 0 means "no more ungrouped items left."
- Have the children sort the dinosaur counters into boxes. They may choose to sort by color, numbers of legs, and so on. There should be no more than 10 counters for any category. Ask the children to put the appropriate Numeral card in front of the box.
- Reintroduce the activity Dinosaur Shop, Level 1. Have the children tell you how to answer by pointing to the numeral on the screen.

Practice

- Challenge the children to sort the dinosaurs in another way and to label each box with the corresponding Numeral card. Tell the children that they may put different numbers of items in the boxes and re-label them.
- Encourage the children to sort numerals as they did on Day 1.
- The children may work on Dinosaur Shop, Level 1. If available, put toy dinosaurs near the computer so the children can solve the problems with physical objects as well.

Reflect/Assess

- Show the numeral 10. *How do you know how to read this numeral?*
  ¿Cómo creen que deben leer este número?
- *How have you seen the numeral 10 used at home, at the store, or other places?*
  ¿Cómo han visto que se usa el número 10 en su casa, en la tienda o en otros lugares?

Music and Movement

- Sing "Apples and Bananas" from the *Where Is Thumbkin?* CD, or play "Platanos y manzanas" from the *Esta es mi tierra* CD.
- Play the Fruit Salad game/Juego de la ensalada de frutas.

Content Connection

Fine Arts

Objective
To use a variety of materials to create original work

Materials to Gather
clay

Activity 1
- At the art easel, challenge children to make the numeral 9 or 10. Emphasize vertical lines and circles.

Activity 2
- Have the children make numerals out of clay.

Reflect on the Day

- *Which activity was your favorite today?*
  ¿Cuál fue su actividad favorita de hoy?
- *What fruits and vegetables have you eaten today?*
  ¿Qué frutas y vegetales han comido hoy?

Suggested Reading

One Lonely Sea Horse by Saxton Freymann
More Than One by Miriam Schlein

Begin the Day

- Sing "Peanut Butter"/"Mantequilla de maní."
- Use the suggestions for Morning Circle offered in the front of this *Teacher's Edition.*

Objective

- To understand that print carries a message by recognizing labels, signs, and other print forms in the environment

Vocabulary

meat	carne
fish	pescado
poultry	aves
nuts	nueces

DLM Materials

- Oral Language Development Card 70
- *Fish Wish/Deseos de un pez*
- *Teacher's Resource Anthology*
  "Peanut Butter"/"Mantequilla de maní"
  "Five Fat Turkeys Are We"/"Somos los cinco pavos gordos"
  animal patterns
  "Silly Nellie: The Story of One Funny Turkey"/"Clotilde Bobilde: La historia de una pavita muy divertida"

Materials to Gather

- chart paper
- four-box food pyramid
- nuts
- construction paper
- paper clips
- coat hanger tube
- yarn
- magnet
- magazines
- fast-food packaging

LITERACY

Focus

- Ask the children about the fruits and vegetables they ate for dinner last night. Make a list on chart paper.
- Have the children look at the food pyramid and briefly review the first two food groups. Tell them that the third box represents the meats and proteins group. *What kinds of foods are in the meat group? ¿Qué tipos de alimentos están en el grupo de las carnes?*

Develop

One Way to Develop the Lesson

- Discuss pork, poultry, fish, and beef. Talk about the source of each type of meat.
- Explain that eggs and nuts are part of this food group because of their high protein content.
- Show Oral Language Card 70. Use the suggestions on the back of the card to stimulate discussion. Remind the children that their bodies need meat/protein every day to stay healthy.
- Ask the children which meats are their favorites. Make a graph depicting their responses.

Reflect/Assess

- Show the numeral 10. *How do you know how to read this numeral?*
  ¿Cómo creen que deben leer este número?
- *How have you seen the numeral 10 used at home, at the store, or other places?*
  ¿Cómo han visto que se usa el número 10 en su casa, en la tienda o en otros lugares?

Music and Movement

- Sing "Apples and Bananas" from the *Where Is Thumbkin?* CD, or play "Platanos y manzanas" from the *Esta es mi tierra* CD.
- Play the Fruit Salad game/Juego de la ensalada de frutas.

Content Connection

Fine Arts

Objective
To use a variety of materials to create original work

Materials to Gather
clay

Activity 1
- At the art easel, challenge children to make the numeral 9 or 10. Emphasize vertical lines and circles.

Activity 2
- Have the children make numerals out of clay.

Reflect on the Day

- *Which activity was your favorite today?*
  ¿Cuál fue su actividad favorita de hoy?
- *What fruits and vegetables have you eaten today?*
  ¿Qué frutas y vegetales han comido hoy?

Suggested Reading

One Lonely Sea Horse by Saxton Freymann
More Than One by Miriam Schlein

Begin the Day

- Sing "Peanut Butter"/"Mantequilla de maní."
- Use the suggestions for Morning Circle offered in the front of this *Teacher's Edition.*

Objective

- To understand that print carries a message by recognizing labels, signs, and other print forms in the environment

Vocabulary

meat	carne
fish	pescado
poultry	aves
nuts	nueces

DLM Materials

- Oral Language Development Card 70
- *Fish Wish/Deseos de un pez*
- *Teacher's Resource Anthology*
  "Peanut Butter"/"Mantequilla de maní"
  "Five Fat Turkeys Are We"/"Somos los cinco pavos gordos"
  animal patterns
  "Silly Nellie: The Story of One Funny Turkey"/"Clotilde Bobilde: La historia de una pavita muy divertida"

Materials to Gather

- chart paper
- four-box food pyramid
- nuts
- construction paper
- paper clips
- coat hanger tube
- yarn
- magnet
- magazines
- fast-food packaging

LITERACY

Focus

- Ask the children about the fruits and vegetables they ate for dinner last night. Make a list on chart paper.
- Have the children look at the food pyramid and briefly review the first two food groups. Tell them that the third box represents the meats and proteins group. *What kinds of foods are in the meat group? ¿Qué tipos de alimentos están en el grupo de las carnes?*

Develop

One Way to Develop the Lesson

- Discuss pork, poultry, fish, and beef. Talk about the source of each type of meat.
- Explain that eggs and nuts are part of this food group because of their high protein content.
- Show Oral Language Card 70. Use the suggestions on the back of the card to stimulate discussion. Remind the children that their bodies need meat/protein every day to stay healthy.
- Ask the children which meats are their favorites. Make a graph depicting their responses.

Another Way to Develop the Lesson

- Sing "Five Fat Turkeys Are We"/"Somos los cinco pavas gordos."
- Sing the song a second time and encourage the children to act it out. *Why are the turkeys hiding?*

  ¿Por qué se esconden los pavos?
- Explain that turkeys are poultry. Ask the children to name other types of poultry. *Which type of poultry is your favorite?*

  ¿Qué tipo de carne de ave es su favorita?

Practice

- Provide nuts for the children to sort.
- Play the Fishing game. Cut fish out of construction paper and place a paper clip on each fish's nose. Provide a fishing pole (coat hanger tube and yarn) with a magnet on the end of it and encourage the children to catch fish for dinner by touching the noses of the fish with the fishing pole magnet.
- Provide magazines and encourage the children to cut out pictures of meat to make meat and protein collages.
- Provide packaging from fast-food restaurants along with plastic foods, play money, and other props. Have the children set up a fast-food restaurant. Tell them to order hamburgers, hot dogs, fish sandwiches, chicken nuggets, and so on.
- Provide the animal patterns and encourage the children to play a game of Concentration.

Preparation

- Gather nuts.
- Make the Fishing game.
- Make the flannel board story, if not already made.
- Make two photocopies of the animal patterns. Color them, cut them out, and laminate them to make an Animal Concentration game.

Second Language Learners

Prepare a pictorial recipe poster describing the ingredients and the steps for making homemade peanut butter. Use packages to make the recipe poster (for example, a partially empty bag of peanuts, an empty bottle for oil, salt shaker). As you make the peanut butter, stress new vocabulary, such as *shell* the peanuts/*cascar* los cacahuates [*maní* outside of Mexico] (have most shelled, but keep some in the husks, so children see where they came from), *grind* the peanuts/*moler* los cacahuates, *spread* the peanut butter/*cubre* (la galleta) con mantequilla de cacahuate. Later, talk about the texture, color, and so on as children eat the peanut butter. **(Allergy Warning)**

Anthology Support

"Counting Rhyme"
"Los pollitos"
"The Baby Chicks"
"To Market, to Market"

DAY 3

Letter Knowledge

English

-  Have the children draw the letter *j* in a sand tray. Point out the *j* in *jelly.*

Spanish

- Have the children draw the letter *l* in a sand tray.

Suggested Reading

Grey Lady and the Strawberry Snatcher by Molly Bang

El Gusto del Mercado Mexicano by Nancy Taylor

Espaguetis para Susi by Peta Coplans

Teacher's NOTE

Be sensitive to the fact that some children may not eat meat. Families may practice vegetarianism as part of their religion or for health or personal reasons.

Reflect/Assess

- *How are chicken and turkey alike? How are they different?*

  ¿En qué se parecen los pollos y los pavos? ¿En qué se diferencian?
- *If you ate a peanut butter sandwich or a grilled cheese sandwich, would you be eating something from this food group (see question above)? Why or why not?*

  Si comen un emparedado de mantequilla de maní o un emparedado de queso a la parrilla, ¿estarían comiendo algo de este grupo (ver la pregunta anterior)? ¿Por qué sí o por qué no?

Literacy Circle

Storytime 1

- Present "Silly Nellie: The Story of One Funny Turkey"/"Clotilde Bobilde: La historia de una pavita muy divertida" flannel board story.

Storytime 2

- Read *Fish Wish/Deseos de un pez.* Discuss the many sea animals eaten by people.

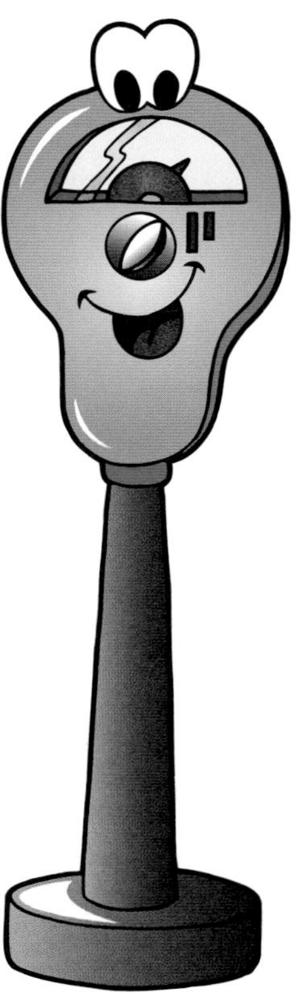

Content Connection

Health and Safety

Objective
To prepare simple healthy snacks

Vocabulary
chop, blend, shell, spread
cortar, mezclar, concha, untar

DLM Materials
- *Teacher's Resource Anthology* homemade peanut butter

Materials to Gather
peanuts (shelled and unshelled), oil, crackers

Activity 1

- **(Allergy Warning)** Provide peanuts in the shells and encourage the children to shell them.

Activity 2

- **(Allergy Warning)** Make homemade peanut butter. Provide crackers for the children to use to sample their peanut butter.

DAY 3

Objectives

- To count by ones to 10 or higher
- To begin to recognize numerals 1 to 10

Vocabulary

numbers to 10 — números hasta 10

DLM Materials

- dinosaur counters
- Rafita and Pepita/Rafita y Pepita
- *Math Resource Guide*
  Numeral Jump/Saltar números
  Numeral cards (1–10)
  Dot cards (1–10)
  Memory Game: Numbers version/ Juego de memoria: versión números
  Places Scenes (dinosaur background)
- *DLM Math* software
- *Where Is Thumbkin?* CD
- *Diez deditos* CD
- *Teacher's Resource Anthology*
  "Five Little Fingers"/"Los dedos de la mano"

Materials to Gather

- tactile numeral cards
- muffin tin

Scaffolding Strategies

More Help In the Memory Game, limit the set of cards that children use to 1 through 5.

Extra Challenge Have children who are able use cards beyond 10.

MATH

Focus

- Teach children "Five Little Fingers"/"Los dedos de la mano."
- Play Numeral Jump/Saltar números. Show a numeral, and then ask the children to read it and jump that many times. Count out the jumps in unison. You may add variety by specifying how the children should jump—slowly, quickly, on 1 foot, and so on. Repeat with several numerals.

Develop

- Explain that Rafita and Pepita are learning how to count, just as the children are, and that they sometimes get confused. Have the puppets take turns trying to verbally count, with the other one trying to help but eventually asking the children to help. Have Rafita and Pepita make the following kinds of mistakes: wrong order (1, 2, 4, 3), skipping numbers (. . . 6, 7, 9, 10), and repeating a number (. . . 4, 5, 6, 6, 7). Encourage the children to show the puppets the correct way to count.

Practice

- Encourage the children to continue to sort numbers as they did on Day 1.
- Invite the children to use the Places Scenes background. Have the children place a Numeral card on each scene, and then match the numeral with that many counters.
- Allow the children to play Memory Game: Numbers version/Juego de memoria: versión números with the cards.
- The children may work on Dinosaur Shop, Level 1.

Reflect/Assess

- *How did you know that Rafita and Pepita were not counting correctly?*
  ¿Cómo sabían que Rafita y Pepita no estaban contando bien?

Music and Movement

- Sing "Peanut Butter" from the *Where Is Thumbkin?* CD, or "Cuando vayas al mercado" from the *Diez deditos* CD.
- Sing "Five Fat Turkeys Are We" from the *Where Is Thumbkin?* CD.

Content Connection

Physical Development

Objectives

To become more able to move from one space to another in different ways

To become more able to move in place

DLM Materials

- *Teacher's Resource Anthology*
  Hopscotch/Rayuela

Activity 1

- Invite the children to play Hopscotch/Rayuela. Encourage them to call out the numeral when they toss their markers.

Activity 2

- Do exercises, 10 of everything: 10 toe touches, 10 jumping jacks, 10 knee bends, and so on. Count each move.

Suggested Reading

The Dinosaur Egg Mystery by M. Christina Butler

The Right Number of Elephants by Jeff Sheppard

Reflect on the Day

- *What was your favorite activity today?*
  ¿Cuál fue su actividad favorita de hoy?
- *What is your favorite kind of meat?*
  ¿Cuál es su tipo de carne favorito?

What Research Suggests

Although some people worry that *talking about mistakes* will teach children errors, studies show that when children help identify and correct counting errors, they develop more reliable skills.

Begin the Day

- Say "Ice Cream Chant"/"La canción del helado."
- Use one of the suggestions for Morning Circle offered in the front of this *Teacher's Edition.*

Objective

- To understand that print carries a message by recognizing labels, signs, and other print forms in the environment

Vocabulary

butter mantequilla
cheese queso
milk leche
yogurt yogur

DLM Materials

- Oral Language Development Card 72
- *The Farm/La granja*
- *Teacher's Resource Anthology*
  "Ice Cream Chant"/"La canción del helado"
  "Drink, Drink, Drink Your Milk"/ "Toma, toma tu leche"
  baggie ice cream
  "Let's Pretend to Bake a Cake"/ "Pretendamos como que horneamos un pastel"
  baggie ice cream rebus card

Materials to Gather

- food pyramid
- dairy products
- magazines
- milk cartons
- chart paper
- brown and various other colors of construction paper

LITERACY

Focus

- Ask the children which meats or proteins they ate for dinner last night. Make a list on chart paper.
- Review the boxes in the food pyramid. Tell the children that dairy products make up the last food group.
- Sing "Drink, Drink, Drink Your Milk"/"Toma, toma tu leche."

Develop

One Way to Develop the Lesson

- Show the dairy products that you brought to class. Invite the children to name as many dairy products as they can. Make a list.
- Display Oral Language Card 72. Use the suggestions on the back of the card to stimulate discussion. Remind the children that their bodies need dairy products every day to stay healthy.
- Play a riddle game about dairy products. For example, *I am thinking of something cold that comes in a cone. I am thinking of something white that comes from a cow.*

  Estoy pensando en algo frío que se sirve en una barquilla. Estoy pensando en algo blanco que proviene de una vaca.

Another Way to Develop the Lesson

- Make baggie ice cream. Encourage the children to follow the directions on the baggie ice cream rebus.

Practice

- Provide magazines. Encourage the children to cut out pictures of dairy products to create a dairy product collage.
- Provide milk carton puzzles made from the sides of milk cartons.
- Provide several different sizes of clean, empty milk cartons and encourage the children to arrange them in order from shortest to tallest and tallest to shortest.
- Place your list of dairy products in the Writing Center and encourage the children to use it as a model to make a grocery list of dairy products.
- Cut ice-cream cones out of brown construction paper and different flavors of ice-cream scoops out of the appropriate colors of construction paper. Write alphabet letters on the cones and matching letters on the scoops of ice cream. Have the children match cones to ice-cream scoops.

Preparation

- Gather examples of dairy products.
- Photocopy the baggie ice cream rebus.
- Gather ingredients for baggie ice cream.
- Cut milk cartons into puzzle pieces.
- Cut cones and scoops of ice cream from construction paper.

Second Language Learners

Be sure to compliment children for including protein in their meal. Mention legumes, tofu, eggs, nuts, and certain food combinations such as beans and rice, in addition to meat and fish. Show empty cartons of these protein foods. Ask children which protein foods they eat at home. Acknowledge all answers and note the language used. Model a sentence such as "Hector's protein is from fish. Anh's protein is from tofu." "La proteína de Héctor viene del pescado. La proteína de Anh viene del tofu."

Anthology Support

"The Purple Cow"
"The Raindrop Song"
"Canción gotas de lluvia"

DAY 4

Letter Knowledge

English

- Have the children make the letter *j* out of play dough.

Spanish

- Have the children make the letter *l* out of play dough.

Suggested Reading

Milk: From Cow to Carton by Aliki
Cloudy with a Chance of Meatballs by Judi Barrett
Gracias a las vacas by Allan Fowler
Sopa de Piedras by Marcia Brown

Reflect/Assess

- *Which food in the dairy group is your favorite?*
  ¿Cuál comida del grupo lácteo es su favorito?
- *How are milk and ice cream alike? How are they different?*
  ¿En qué se parecen la leche y el helado? ¿En qué se diferencian?

Literacy Circle

Storytime 1

- Read *La granja/The Farm*. Discuss the importance of farming and agriculture in helping provide people with food to eat: *Can you think of foods we get from farms?*
  ¿Pueden pensar en otros alimentos que obtenemos de las granjas?

Storytime 2

- Have the children participate in the action story "Let's Pretend to Bake a Cake"/"Pretendamos como que horneamos un pastel." *Which dairy products go into the cake?*
  ¿Qué productos lácteos se usan en la torta?

Content Connection

Fine Arts

Objective
To use different colors, surface textures, and shapes to create form and meaning

Vocabulary
buttermilk
leche cortada

Materials to Gather
finger-paint paper, colored chalk, buttermilk, plastic knifes, cookie cutters, cheese slices, crackers

Activity 1

- Give each child a piece of finger-paint paper and a piece of colored chalk. Place a tablespoon of buttermilk on each child's paper. Demonstrate rubbing the chalk in the buttermilk to create a paint stick. *How are these pictures different from regular chalk pictures?* *¿En qué se diferencia este dibujo de uno común hecho con tiza?*

Activity 2

- Provide plastic knives and cookie cutters and have the children cut shapes out of cheese slices. Serve the cheese on crackers for snack.

DAY 4

Objectives
- To match numerals to collections of items
- To recognize numerals

Vocabulary
numbers to 10 números hasta 10

DLM Materials
- dinosaur counters
- Rafita and Pepita/Rafita y Pepita
- *Math Resource Guide*
  Mystery Box
  Numeral cards (1–10)
  Dot cards (1–10)
  Memory Game: Numbers version/ Juego de memoria: versión números
  Places Scenes (dinosaur background)
- *DLM Math* software
- *Teacher's Resource Anthology*
  "Five Little Fingers"/"Los dedos de la mano"
  Who Took the Cookie from the Cookie Jar?/¿Quién se comió la galleta?
  "Farmer in the Dell"/"El granjero en la cañada"
  Hopscotch/Rayuela

Materials to Gather
- tactile numeral cards (1–10)
- connecting cubes
- small containers

MATH

Focus
- Recite "Five Little Fingers"/"Los dedos de la mano" with the children.
- Play Who Took the Cookie from the Cookie Jar?/¿Quién se comió la galleta? with the children.

Develop
- Have Rafita and/or Pepita make mistakes in verbal counting as on Day 3. Then begin to include mistakes in object counting, such as skipping objects, saying 1 number word while pointing to 2 items, saying 2 number words while pointing to 1 item, pointing once but indicating more than 1 object, or pointing more than once to 1 object. Rafita's and Pepita's errors are all one-to-one correspondence errors. Even if children can count verbally, they often make one-to-one correspondence errors somewhere between saying the number, pointing, and touching an object.
- Secretly hide 2 connecting cubes in the Mystery Box. Have a child feel them and tell how many. Encourage the children to tell how they figured out how many cubes they were feeling.

Practice
- Have the children continue sorting and labeling dinosaurs into small containers.
- Encourage a small group of children to continue the Mystery Box activity.
- Invite the children to play Memory Game: Numbers version/Juego de memoria: versión números with the cards.
- Encourage the children to continue to work with the Places Scenes background.
- The children may work on Dinosaur Shop, Level 1.

Reflect/Assess

- Show the numeral 8 either upright or turned on its side. *How do you know how to read this numeral?*
  ¿Cómo creen que se debe leer este número?

Content Connection

Fine Arts

Objectives

To use a variety of materials to create original work

To use different colors, surface textures, and shapes to create form and meaning

Materials to Gather

vegetables, leaves, seeds, paint

Activity 1

- Have the children use natural objects such as vegetables, leaves, and seeds to create prints with paint. Help the children notice how each object appears. Is it a complete print, a shape, or only part of a shape? Why?

Activity 2

- Encourage the children to make crayon rubbings of leaves, seeds, and vegetable skins. Call attention to each rubbing. Is it a complete print, a shape, or only part of a shape?

Reflect on the Day

- *What have you learned today?*
  ¿Qué han aprendido hoy?
- *What is your favorite kind of ice cream?*
  ¿Cuál es su sabor de helado favorito?

Music and Movement

- Play and sing "Farmer in the Dell"/"El granjero en la cañada."
- Play Ice-Cream Hopscotch/ Rayuela. Instead of putting numerals on the hopscotch grid, use colored chalk to make different flavors of ice-cream cones.

Suggested Reading

Lunch by Denise Fleming
Mouse Mess by Linnea Asplind Riley
Rooster's Off to See the World by Eric Carle

Begin the Day

- Sing "Raindrop Song"/"Canción gotas de lluvia." Perform the "Little Red Apple"/"Manzanita roja" finger play. *Which foods in the song and finger play are healthful foods?*
  ¿Qué comidas en la canción y en el juego con los dedos son saludables?
- Use one of the suggestions for Morning Circle offered in the front of this *Teacher's Edition.*

Objective

- To understand that print carries a message by recognizing labels, signs, and other print forms in the environment

Vocabulary

junk food — alimentos, comida no saludable
healthful food — alimentos, comida saludable

DLM Materials

- Oral Language Cards 68–72
- *SRA Alphabet Book*
- *Los niños alfabéticos*
- *Teacher's Resource Anthology*
  "Raindrop Song"/"Canción gotas de lluvia"
  "Little Red Apple"/"Manzanita roja"
  "The Donut Song"/"La canción de la rosca"
  "The Donut Machine"/"La máquina de donas"
  junk food and healthful food patterns
  "Candy Land Journey"/"Un viaje a la tierra del dulce"

Materials to Gather

- examples of healthful and unhealthful food
- food pyramid
- magazines
- fast food packaging
- plastic food
- play money

LITERACY

Focus

- Ask the children about the dairy products they had for dinner last night. Make a list.
- Tell the children that today they will learn about healthful and unhealthful food.

Develop

One Way to Develop the Lesson

- Show the foods that you brought to the circle. Let the children help you sort the foods into healthful and unhealthful categories.
- Point out that the healthful foods are all in the basic food groups represented by the box pyramid. Point out that the other foods such as cookies, cakes, donuts, and candies do not show up on the pyramid because they do not contain a sufficient amount of the vitamins and minerals that people need. Be sure that the children understand that it is okay to eat unhealthful foods once in a while but that they should not make a habit of including them in their regular diets.
- Show Oral Language Cards 68–72. Explain that all the foods in these photos are healthful foods.
- Explain that people need healthful foods to live, grow, be strong and healthy, and for energy to think.

Another Way to Develop the Lesson

- Discuss the food people buy at fast-food restaurants. Explain that most of it is not considered healthful because it is high in fat and low in vitamins and nutrients. Ask the children which foods they eat from fast-food restaurants.
- Sing "The Donut Song"/"La canción de la rosca."
- Present "The Donut Machine"/"La máquina de donas" flannel board story. *What could the baker make that would be a good food for us to eat?*

  ¿Qué podría hacer el pastelero que sería saludable para nosotros?
- Discuss why donuts are not healthful. Explain that they have a high sugar content, limited nutrients, and high fat content. Be sure that children understand that it is fine to eat somewhat unhealthful foods every once in a while.

Practice

- Pass out the junk food and healthful food pattern cards. Invite the children to sort the foods into categories of *good for me* and *not good for me*. Make sorting mats labeled *Junk Food* and *Good Food*. Add pictures to each mat so that the children will be able to discern the differences.
- Provide packaging from fast-food restaurants along with plastic food, play money, and other props and have the children set up a fast food restaurant. Have them order hamburgers, hot dogs, fish sandwiches, chicken nuggets, and so on.
- Invite the children to draw pictures of their favorite junk food.

Preparation

- Gather examples of healthful and unhealthful food.
- Prepare the flannel board story, if not already made.
- Find magazine pictures of unhealthful foods.
- Make photocopies of the junk food and healthful food patterns. Color them, cut them out, and laminate them.

Second Language Learners

Ask parents to send healthful foods from the food pyramid. Have a healthful food feast in the classroom, served family style. Make sure all children know the names of all the foods. Ask the children to describe the food sent from home. Before eating, discuss polite language used at the table: "Please pass the (rice)/Por favor, pásame el (arroz)." "May I please have more (chicken)/Más (pollo), por favor." "May I be excused?/¿Me puedo levantar de la mesa?"

Anthology Support

"Little Red Apple"
"Manzanita roja"
"Drink, Drink, Drink Your Milk"
"Toma, toma tu leche"

DAY 5

Letter Knowledge

English

- Point out the letter *j* in *junk food.* Make sandpaper letter *j*s. Invite the children to trace the letters with their fingers (point out the *f* in *fingers*) and then make crayon rubbings of the letter.

Spanish

- Make sandpaper letter *l*s. Invite the children to trace the letters with their fingers and then make crayon rubbings of the letter.

Suggested Reading

The Chocolate-Covered-Cookie Tantrum by Deborah Blumenthal
Lunch by Denise Fleming
Gordito, gordón gato Galano by Donald Charles

Teacher's NOTE

Be sensitive to the fact that most children have little control over their diets.

Reflect/Assess

- *What is your favorite junk food? Can you think of a healthful food you might try to eat instead?*
  ¿Cuál es su comida no saludable favorita? ¿Podrían pensar en una comida saludable que probarían en su lugar?
- *What is your favorite healthful food to eat?*
  ¿Cuál es la comida saludable que más les gusta comer?

Literacy Circle

Storytime 1

- Invite the children to participate in the "Candy Land Journey"/ "Un viaje a la tierra del dulce" action story.

Storytime 2

- Read "Crusty Corn Bread" or "Popping Popcorn" from the *SRA Alphabet Book,* or "La piña" from *Los niños alfabéticos.* Discuss why these foods are important.

Content Connection

Personal/Social

Objective
To begin to be responsible for individual behavior and actions

Vocabulary
please, thank you, manners
por favor, gracias, modales

DLM Materials
- *Teacher's Resource Anthology*
  "Table Manners"/"Modales de mesa"
  "Pimpón"
  American Sign Language

Activity 1

- Read "Table Manners"/"Modales de mesa" or "Pimpón." Discuss the examples of bad manners described in the poem and ask the children to name other behaviors that make people uncomfortable. Talk about manners that change depending on the situation. For example, people might eat with their fingers at home but not at a restaurant.
- Remember that mealtime manners differ with situations and cultures. Encourage the children to talk about the differences among situations and cultures in foods, utensils, table settings, and so on.

Activity 2

- Read "Table Manners"/"Modales de mesa" or "Pimpón" again. Have the children brainstorm a list of manners that people use when they're eating. Post the list near the snack area.
- Teach the children to say *please* and *thank you* in American Sign Language.

DAY 5

Objectives

- To match numerals to collections of items
- To use a variety of software packages with audio, video, and graphics to enhance learning experiences

Vocabulary

numbers to 10 números hasta 10

DLM Materials

- dinosaur counters
- Rafita and Pepita/Rafita y Pepita
- *Math Resource Guide*
  Numeral Jump/Saltar números
  Mystery Box
- *DLM Math* software
- *Four Baby Bumblebees* CD
- *Teacher's Resource Anthology*
  "Ten Little Fingers"/"Diez deditos"
  Who Took the Cookie from the Cookie Jar?/¿Quién se comió la galleta?

Materials to Gather

- muffin tins
- paper or foam numerals
- see Day 4

More Help Suggest that the children count as they take the cubes apart one at a time and place them outside the Mystery Box.

Extra Challenge Have the children feel a connecting cube tower, add one inside the Mystery Box, and then tell how many.

MATH

Focus

- Say "Ten Little Fingers"/"Diez deditos" verses 1 to 8. Teach verses 9 and 10.
- Play Numeral Jump/Saltar números as on Days 2 and 3.

Develop

- Review counting by having Rafita and Pepita/Rafita y Pepita make any mistakes you have already used. You may wish to add the mistake of saying the wrong number as the final count, for example, counting 3 objects correctly but then saying, "There are 4"/"Hay 4."

Practice

- Invite the children to play Numeral Jump/Saltar números with a friend. Use the Numeral cards.
- Encourage the children to continue to sort numerals into muffin tins as they did on Day 1.
- Have the children continue sorting and labeling dinosaurs into small containers.
- Encourage the children to continue to work with the Mystery Box by secretly hiding 10 or fewer connecting cubes for a friend to see if he or she can feel them and tell how many.
- Have the children work on Dinosaur Shop, Level 1.

Reflect/Assess

- *At the computer, how did you figure out how many were hidden under the napkin?*

  En la computadora, ¿cómo determinaron cuántos había escondidos debajo de la servilleta?
- *How did you know how many cubes there were in the Mystery Box?*

  ¿Cómo sabían cuántos cubos había en la Caja misteriosa?

Music and Movement

- Play Who Took the Cookie from the Cookie Jar?/¿Quién se comió la galleta?
- Play "On the Good Ship Lollipop" from the *Four Baby Bumblebees* CD. Invite the children to dance and sing along. *Who can name all the candies mentioned in the song?*

  ¿Quién puede nombrar todos los caramelos mencionados en la canción?

Content Connection

Fine Arts/Personal and Social Development

Objectives

To use different colors, surfaces, and shapes to create form and meaning

To begin to express thoughts, feelings, and ideas through language as well as through gestures and actions

Materials to Gather

finger paint, lemon drops, gumdrops

Activity 1

- Provide finger paint. Encourage the children to make finger prints over numerals that you have written on index cards.

Activity 2

- Encourage the children to serve a snack to a friend. Have each child use a plastic spoon to spoon 2 lemon drops and 3 gumdrops onto a napkin for his or her friend. Remind the children to ask each other which colors of gumdrops they would like to have.

Reflect on the Day

- *What kinds of food have we talked about this week?*

  ¿Qué tipos de comida hemos comentado esta semana?
- *Which kind of food do you need to eat more of?*

  ¿De qué tipo de comida tienen que comer más?

Suggested Reading

Numblers by Suse MacDonald and Bill Oakes

Looking Ahead

Connecting to the Theme: Nursery Rhymes

Hopefully, most preschool children are developing a love of spoken language. Nursery rhymes can be a traditional way to motivate children and to have fun discovering language. Nursery rhymes and other rhymes also assist in a child's comprehension of real and imaginary.

	Objectives	DLM Materials	Materials to Gather
DAY 1	• To begin to identify rhymes and rhyming words, participate in rhyming games,and repeat rhyming songs and poems • To begin to perform simple investigations	• *Humpty Dumpty Dumpty* • *Teacher's Resource Anthology*	• bowl • cottage cheese • pipe cleaners • spoon • white yarn • bandages • inclined plank • plastic lids
DAY 2	• To begin to identify rhymes and rhyming words, participate in rhyming games, and repeat rhyming songs and poems • To move within a space of defined boundaries, changing body configurations to accommodate the space	• *The Little Ants/Las hormiguitas* • *Humpty Dumpty Dumpty* • *Teacher's Resource Anthology*	• construction-paper moon • mitten templates • mittens • wallpaper samples • masking tape • yarn
DAY 3	• To begin to identify rhymes and rhyming words, participate in rhyming games, and repeat rhyming songs and poems • To become more able to move from one space to another in different ways	• *Teacher's Resource Anthology*	• pipe cleaners • eyedroppers • food coloring • coffee filters • baby doll and night clothes • beanbags
DAY 4	• To begin to identify rhymes and rhyming words, participate in rhyming games, and repeat rhyming songs and poems • To use different colors, surface textures, and shapes to create form and meaning	• *The Itsy Bitsy Spider/La araña pequeñita* • *Teacher's Resource Anthology*	• chocolate • milk • rock salt • shoes • tweezers • tea party props • star templates • *The Starry Night* print • white felt stars and moon
DAY 5	• To begin to identify rhymes and rhyming words, participate in rhyming games, and repeat rhyming songs and poems • To count concrete objects to five or higher	• *Teacher's Resource Anthology*	• chocolate bar • doll • class book of nursery rhymes • gift bag • long stick • mitten • pie tin • spider • ten paper plates • fish crackers

(See individual lesson pages for complete lists of materials.)

Learning Centers

DRAMATIC PLAY

Nursery Rhyme Theater

Objective
To begin to engage in dramatic play with others

Materials to Gather
candlestick, cat, cow, dish, dog, fiddle, pie tins, spider, spoon

Develop
Place any of the nursery rhyme props you can locate from the Materials list in the Dramatic Play Center. Encourage the children to dramatize the rhymes they are learning during the week.

Reflect/Assess
Which nursery rhyme do you enjoy acting out the most?
¿Cuál canción/rima de cuna les gusta más representar?

LIBRARY

Remembering and Respecting Rhymes

Objective
To understand that books and other print resources are handled in specific ways

Materials to Gather
nursery rhyme books

Develop
Fill the Library Center with nursery rhyme books. Read some rhymes to the children and/or let the children recall some rhymes for you. Model and discuss with them how to handle all books properly.

Reflect/Assess
Which rhyme or book do you like to listen to the best?
¿Cuál rima o libro les gusta escuchar más?

WRITING

Copying Words

Objective
To begin to associate the names of letters with their shapes

Materials to Gather
magnetic letters, markers, paper

Develop
Post charts of the nursery rhymes that you will be creating each day in the Writing Center. Invite the children to copy the rhymes or some rhyming words using paper and markers or magnetic letters.

Reflect/Assess
Do you prefer to use the markers and crayons or the magnetic letters? Why?
¿Prefieren usar los marcadores y creyones o las letras imantadas? ¿Por qué?

What Research Suggests

Rhyme is a language pattern. Our cognitive structures are based on patterns. The more patterns children develop in their understanding of language, the greater their ability to relate to future learning. This also increases their ability to manipulate language into new creations.

Begin the Day

- Sing the "Nursery Rhyme Rap"/ "El rap infantil."
- Use a suggestion for Morning Circle found in the front of this *Teacher's Edition.*

Objective

- To begin to identify rhymes and rhyming sounds in familiar words, participate in rhyming games, and repeat rhyming songs and poems

Vocabulary

crown	corona
curds	cuajadas
fetch	traer
nursery rhyme	canción de cuna
pail	cubo
tuffet	silla baja
whey	suero (de la leche)

DLM Materials

- *Humpty Dumpty Dumpty*
- *Teacher's Resource Anthology*
  "Little Miss Muffet"/"La Señorita Mufete" flannel board story
  Nursery Rhyme Concentration game

Materials to Gather

- bowl
- cottage cheese ("curds and whey")
- pipe cleaners ("the spider")
- spoon
- white yarn
- bandages

LITERACY

Focus

- Tell the children that they will be learning nursery rhymes this week. Explain that nursery rhymes are stories that have been around for a long time and that most of the stories rhyme.
- Explain that, each day, the children should say the rhymes they learn to their families. They will be excited to learn that their families can say some of the rhymes with them.

Develop

One Way to Develop the Lesson

- Teach the children "Jack and Jill"/"Jack y Jill" or "Sana, sana." Read the rhyme from the chart you prepared and point to each word as you read.
- Read the rhyme again. Help children fill in the rhyming words.
- Point out the alliteration in "Jack and Jill"/"Jack y Jill." Discuss the unusual vocabulary in the rhyme such as *fetch, pail,* and *crown.* Ask the children why they think Jack fell and what made Jill fall.
- Point out the alliteration in "Sana, sana." Discuss whether a little frog's tail really helps you heal.

Another Way to Develop the Lesson

- Present the "Little Miss Muffet"/"La Señorita Mufete" flannel board story.
- Invite the children to identify the rhyming words.
- Present the alternative second verse to the rhyme. Ask: *Which ending do you like best and why? What made the endings different?*

  ¿Cuál final les gustó más y por qué? ¿Qué hizo que los finales fueran diferentes?
- Tell the children that they are going to make a big spider web. Sitting in a circle, have the children roll a ball of white yarn randomly to one another as they say the rhyme. Continue until each child is holding a piece of yarn.

Preparation

- Write "Jack and Jill"/"Jack y Jill" or "Sana, sana" on chart paper.
- Prepare the "Little Miss Muffet"/"La Señorita Mufete" flannel board story.
- Prepare the Nursery Rhyme Concentration game. Photocopy two nursery rhyme patterns. Color the patterns, cut them out, and then laminate them.
- Get cottage cheese.

Practice

- Have the children play the Nursery Rhyme Concentration game.
- Place the "Little Miss Muffet"/"La Señorita Mufete" flannel board story in the Language Center. Invite the children to retell the rhyme or to make up a new version.
- Encourage children to illustrate one of the rhymes. Collect their drawings to make a class nursery rhyme book later in the week.
- Provide a bowl, a spoon, and a spider made of pipe cleaners. Have the children act out "Little Miss Muffet"/"La Señorita Mufete."
- Provide curds and whey (cottage cheese). Let the children sample it.
- Give the children bandages and let them practice nursing each other's pretend wounds.

Scaffolding Strategies

More Help Have the children perform various nursery rhymes.

Extra Challenge Help the children compare two nursery rhymes.

Second Language Learners

Do the "Little Miss Muffet"/"La Señorita Mufete" flannel board story several times. First, pantomime the story. Children can do the actions as you recite story lines. Then use flannel board figures. Invite children to recite with you. Finally, tell the story as a group and audiotape it. Put the flannel board, its figures, and audiotape in a center. Have the children place figures on the board following the tape.

DAY 1

Letter Knowledge

English

- Introduce the letter *k* using the "Katie" story from the *English Phonics Resource Guide.*

Spanish

- Introduce the letter *d* using the "David" story from the *Spanish Phonics Resource Guide.*

Suggested Reading

Animal Crackers by Jane Dyer
Tomie de Paola's Mother Goose Favorites by Tomie de Paola
The Three Little Pigs by James Marshall

Teacher's NOTE

Mother Goose rhymes are from England and were written in the 1700s. Originally, the rhymes were used to pass information along to the commoners about the goings-on in the king's court.

Anthology Support

"The Grand Old Duke of York"
"Pin uno"

Reflect/Assess

- *What makes a nursery rhyme a nursery rhyme?*
  ¿Qué hace que una canción sea una canción de cuna?
- *Did you like how the curds and whey tasted?*
  ¿Les gustó el sabor de las cuajadas y el suero de leche?

Literacy Circle

Storytime 1

- Read *Humpty Dumpty Dumpty* to the children. Stop just before the part of the story where Mr. Moore fixes the broken egg.
- Ask the children if they can think of a way to help Humpty Dumpty. Finish reading the story. Discuss Mr. Moore's solution to the problem.

Storytime 2

- Read another version of "Humpty Dumpty." Help the children compare the two versions. You may also write "Él/ella compró un huevito" on a sheet of chart paper to read to the children.

Content Connection

Science

Objective
To begin to perform simple investigations

Vocabulary
inclined plank
tabla inclinada

Materials to Gather
heavy objects, inclined plank, light objects, plastic lids

Activity 1

- Have the children roll small plastic lids (shaving cream can lids, deodorant) down inclined planks to imitate the pail that followed Jack and Jill down the hill. Ask: *What makes the lids roll? Do the lids roll faster on an inclined plank (hill) or on the level floor?*
  ¿Qué hace que las tapas rueden? ¿Las tapas ruedan más rápidamente en una tabla inclinada (colina) o en un piso nivelado?

Activity 2

- Give the children light objects (small paper plates, cups) and heavier objects (buttons, pennies) to roll down the inclined plank. Discuss which items roll faster and where the items roll faster: on the incline, at the top, or near the bottom. Ask children: *Do you think Jack or his pail reached the bottom of the hill first?*
  ¿Creen que Jack o su cubo llegará primero al pie de la colina?

DAY 1

Objectives

- To begin to investigate and predict the results of putting together two or more shapes
- To start, use, and exit software programs

Vocabulary

triangle	triángulo
square	cuadrado
rectangle	rectángulo
circle	círculo
hexagon	hexágono
trapezoid	trapecio
rhombus	rombo

DLM Materials

- pattern blocks
- *Math Resource Guide*
  Shape Set (several sets)
  Pattern Block Cutouts
  Guessing Bag
- *DLM Math* software
- *Making Music with Thomas Moore* CD
- *Teacher's Resource Anthology*
  gelatin jigglers

Materials To Gather

- soup can or other geometric object

Preparation

- Photocopy several Shape Sets or Pattern Block Cutouts onto construction paper. Make rhombuses blue and tan and trapezoids red.
- Place a soup can or other geometric object in the Guessing Bag.

MATH

Focus

- This week begins with a brief review of geometric shapes. Hold up a rectangle, circle, square, and triangle one at a time from the Shape Set and encourage children to tell you their names.
- From the Shape Set, hold up the rhombus. Ask children to describe it.
- Accept and encourage children's own descriptions. Encourage them to compare it to objects in their homes or other places in the world.
- Tell children that mathematicians call it a "rhombus."
- Repeat with the trapezoid.

Develop

- Tell the children there are new shapes to explore.
- Show the pattern block shapes one after another, having students name each one. Focus on the two rhombuses (blue and tan) and the trapezoid (red).
- Demonstrate Mystery Toys, Level 3. At this level, the children match a wider variety of shapes than in Level 1. When they have completed Mystery Toys, they may play Memory—Geometry, Level 3.

Practice

- Provide Shape Sets or Pattern Block Cutouts. Challenge the children to make pictures out of them by combining shapes in different ways. Encourage the children to ask their friends for the shapes they need using the names of the shapes.
- Invite the children to feel the object in the Guessing Bag. Encourage them to share their guesses.
- Have the children work on Mystery Toys, Level 3, and Memory—Geometry, Level 3.

Reflect/Assess

- *How did you remember the names of the shapes?*
  ¿Cómo recordaron los nombres de las figuras?

Content Connection

Science

Objective
To use one or more senses to observe and learn about objects, events, and organisms

DLM Materials
Guessing Bag
Teacher's Resource Anthology
gelatin jigglers

Materials to Gather
gelatin, cookie cutters, plastic knife

Activity 1

- With a "mystery object" already hidden in the Guessing Bag, challenge children to feel it over the next couple of days and guess what it might be based on its shape and so on. Tell them to secretly tell friends what they think is in the bag after each friend has had a chance to feel it, but don't say it out loud!

Activity 2

- Allow children to help mix gelatin to make gelatin jigglers. When the gelatin sets, invite the children to cut it into geometric shapes.

Music and Movement

- Have the children do the Humpty Dumpty from the *Making Music with Thomas Moore* CD.
- Invite the children to do Humpty Dumpty rolls (forward rolls) on carpet or outdoors in the grass.

Suggested Reading

Look, Look, Look by Tana Hoban

Reflect on the Day

- *Which of the rhymes did you like best today? Can you say it?*
  ¿Cuál rima les gustó más hoy? ¿La pueden repetir?
- *Say today's nursery rhymes to your family tonight. See who can join you in the rhyme.*
  Díganles las rimas o canciones de cuna a sus familias esta noche. Fíjense quién puede acompañarlos a decirlas.

Home Connection

From the *Home Connections Resource Guide*, send home with the children the Shapes letter and the Nursery Rhyme letter. The nursery rhyme letter will allow families to become familiar with the rhymes the children are learning this week.

Begin the Day

- Sing the "Nursery Rhyme Rap"/"El rap infantil."
- Use one of the suggestions for Morning Circle offered in the front of this *Teacher's Edition*.

Objective

- To begin to identify rhymes and rhyming sounds in familiar words, participate in rhyming games, and repeat rhyming songs and poems

Vocabulary

fiddle	violín
naughty	travieso
nursery rhyme	canción de cuna

DLM Materials

- *The Little Ants/Las hormiguitas*
- *Humpty Dumpty Dumpty* book and listening tape
- *Teacher's Resource Anthology*
  Nursery Rhyme card patterns
  Nursery Rhyme Concentration game

Materials to Gather

- construction-paper moon
- mitten templates
- mittens
- wallpaper samples

Preparation

- Write "Hey Diddle Diddle"/"¡Eh, chin, chin!" or "La boca" on chart paper.
- Cut a moon out of construction paper.
- Make mitten templates.

LITERACY

Focus

- Discuss the nursery rhymes that were introduced yesterday. Say each of them with the children.
- Tell the children that we will learn more rhymes today.

Develop

One Way to Develop the Lesson

- Read "Hey Diddle Diddle"/"¡Eh, chin, chin!" or "La boca" to the children from the chart paper.
- Help them identify the rhyming words.
- Read the rhyme a second time, allowing the children to fill in the rhyming words.
- For "Hey Diddle Diddle"/"¡Eh, chin, chin!" ask the children: *What made the dog laugh? Which two things in the story ran away together?*
  ¿Qué hizo reír al perro? ¿Cuáles dos cosas en el cuento salieron corriendo juntas?
- For "La boca," discuss with the children whether their eyes and ears sleep when they sleep.

Another Way to Develop the Lesson

- Read "Three Little Kittens"/"Los tres gatitos" to the children. Remind them to listen carefully. Read the rhyme a second time. Invite the children to fill in the rhyming words.
- Write the words *kittens* and *mittens* on a piece of chart paper. Have the children look at the two words and tell you how they are different. Then discuss how the two words are alike.
- Ask: *Why did the kittens get in trouble? Have you ever lost something and gotten in trouble for it? Which other nursery rhyme has a pie in it?*

  ¿Por qué se metieron en problemas los gatitos? ¿Alguna vez han perdido algo y se han metido en un problema por eso? ¿Cuál otra canción de cuna habla también de un pastel?

Practice

- Have children play the Nursery Rhyme Concentration game.
- Encourage the children to illustrate one of the nursery rhymes. Save their drawings for the nursery rhyme book that will be made on Thursday.
- Give the children mitten templates and wallpaper samples. Have them trace the templates onto the wallpaper to make mitten pairs.
- Place the *Humpty Dumpty Dumpty* book and listening tape in the Listening Center. Encourage the children to listen to the story again.
- Hide mittens in the classroom and have the children find them.
- Cut a moon out of construction paper (you may also use posterboard). Place it in the Blocks Center. Have children jump over it.
- Have the children draw faces. How many noses, ears, eyes, and mouths should each face have? Have them say "La boca" while they draw.

Scaffolding Strategies

More Help Invite the children to perform a nursery rhyme.

Extra Challenge Help the children look for similarities in all the rhymes to which they have been introduced. Encourage them to think about characters, names, and rhyme structure.

Second Language Learners

In the Listening center, invite children to recite "Little Miss Muffet"/"La Señorita Mufete" to a stuffed animal. Depending on their proficiency level and familiarity with the story, children may recall the rhythm and key words of the entire rhyme. Note language used.

Anthology Support

"Fiddle-I-Fee"
"Riqui-riqui-ra"
"Frog Went a-Courtin'"
"El sapo fue a cortejar"

DAY 2

Letter Knowledge

English

- Read the *k* selection entitled "Keepsakes" from the *SRA Alphabet Book.* Explain that the word *kittens* begins with the letter *k.*

Spanish

- Read the *d* selection entitled "Daniel" from *Los niños alfabéticos.*

Suggested Reading

Babushka's Mother Goose by Patricia Polacco
Richard Scarry's Best Mother Goose Ever
Tortillitas Para Mama compiled by Margot Griego

Reflect/Assess

- *Do you know anyone who plays a fiddle?*
  ¿Conocen a alguien que toque violín?
- *Which animal was in both rhymes?*
  ¿Qué animal estaba en ambas canciones?

Literacy Circle

Storytime 1

- Read *The Little Ants/Las hormiguitas.* Ask: *Can you think of a song that is similar to this book?*
  ¿Pueden pensar en una canción que se parezca a este libro?
- Invite the children to attempt the dance moves that the ants used.

Storytime 2

- Read *Humpty Dumpty Dumpty* again. Compare the dances of the children in this story to the dance of the ants in *The Little Ants/Las hormiguitas.*

Content Connection

Physical Development

Objective
To move within a space of defined boundaries, changing body configurations to accommodate the space

Vocabulary
slink, stalk, stretch,
escabullir, caminar cautelosamente, estirarse

Materials to Gather
masking tape, yarn

Activity 1
- Provide a piece of masking tape on the floor or a balance beam. Have the children walk safely on the masking tape line or the balance beam. Encourage them to move like a cat. Ask: *Can you stalk? Can you stretch?*
  ¿Pueden caminar cautelosamente? ¿Pueden estirarse?

Activity 2
- Dangle a piece of yarn in front of the children. Explain that they should chase it like kittens and cats do.

Objectives

- To begin to recognize, describe, and name shapes
- To begin to recognize when a shape's position or orientation has changed

Vocabulary

rhombus	rombo
triangle	triángulo
square	cuadrado
rectangle	rectángulo
circle	círculo
diamond	diamante

DLM Materials

- pattern blocks
- *Math Resource Guide*
  Shape Step/Paso de figuras
  Shape Set (several sets)
  Pattern Block Cutouts
  Guessing Bag
- *DLM Math* software
- *Teacher's Resource Anthology*
  "My Hat, It Has Three Corners"
  Duck, Duck, Goose/Pato, pato, ganso
  "Miss Mary Mack"/"La Señorita María Marao"
  "Hey Diddle Diddle"/"¡Eh, chin, chin!"

Materials to Gather

- three-dimensional object

Preparation

- Place the 3-dimensional object in the Guessing Bag.

MATH

Focus

- Count in groups of two from 1 to 20, jumping with each count.
- Sing "My Hat, It Has Three Corners" with the children. Ask what shape a corner is similar to. Ask them what shape the hat was.

Develop

- Show the children shapes from the Shape Set, casually naming the shapes as you go.
- Tell the children you have a new shape for them to explore. Show the rhombuses from the Shape Set, using different orientations. Give the children time to manipulate these shapes. Ask them to describe these shapes. They may notice that all four sides are the same length or that there are two pairs of parallel sides. A rhombus has two pairs of parallel sides, and all the sides are the same length. The focus should be on distinguishing one shape from another, not necessarily on naming the shapes.
- Compare the square to the rhombuses. Children may respond that it is a diamond. Accept this answer. You may mention that mathematicians call it a *rhombus*. Ask what is the same and what is different about the rhombuses.
- Hold up a trapezoid from the Shape Set and one from the pattern blocks. Hold them in different orientations. Ask the children to name and describe the shapes.

Practice

- Invite children to explore the Shape Sets or the pattern blocks. Encourage them to find any of these shapes in the classroom. Encourage them to discuss and name shapes.
- Invite the children to play Shape Step/Paso de figuras with a friend (see Color, Shape, and Size, Day 1).
- Encourage the children to feel the object in the Guessing Bag and secretly tell their friends what they think it is.
- Have the children work on Mystery Toys, Level 3.

Reflect/Assess

- Show two of the pattern block rhombuses. *What is the same about these two shapes? What is different?*

  ¿En qué se parecen estas dos figuras? ¿En qué se diferencian?

Music and Movement

- Play Dish, Dish, Spoon/Fuente, fuente, cuchara the same way you would play Duck, Duck, Goose/Pato, pato, ganso.
- Sing "Miss Mary Mack"/"La Señorita María Marao." Discuss what happens in the song that is similar to the cow jumping over the moon in "Hey Diddle Diddle"/"¡Eh, chin, chin!"

Content Connection

Fine Arts

Objective

To begin to create or re-create stories, moods, or experiences through dramatic representation

DLM Materials

The Itsy Bitsy Spider/ La araña pequeñita

Teacher's Resource Anthology

"Little Miss Muffet"/ "La Señorita Mufete"

Activity 1

- Read *The Itsy Bitsy Spider*. Use silhouettes to identify key elements (the pipe, the spider web) and what shape they are. Act out the story.

Activity 2

- Use silhouettes to identify key elements (the spider, the tuffet, the spoon) in "Little Miss Muffet"/"La Señorita Mufete."

Suggested Reading

Itsy Bitsy Spider by Iza Trapani

A Fishy Shape Story by Joanne Wylie and David Graham

Reflect on the Day

- *Which of the rhymes did you like best today? Can you say it?*

  ¿Cuál de las rimas les gustó más hoy? ¿La pueden repetir?
- *Say today's nursery rhymes to your family tonight. See who can join you in the rhyme.*

  Díganles las rimas o canciones de cuna a sus familias esta noche. Fíjense quién puede acompañarlos a decirlas.

What Research Suggests

One advantage of the computer storing records is that it provides individualized practice for each child so that he or she can work on specific shapes.

Begin the Day

- Sing the "Nursery Rhyme Rap"/"El rap infantil."
- Use a suggestion in the front of this *Teacher's Edition* for Morning Circle.

Objective

- To begin to identify rhymes and rhyming sounds in familiar words, participate in rhyming games, and repeat rhyming songs and poems

Vocabulary

nimble   ágil/ligero

DLM Materials

- Metamorphosis Sequence Cards
- *Teacher's Resource Anthology*
  "Wee Willie Winkie"/"Muchachito dormilón"
  "Está la mariposa"
  "This Is the House That Jack Built"/"Ésta es la casa que Juan construyó"
  Nursery Rhyme Concentration game
  Nursery Rhyme card patterns

Materials to Gather

- blocks
- pipe cleaners
- eyedroppers
- food coloring
- coffee filters
- baby doll and night clothes

LITERACY

Focus

- Discuss the nursery rhymes that were introduced yesterday. Say each of them with the children.

Develop

One Way to Develop the Lesson

- Teach the children "Wee Willie Winkie"/"Muchachito dormilón." Read the rhyme from the chart you have prepared. Be sure to point to each word as you read it so the children can follow along.
- Read the rhyme again. Help children fill in the rhyming words.
- Read the rhyme a third time and encourage the children to clap out the rhythm of the rhyme.

Another Way to Develop the Lesson

- Discuss other rhymes children have learned that have a boy named Jack in them. Ask: *Why do you think the name Jack is used often?*
  ¿Por qué creen que el nombre Jack se usa a menudo?
- Read "Jack was nimble" on page 22 of the *SRA Alphabet Book*. Discuss it with the children.
- Read "Esta la mariposa" from the chart paper. Discuss the words used to describe the butterfly.
- Ask the children to identify the rhyming words. Read the rhyme a second time. Encourage the children to fill in the rhyming words.

Practice

- Have the children play the Nursery Rhyme Concentration game.
- Invite the children to illustrate one rhyme. Collect their drawings for the class nursery rhyme book to be made tomorrow.
- Cut out a large paper oval. Draw details on the oval to make Humpty Dumpty. Cut your Humpty Dumpty into puzzle pieces. Have the children put Humpty Dumpty together again.
- Invite the children to make butterflies by using an eyedropper to drop diluted food coloring on coffee filters. When the filters are dry, use a pipe cleaner to gather the filter in the middle and create a body and antennae.
- Provide a baby doll and night clothes. Encourage the children to put the baby to bed.
- Invite the children to sequence the Metamorphosis Sequence Cards.

Preparation

- Write "Wee Willie Winkie"/"Muchachito dormilón" or "Está la mariposa" on chart paper.
- Mix play dough.
- Make "This Is the House That Jack Built"/"Ésta es la casa que Juan construyó" flannel board story.

Scaffolding Strategies

More Help Encourage the children to perform one of the nursery rhymes.

Extra Challenge Continue helping the children compare the characters, names, and structure of various nursery rhymes.

Second Language Learners

Based on "The Itsy Bitsy Spider"/"La araña pequeñita," allow the children to pretend to be spiders trying to climb up the spout. Recite the poem using a child's name: *Itsy Bitsy (Kelly) went up the water spout,* and so on. Allow a turn for each child.

Anthology Support

"Jack and the Beanstalk"
"Jaime y los frijoles mágicos"
"Jack Sprat"
"Metamorphosis"
"Mariposa Linda"

DAY 3

Letter Knowledge

English

- Have the children find the letter *k* in magazines and newspapers.

Spanish

- Have the children find the letter *d* in magazines and newspapers.

Suggested Reading

Big Fat Hen by Keith Baker
My Mother Goose Library by Iona Opie

Reflect/Assess

- *What else could Wee Willie Winkie be doing in his nightgown?*

  ¿Qué más podría hacer el muchachito dormilón en su camisón?
- *Who can remember a set of rhyming words from "Wee Willie Winkie"/"Muchachito dormilón"?*

  ¿Quién puede recordar un par de palabras que riman de "Wee Willie Winkie"/"Muchachito dormilón"?

Literacy Circle

Storytime 1

- Present the "This Is the House That Jack Built"/"Ésta es la casa que Juan construyó" flannel board story. Explain that this story is a Mother Goose rhyme. Discuss what this rhyme has in common with the other rhymes that were introduced today. Help the children think about the cause-and-effect relationship of the characters in this rhyme.

Storytime 2

- Present the "El burrito enfermo"/"My Sick Little Donkey" flannel board story. Compare the cumulative text of this original Spanish rhyme with "This Is the House That Jack Built"/"Ésta es la casa que Juan construyó."

Content Connection

Physical Development

Objective
To become more able to move from one space to another in different ways

Vocabulary
broad jumps, jumping jacks
saltos largos, buscapiés

Materials to Gather
beanbags, masking tape

Activity 1

- Teach the children how to do Jack Jumps, similar to the way they would do broad jumps. Make a starting line using masking tape. Provide a beanbag to mark the length of their jumps.

Activity 2

- Show or teach the children how to do jumping jacks.

DAY 3

Objectives

- To begin to recognize, describe, and name shapes
- To begin to recognize when a shape's position or orientation has changed

Vocabulary

rhombus	rombo
hexagon	hexágono
triangle	triángulo
square	cuadrado
rectangle	rectángulo
circle	círculo
diamond	diamante

DLM Materials

- pattern blocks
- *Math Resource Guide*
  Shape Set (several sets)
  Pattern Block Cutouts
  Guess My Rule/Adivina mi regla
  Guessing Bag
- *DLM Math* software
- *Making Music with Thomas Moore* CD
- *Teacher's Resource Anthology* "Dance, Thumbkin, Dance"

Materials to Gather

- three-dimensional object

- Fill the Guessing Bag.

MATH

Focus

- Ask the children to help you sort the shapes into two sets—hexagons and all other shapes.

Develop

- Show the rhombuses again. Then show a square. Give the children time to manipulate these pieces. Ask them to compare the rhombuses with a square in terms of their likenesses and differences.
- Play Guess My Rule/Adivina mi regla (see Color, Shape, and Size, Day 5). Tell the children you are going to sort shapes into piles and they have to guess your rule for sorting.
- One by one, place a square shape in one spot, then a non-square shape in another spot. Continue until 2 or more squares are together and 2 or more non-squares are together.
- Pick up a new shape with a quizzical look and ask the children to tell you in which pile it belongs. Place the shape in the correct pile. Repeat with other shapes.
- Ask the children to guess your rule for sorting (squares and not squares).
- Repeat the activity with new rules.

Practice

- Invite a small group of children to play Guess My Rule/Adivina mi regla.
- Have the children feel the object in the Guessing Bag (see Day 2).
- Encourage children to explore Shape Sets and pattern block shapes. Copy or memorize any of the children's designs that contain symmetry or linear patterns to show the group later this week.
- Have the children work on Memory—Geometry, Level 3.

Reflect/Assess

- *How did you know which rule I used?*
  ¿Cómo saben qué regla usé?
- *What shapes are you using to build designs or pictures? Why?*
  ¿Qué figuras usan para hacer diseños o dibujos? ¿Por qué?

Music and Movement

- Do "Dance, Thumbkin, Dance." Explain that this is an original Mother Goose rhyme.
- Do some exercises to an instrumental selection from the *Making Music with Thomas Moore* CD. Be sure to do some jumping jacks.

Content Connection

Fine Arts

Objective
To use a variety of colors, surface textures, and shapes to create form and meaning

Materials to Gather
sponges (triangular and circular shapes)

Activity 1
- Invite the children to use triangular sponges to make pictures and designs.

Activity 2
- Invite the children to use circular sponges to make pictures and designs.

Suggested Reading

The Shape of Things by Dayle Ann Dodds
All Shapes and Sizes by Shirley Hughes

Reflect on the Day

- *Which of the rhymes did you like best today? Can you say it?*
  ¿Cuál de las rimas les gustó más hoy? ¿Pueden repetirla?
- *Say today's nursery rhymes to your family tonight. See who can join you in the rhyme.*
  Díganles las rimas o canciones de cuna a sus familias esta noche. Fíjense quién puede acompañarlos a decirlas.

Home Connection

If family members work in the arts or in an art-related field (such as quilting), invite them in to discuss the shapes they use in their art.

Begin the Day

- Sing the "Nursery Rhyme Rap"/"El rap infantil."
- Use one of the suggestions for Morning Circle found in the front of this *Teacher's Edition*.

Objective

- To begin to identify rhymes and rhyming sounds in familiar words, participate in rhyming games, and repeat rhyming songs and poems

Vocabulary

bat	bate
chocolate	chocolate
nursery rhymes	canciones infantiles
out	fuera
shout	gritar
spout	declamar/hablar
stout	robusto/incansable

DLM Materials

- *The Itsy Bitsy Spider/La araña pequeñita*
- *Teacher's Resource Anthology*
  "El burrito enfermo"/"My Sick Little Donkey" flannel board story
  "I'm a Little Teapot"
  Nursery Rhyme card patterns
  Nursery Rhyme Concentration game

Materials to Gather

- chocolate (allergy warning)
- index cards
- milk (allergy warning)
- rock salt
- shoes (with a variety of fasteners)
- tweezers
- tea party props

LITERACY

Focus

- Discuss the nursery rhymes that were introduced yesterday. Say each of them with the children.
- Tell the children that many nursery rhymes have been put to music and are now songs. Often, the songs are more familiar to us. Tell them we will learn about musical rhymes today.

Develop

One Way to Develop the Lesson

- Read "I'm a Little Teapot" from the chart. The children should recognize this nursery rhyme. This song is also easy to learn in a second language.
- Help the children identify the rhyming words. Show them the words on the chart or in the book. Read the rhyme again. Invite the children to fill in the rhyming words.
- Write *stout, spout, shout,* and *out* on a piece of chart paper. Ask the children to find the three letters that are the same in each word.
- Sing the rhymes as songs with the children. Teach them the hand motions that go with each song.

Another Way to Develop the Lesson

- Say "Twinkle, Twinkle Little Star"/"Brilla, brilla, estrellita." This is a nursery rhyme/song that the children should recognize.
- Encourage the children to name the rhyming words they hear in the song. Read the rhyme again and have the children fill in the rhyming words. This should be easy if the children know the song.
- Teach the children the second verse of the "Twinkle, Twinkle Little Star"/"Brilla, brilla, estrellita" rhyme/song. Again, you may have them fill in the rhyming words.

Practice

- Have the children play the Nursery Rhyme Concentration game.
- Invite the children to make a drawing about one nursery rhyme.
- Help the children make chocolate milk and drink it. (Allergy)
- Give each child an index card with the word *star* written on it. Provide rock salt ("diamonds from the sky"), glue, and tweezers. Help them trace the letters of the word *star* with the glue. They can use the tweezers to move the rock salt onto the glue outline.
- Let the children have a tea party in the Dramatic Play Center.

Preparation

- Print the words from "I'm a Little Teapot" on chart paper.
- Write the word *star* on several index cards.
- Gather the milk and chocolate.
- Ask for the children's nursery rhyme drawings at the end of the day. Put them in a plastic bag book for the Library Center.
- Make the Nursery Rhyme Concentration game by copying, cutting out, and laminating the Nursery Rhyme card patterns.

Scaffolding Strategies

More Help Sing the songs before you introduce the nursery rhymes.

Extra Challenge Invite the children to make up a new verse to a rhyme.

Second Language Learners

Show a teapot before teaching "I'm a Little Teapot." Talk about the handle and the spout. Point them out on the teapot. Perform the rhyme and then have the children act it out with you. Note if they mouth the words of the rhyme. Repeat this throughout the day.

DAY 4

Letter Knowledge

English

- Have the children make the letter *k* in a sand tray.

Spanish

- Have the children make the letter *d* in a sand tray.

Suggested Reading

To Market, to Market by Anne Miranda
The Real Mother Goose by Blanche Fisher Wright

Anthology Support

"Little Miss Muffet"
"La Señorita Mufete"
"Sana, sana"
"Where Is Thumbkin?"
"¿Dónde está Pulgarcito?"
"Naranja dulce"
"Sweet Orange"

Reflect/Assess

- *How are the nursery rhymes we learned today alike? How are they different?*
  ¿En qué se parecen las canciones de cuna que aprendimos hoy? ¿En qué se diferencian?
- *Who can remember one of the words that went with* stout?
  ¿Quién puede recordar una de las palabras que concordaba con robusto?

Literacy Circle

Storytime 1

- Read *The Itsy Bitsy Spider/La araña pequeñita*. This is a traditional rhyme. Ask: *Which of the Mother Goose rhymes was about a spider?*
  ¿Cuáles rimas de Mother Goose trataban de una araña?

Storytime 2

- Present the "El burrito enfermo"/"My Sick Little Donkey" flannel board story. Teach the children to sing this rhyme.

Content Connection

Fine Arts

Objective
To use different colors, surface textures, and shapes to create form and meaning

Vocabulary
rubbings, star-filled sky
calcos/bronce pulido, cielo lleno de estrellas

Materials to Gather
star templates, *Starry Night* print (optional), white felt stars and moon

Activity 1

- Provide star templates and encourage the children to make rubbings of the stars or to trace them. If available, show the children a copy of Vincent van Gogh's *Starry Night* painting. You may be able to obtain a copy from the library.

Activity 2

- Provide the children with white felt stars. Encourage them to place the stars on the flannel board in creative patterns. Explain that they have made their own starry sky. Don't forget to provide a moon.

DAY 4

Objectives

- To begin to recognize, describe, and name shapes
- To put together puzzles of increasing complexity

Vocabulary

rhombus	rombo
hexagon	hexágono
triangle	triángulo
square	cuadrado
rectangle	rectángulo
circle	círculo
diamond	diamante

DLM Materials

- pattern blocks
- *Math Resource Guide*
  Shape Set (several sets)
  Guess My Rule/Adivina mi regla
  Mystery Box
  Memory Game: Geometry version/ Juego de memoria: versión geométrica
  Memory Game: Geometry cards (Set B)
- *DLM Math* software
- *Making Music with Thomas Moore* CD
- *Teacher's Resource Anthology*
  Spider Walk/Camina como la araña

Materials to Gather

- building blocks

Preparation

- Place a pattern block in the Mystery Box.

MATH

Focus

- Count in groups of 4 from 1 to 20, beating a drum softly with each count. Give the children opportunities to beat the drum.
- Play Guess My Rule/Adivina mi regla. You may wish to make a set of just 2 shapes to sort, such as hexagons and rhombuses or triangles and rhombuses.

Develop

- Put a pattern block in the Mystery Box. Challenge the children to identify it. Have them explain how they guessed.
- Using the pattern blocks, make a design as the children watch. You may choose a pattern that builds out from the center or one that is linear. Give the children pattern blocks and challenge them to create similar designs.
- Review Memory Game: Geometry version/Juego de memoria: versión geométrica with the children.

Practice

- Invite a small group of children to play Guess My Rule/Adivina mi regla with an adult.
- Encourage pairs or small groups of children to explore the Mystery Box with a set of building blocks of various shapes and sizes.
- Challenge the children to continue making designs with the Shape Sets or pattern blocks. Encourage them to discuss the shape names and attributes.
- Have the children play Memory Game: Geometry version/Juego de memoria: versión geométrica.
- Have the children work on Mystery Toys, Level 3.

Reflect/Assess

- *How are rectangles and squares the same? How are they different?*

  ¿En qué se parecen los rectángulos y cuadrados? ¿En qué se diferencian?

Content Connection

Physical Development

Objective
To show an awareness of name, location, and relationship of body parts

Materials to Gather
construction paper, mirrors, felt, flannel board

Activity 1

- Using paper shapes of appropriate ethnic colors, have children look into mirrors and create representations of their faces. Talk about face parts. How are we the same and different?

Activity 2

- Provide felt shapes in appropriate ethnic colors. Encourage the children to create faces on the flannel board. Which features are there 2 of?

Music and Movement

- Teach the children how to do the Spider Walk/Camina como la araña. They should sit on the floor and lean back on their arms, then support their weight with their arms and legs in order to walk on all four limbs.
- Encourage the children to dance creatively to "Twinkle, Twinkle, Little Star" from the *Making Music with Thomas Moore* CD.

Reflect on the Day

- *Which of the rhymes did you like best today? Can you say it?*

  ¿Cuál de las rimas les gustó más hoy? ¿Pueden repetirla?
- *Say today's nursery rhymes to your family tonight. See who can join you in the rhyme.*

  Díganles las rimas o canciones de cuna a sus familias esta noche. Fíjense quién puede acompañarlos a decirlas.

Home Connection

- Next week, we will be studying sound and movement. Notify families that the children will be asked to bring an item to school that both moves and makes a sound.
- Send home take-home book packs with four children. You will find the directions and a recording sheet for this activity in the *Home Connections Resource Guide*.

Begin the Day

- Sing the "Nursery Rhyme Rap"/"El rap infantil."
- Use a suggestion for Morning Circle offered in the front of this *Teacher's Edition*.

Objective

- To begin to identify rhymes and rhyming sounds in familiar words, participate in rhyming games, and repeat rhyming songs and poems

Vocabulary

nursery rhymes   canciones infantiles

DLM Materials

- *Teacher's Resource Anthology*
  "One, Two, Buckle My Shoe"/"Uno, dos, ata los zapatos"
  "Pin uno" or "Counting Rhyme"
  Nursery Rhyme Concentration game
  Nursery Rhyme card patterns

Materials to Gather

- candlestick
- chocolate bar
- class book of nursery rhymes
- construction paper
- counters
- doll
- fake egg
- gift bag
- long stick
- mitten
- pie tin
- shoes
- small magnet
- spider
- ten paper plates
- yarn

LITERACY

Focus

- Discuss the nursery rhymes that were introduced yesterday. Sing each of them again with the children.
- Tell the children that today's rhymes are about numbers.

Develop

One Way to Develop the Lesson

- Read "One, Two, Buckle My Shoe"/"Uno, dos, ata los zapatos" or "Counting Rhyme" and "Pin uno" from your chart.
- Encourage the children to help you find the rhyming words.
- Read the poem again. Help the children fill in the rhyming words.

Another Way to Develop the Lesson

- Read "Pin uno" or "Counting Rhyme" from the chart.
- Again, encourage the children to help you find the rhyming words.
- Read the poem again. Help the children fill in the rhyming words.
- Teach the children how to express the numerals 1 through 10 using American Sign Language.

Practice

- Have the children play the Nursery Rhyme Concentration game.
- Place the class book of nursery rhymes in the Library Center. Encourage the children to find their contribution to the book.
- Give the children ten paper plates with the numerals 1 to 10 written on them. Provide counters and allow the children to count the correct number of counters onto each plate.
- Provide a variety of shoes with different fastening methods. Try to include shoes that buckle, tie, and tighten with hook and loop tape. Have the children sort the shoes by the way they fasten.
- Provide a fishing pole and fish for children. Ask them to catch the fish in numerical order. Have the children sort the fish using the *so* and *go* sides after they are caught.

Preparation

- Print "One, Two, Buckle My Shoe"/"Uno, dos, ata los zapatos" and "Pin uno" or "Counting Rhyme" on chart paper.
- Make a fishing pole. Attach one end of a piece of yarn to a long stick and the other end to a magnet. Cut fish from construction paper and number them one to ten. Write the words *so* and *go* on the other side of the fish. Attach paper clips to their tail fins.
- Write the numerals 1 through 10 on paper plates.

Scaffolding Strategies

More Help Reduce the number of fish and plates to fewer than five.

Extra Challenge Invite the children to change the items in the rhyme. ("One, two, color me blue; Three, four, give me more," for example.)

Second Language Learners

How do the children's shoes fasten? Discuss various ways to secure a shoe. After the children learn the first line of "One, Two, Buckle My Shoe"/"Uno, dos, ata los zapatos," adapt it to their shoes: *One, two, tie my shoe; One, two, fasten my shoe; One, two, slip on my shoe,* etc.

DAY 5

Letter Knowledge

English

- Using the Think, Pair, Share game, ask the children to think of ways to make the letter *k* with their bodies.

Spanish

- Ask the children to think of ways to make the letter *d* with their bodies using the Piensa, aparea, comparte.

Suggested Reading

Over the Moon by Rachel Vail

Los pollitos dicen by Nancy Abraham Hall

Anthology Support

"Five Little Monkeys"

"Cinco monitos"

"Mi tía"

Reflect/Assess

- *What is your favorite rhyme that we learned today?*

  ¿Cuál es su canción o rima favorita que aprendimos hoy?
- *How are the rhymes we learned today alike? How are they different?*

  ¿En qué se parecen las rimas/canciones que aprendimos hoy? ¿En qué se diferencian?

Literacy Circle

Storytime 1

- Invite the children to listen to "Three Little Kittens"/"Los tres gatitos." Ask: *Who can remember the rhyming words used in the rhyme?*

  ¿Quién puede recordar las palabras que riman que se usaron en la rima?

Storytime 2

- Provide a gift bag with a mitten, spider (you can use the pipe cleaner spider), fake egg, candlestick, pie tin, chocolate bar, and doll (for Spanish-speaking children) inside of it. Ask the children to choose an item from the bag, then have them say the item's corresponding rhyme.

Content Connection

Math

Objective
To count concrete objects to five or higher

Vocabulary
count, numbers
contar, números

Materials to Gather
blue construction paper, fish crackers

Activity 1

- Cut blue construction paper into five ponds. Help the children count fish crackers onto one of the pieces of blue construction paper. Write the numerals 1 through 5 on the pond papers. Encourage the children to match the number of fish to the corresponding numeral.

Activity 2

- Teach the children "Over in the Meadow"/"Sobre la pradera."

DAY 5

Objectives

- To begin to recognize, describe, and name shapes
- To begin to recognize when a shape's position or orientation has changed

Vocabulary

rhombus	rombo
hexagon	hexágono
triangle	triángulo
square	cuadrado
rectangle	rectángulo
circle	círculo
diamond	diamante

DLM Materials

- pattern blocks
- *Math Resource Guide*
  Shape Set (several sets)
  Guess My Rule/Adivina mi regla
  Mystery Box
  Memory Game: Geometry version/ Juego de memoria: versión geométrica
  Memory Game: Geometry cards (Set B)
- *DLM Math* software
- *Where Is Thumbkin?* CD
- *Teacher's Resource Anthology*
  "To Be a Kite"
  "Tillie Triangle"/"El Triángulo Tilín

Materials to Gather

- three-dimensional object

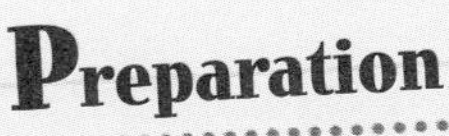

- Prepare the flannel board story.

MATH

Focus

- Recite "To Be a Kite" with the children. Draw a simple kite on the board. Ask the children what shape a kite is (diamond). Ask them if they have seen other shapes of kites (triangle, rhombus).
- Present the flannel board story "Tillie Triangle"/"El Triángulo Tilín." Give each child several triangles and encourage them to show something they can make with them.

Develop

- Play Guess My Rule/Adivina mi regla as you did on Day 3.
- Complete a task from Mystery Toys, Level 3, with the children. Talk about the various shapes in the pictures.

Practice

- Encourage the children to play Guess My Rule/Adivina mi regla with an adult.
- Invite children to feel an object in the Mystery Box and secretly tell friends what they think it is. After everyone has had a chance to feel the object, take it out for children to see.
- Invite the children to explore the Shape Sets in one center and the pattern blocks in another center. Encourage them to name and discuss the shapes.
- Have the children play Memory Game: Geometry version/Juego de memoria: versión geométrica.
- Have the children work on Mystery Toys, Level 3, and Memory—Geometry, Level 3, in the Computer Center.

Reflect/Assess

- *What shapes did you put together? What did they make?*
  ¿Qué figuras unieron? ¿Qué formaron?

Music and Movement

- Sing "Roll Over" from the *Where Is Thumbkin?* CD.
- Sing "Five Little Ducks" from the *Where Is Thumbkin?* CD.

Content Connection

Social Studies/Physical Development

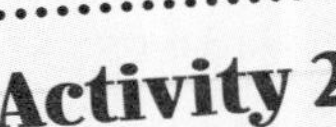

Objectives
To identify common features of local landscape
To begin to participate in group games involving movement

Activity 1

- Brainstorm with children where they see rhombuses and trapezoids in the world. Have pictures of buildings for them to look through.

Activity 2

- Take the children outdoors for a simplified game of baseball. Call attention to the shape of the infield when the bases have been laid out.

Suggested Reading

The Greedy Triangle by Marilyn Burns and Gordon Silveria
The House That Makes Shapes by Jim Potts

Reflect on the Day

- *Which of the rhymes did you like best today? Can you say it?*
  ¿Cuál de las rimas les gustó más hoy? ¿Pueden repetirla?
- *Say today's nursery rhymes to your family tonight. See who can join you in the rhyme.*
  Díganles las rimas o canciones de cuna a sus familias esta noche. Fíjense quién puede acompañarlos a decirlas.

Home Connection

Remind the children to bring an item from home that both moves and makes sounds.

Looking Ahead

Connecting to the Theme: Sound and Movement

As preschoolers exude much energy, it is necessary to provide a channel for that restlessness. **Sound and Movement** activities will teach children the relationship that words and music share with physical movement. Some lessons in this theme will allow them to examine indoor and outdoor noises, learn about safety rules, and discuss cause and effect.

	Objectives	DLM Materials	Materials to Gather
DAY 1	• To ask questions and make comments related to the current topic of discussion • To begin to understand cause-and-effect relationships • To begin to examine a situation from another perspective • To recognize and reproduce simple patterns of concrete objects • To start, use, and exit software programs	• *Teacher's Resource Anthology* • *The Little Ants/Las hormiguitas* • pattern blocks • *Math Resource Guide* • *DLM Math* software • *Four Baby Bumblebees* CD • *This Old Man Is Rockin' On/Este viejito tiene mucho ritmo*	• chart paper • tape recorder • cassette tape • tapes from families • empty paper-towel tubes • can telephones • tag board
DAY 2	• To ask questions and make comments related to the current topic of discussion • To begin to understand cause-and-effect relationships • To imitate pattern sounds and physical movement • To recognize and reproduce simple patterns of concrete objects	• Oral Language Cards 6–31 • *The Farm/La granja* • *Teacher's Resource Anthology* • *DLM Math* software • *Four Baby Bumblebees* CD • *Where Is Thumbkin?* CD • *Esta es mi tierra* CD	• cassette tape of animal sounds • plastic animals • books about animal sounds and movements • stringing beads • nature items
DAY 3	• To listen with increasing attention • To begin to understand cause-and-effect relationships • To recognize and reproduce simple patterns of concrete objects • To begin to predict what comes next when patterns are extended	• *Teacher's Resource Anthology* • pattern blocks • *Math Resource Guide* • *DLM Math* software • *Diez deditos* CD	• ticking clock • spray bottle • cookie sheet • magazines • connecting cubes • stringing beads
DAY 4	• To listen for different purposes • To begin to understand cause-and-effect relationships • To begin to use art as a form of self-expression • To recognize and reproduce simple patterns of concrete objects • To imitate sounds and physical movements	• *This Old Man Is Rockin' On/Este viejito tiene mucho ritmo* • *Animal Orchestra/La orquesta de los animales* • *Teacher's Resource Anthology* • *DLM Math* software • *Making Music with Thomas Moore* CD	• noisemakers • straws • pennies • small washers • tongue depressors • sandpaper • rubber mat • aluminum foil
DAY 5	• To understand that reading and writing are ways to obtain information and knowledge, generate and communicate thoughts and ideas, and solve problems • To recognize and reproduce simple patterns of concrete objects • To use one or more senses to observe and learn about objects, events, and organisms	• *Four Baby Bumblebees* CD • *Esta es mi tierra* CD • *This Old Man Is Rockin' On/Este viejito tiene mucho ritmo* • *Humpty Dumpty Dumpty* • *Teacher's Resource Anthology* • *Making Music with Thomas Moore* CD	• light source • music (various tempos) • washers • paper plates • crepe paper streamers

(See individual lesson pages for complete lists of materials.)

Learning Centers

DISCOVERY

Creating Moving Things

Objective
To use one or more senses to observe and learn about objects, events, and organisms

Materials to Gather
collection of mechanical parts and pieces of various mechanical items, plastic toy screwdrivers, plastic toy pliers, pulley (optional)

Develop
Place the collected items on a table and allow the children to explore them. Have them use the plastic toy screwdrivers and pliers to investigate the parts and the ways they move. Encourage them to put the items together in new ways to create moving things. Introduce at least one new item each day. If you have a pulley, hang it in the center for the week.

Reflect/Assess
Which items on the table interest you the most? Why?
¿Qué objetos en la mesa les interesan más? ¿Por qué?

GROSS MOTOR

Exploring Movement

Objective
To participate in group games involving movement

Materials to Gather
beanbags, baskets, balance beam, table tennis balls, masking tape, paper plates, straws, basters

Develop
Provide a movement game for each day, such as Twister, walking the balance beam, tossing beanbags into baskets, or rolling small balls back and forth.

Try a table tennis ball race. Place two strips of masking tape about 6 feet apart to create start and finish lines. Place two table tennis balls on the start line and invite two children to move the balls from the start line to the finish line without touching them. They can blow on the balls, fan the balls with paper plates, or use a baster to blow on the balls. Provide a variety of materials to use and let the children choose the items they think will help them move the balls.

Reflect/Assess
Is it easy or difficult to move the balls without touching them?
¿Es fácil o difícil mover las pelotas sin tocarlas?

SCIENCE

Identifying Sounds

Objective
To begin to observe changes in size, color, position, weather, and sound

Materials to Gather
items that make sounds (music boxes, clocks, and so on), small items (paper clips, gravel, marbles, and so on), containers (cups, cans, canisters, and so on)

Develop
Fill the center with items that make sounds, such as clocks, music boxes, metronomes, jack-in-the-boxes, and so on. Encourage the children to explore the items. Provide materials, such as paper clips, gravel, and seeds along with film or pill canisters, small cans with lids, and cups. Have the children fill the containers to create sound makers.

Reflect/Assess
Can you make sounds that are both high and low or fast and slow?
¿Pueden producir sonidos altos y bajos o rápidos y lentos?

What Research Suggests

Hearing begins to develop during the fifth month of pregnancy. Children are exceptionally sensitive to sounds until around the age of five. This period of time provides opportunities to increase children's auditory discrimination skills. Every sound experience during this time allows neural connections to expand and strengthen.

Begin the Day

- Sing "If You're Happy & You Know It"/ "Si estás contento." Add new body sound responses; try snapping, whistling, and tapping.
- Use the suggestions for Morning Circle offered in the front of this *Teacher's Edition.*

Objectives

- To ask questions and make comments related to the current topic of discussion
- To begin to understand cause-and-effect relationships

Vocabulary

clap	aplaudir
snap	chasquear
tap	golpear
whistle	silbar
whisper	murmurar

DLM Materials

- *Teacher's Resource Anthology*
  "If You're Happy & You Know It"/ "Si estás contento"
  "The Little Ants"/"Las hormiguitas"
  "Calliope Song"
  Body Sound card patterns
  "Hush, Little Baby"/"Sh, mi bebé"
  "Tortoise Wins the Race"/"La tortuga gana la carrera"
  sound shakers

Materials to Gather

- chart paper
- tape recorder
- cassette tape
- tapes from families
- empty paper-towel tubes
- can telephones

LITERACY

Focus

- Sing "The Little Ants"/"Las hormiguitas" or read the book. Discuss the movements of the ants. *Do you think ants make sounds when they move?*

  ¿Creen que las hormigas producen sonidos al moverse?
- Tell the children that they are going to learn about sound and movement this week.

Develop

One Way to Develop the Lesson

- Invite the children to place their hands on their throats and whisper their names. Ask if they feel movement in their throats when they whisper. Next, have them place their hands on their throats and say their names out loud. Ask if they feel movement in their throats this time. Explain that sound is created when the vocal chords rub together.
- Ask the children to think of other sounds people can make with their bodies. Invite them to demonstrate the body sounds as they suggest them. Make a list of their ideas on chart paper.
- Invite the children to work with partners to make patterns using body sounds. For example, they might clap twice, snap once, and stomp their feet three times. Encourage the pairs to demonstrate their body sound patterns for the class.

Another Way to Develop the Lesson

- Teach "Calliope Song." Add body movement to each sound. For example, group one might bend up and down at the knees while saying *"Um pa pa, um pa pa . . .,"* group two might turn in a circle while saying *"Um tweedli-dee, um tweedli-dee . . .,"* group three might move up and down on their toes while saying *"Um shhh, um shhh, um shhh . . .,"* and group four might sway from side to side while humming the "Circus Song."
- Discuss the body movements and the sounds that each group makes.

Practice

- Provide a tape recorder. Encourage the children to tape sounds or their body sound patterns and then have them play the sounds back.
- Provide one of the tapes created by the children's families and invite the children to listen to the tape.
- Give the children empty paper-towel tubes and sets of can telephones to explore. *How does sound change when it is channeled through an object? ¿Cómo cambia el sonido cuando se conduce a través de un objeto?*
- Invite the children to play the Body Sounds Concentration game.
- Have the children match the sound shakers.

Preparation

- Prepare the "Tortoise Wins the Race"/"La tortuga gana la carrera" flannel board story and the "Hush, Little Baby"/"Sh, mi bebé" flannel board story, if not already made.
- Make the Body Sounds Concentration game by photocopying two sets of the body sounds card patterns.
- Make can telephones (see Friends for directions).
- Make sound shakers, if not already made.

Scaffolding Strategies

More Help Say "I Can, You Can!"/"¡Yo puedo, tú puedes!"

Extra Challenge Invite the children to create new movements to "Calliope Song."

Second Language Learners

Stand in a circle. First, clap the syllables of all children's names (Sa-ra; En-ri-que; Wei-Min). Then ask children to think of a movement for each clap. For example, Sujin might put her hands on her head for the syllable *Su-* and raise her hands in the air for the syllable *–jin*. All children then repeat the movements for each syllable.

DAY 1

Letter Knowledge

English

- Introduce the letter *l* using the story "Lu" from the *English Phonics Resource Guide*.

Spanish

- Introduce the letter *r* using the story "Ratón" from the *Spanish Phonics Resource Guide*.

Suggested Reading

Fox Be Nimble by James Marshall
The Napping House by Audrey Wood
La casa adormecida by Audrey Wood

Anthology Support

"Open, Shut Them"
"Ábranlas, ciérrenlas"
"Thelma Thumb"
"Pulgarcito"

Reflect/Assess

- *Who can put a body sound and movement together for me?*
  ¿Quién puede mostrarme un sonido del cuerpo con su movimiento?
- *Do you think you can make more sounds with your hands or your feet? Why?*
  ¿Creen que pueden hacer más sonidos con las manos o con los pies? ¿Por qué?

Literacy Circle

Storytime 1

- Present the "Hush, Little Baby"/"Sh, mi bebé" listening story.
- Discuss the sounds made when people cry. *Does it sound different when a baby cries than when an adult cries? Does the sound of crying change depending on the person?*
  ¿Es diferente el sonido que produce un bebé que un adulto cuando llora? ¿El sonido al llorar cambia según la persona?

Storytime 2

- Present the "Tortoise Wins the Race"/"La tortuga gana la carrera" flannel board story. Discuss the sound and movement in the story. *Which animal normally moves faster?*
  ¿Qué animal se mueve más rápidamente?
  How do the family and friends of the tortoise use their voices to fool the deer?
  ¿Cómo usan su voz la familia y los amigos de la tortuga para engañar al venado?

Content Connection

Health/Safety

Objectives

To become aware of routine healthy behaviors

To begin to examine a situation from another person's perspective

Vocabulary

ears, loud, soft

orejas, fuerte, suave

DLM Materials

- *Teacher's Resource Anthology*
  Gossip/Chismes
  American Sign Language patterns

Activity 1

- Discuss loud and soft sounds. Make a list of loud sounds such as train whistles and rock music. Discuss the damage loud sounds can inflict on people's ears.
- Play a game of Gossip/Chismes. Discuss how a person must listen carefully to hear soft sounds.
- Discuss deafness. Ask the children to imagine not being able to hear. Ask: *How would you know what someone was trying to tell you if you couldn't hear him or her?*
  ¿Cómo sabrían lo que una persona estaría tratando de decirles si no pudieran oírla?
  Teach the children some American Sign Language.

Activity 2

- Discuss how people care for their ears. Discuss staying away from loud sounds, not sticking things in one's ears, and protecting one's ears from cold weather.
- Invite the children to make up a song to the tune of "The Mulberry Bush" about how to take care of their ears.

DAY 1

Objectives

- To recognize and reproduce simple patterns of concrete objects
- To start, use, and exit software programs

Vocabulary

repeating pattern   patrón periódico

DLM Materials

- pattern blocks
- *Math Resource Guide*
  Listen and Copy/Escucha e imita
  Pattern Strips (Level 1)
- *DLM Math* software
- *Four Baby Bumblebees* CD

Materials to Gather

- tag board

Preparation

- Make photocopies of the Pattern Strips. Cut apart, glue to tag board, and color to match pattern blocks. Laminate for durability.

MATH

Focus

- Play Listen and Copy/Escucha e imita.
- Tell the children they will be dancing a pattern. Vocalize and demonstrate clap, stomp, clap, stomp, clap, stomp. Invite the children to join.

Develop

- Introduce the children to the Pattern Strips. Show them the first Pattern Strip and encourage them to describe the pattern on the strip (square-triangle-square-triangle-square-triangle).
- Have the children help you copy the pattern by placing pattern blocks directly on the Pattern Strips. Have them chant the pattern as you point to each block.
- Introduce Build Stairs, Level 1 on the computer. Children help Builder Bear build stairs by telling her which step (number) comes next. Level 1 is just counting, but this involves an important "number after" or "plus 1" pattern that you will be developing.

Practice

- Encourage the children to copy the patterns on the Pattern Strips with pattern blocks.
- Have the children explore making their own patterns with pattern shapes.
- Children may work on Build Stairs, Level 1. When they finish, they may start, use, and exit Memory—Number, Level 1.

Reflect/Assess

- *Where do you see patterns?*
  ¿Dónde se ven patrones?
- *How do you know something is a pattern?*
  ¿Cómo saben que algo es un patrón?

Music and Movement

- Play "Whistle While You Work" from the *Four Baby Bumblebees* CD. Invite the children to whistle along.
- Sing "Hush, Little Baby" from the *Four Baby Bumblebees* CD. Use the flannel board illustrations from the story with the song.

Suggested Reading

My Mom and Dad Make Me Laugh by Nick Sharratt

Content Connection

Fine Arts

Objective

To begin to engage in dramatic play with others

DLM Materials

This Old Man Is Rockin' On/Este viejito tiene mucho ritmo
The Little Ants/Las hormiguitas

Activity 1

- Read *This Old Man Is Rockin' On/Este viejito tiene mucho ritmo*.
- Invite the children to role-play the story.
- Ask them to identify the patterns in the story.

Activity 2

- Read *The Little Ants/Las hormiguitas*.
- Invite the children to role-play the story/song.
- Encourage them to identify the patterns.

Reflect on the Day

- *If we want someone to know we enjoy something, how can we show him or her by using our bodies but not clapping our hands?*
  Si queremos que alguien sepa que nos gusta algo, ¿cómo podemos demostrarlo usando nuestros cuerpos pero sin aplaudir?
- *Can someone show me some of the sounds we made with our bodies today?*
  ¿Alguien puede mostrarme algunos de los sonidos que hicimos con nuestros cuerpos hoy?

Begin the Day

- Sing and act out "Five Little Speckled Frogs"/"Cinco ranitas manchadas." Discuss the sounds and movements of the frogs.
- Use one of the suggestions for Morning Circle offered in the front of this *Teacher's Edition*.

Objectives

- To ask questions and make comments related to the current topic of discussion
- To begin to understand cause-and-effect relationships

Vocabulary

fly	volar
swim	nadar
hop	brincar
jump	saltar

DLM Materials

- Oral Language Development Cards 6–31
- *The Farm/La granja*
- Rafita and Pepita
- *Teacher's Resource Anthology*
  "Five Little Speckled Frogs"/"Cinco ranitas manchadas"
  "Old MacDonald"/"El viejo MacDonald"
  Mother, May I?/Mamá ¿puedo?
  "Sweetly Sings the Donkey"/"Dulcemente canta el burro"
  "Hear the Lively Song"/"Oye la alegre canción"
  "Six White Ducks"/"Los seis patos blancos"
  Animal card patterns
  "Cat and Mouse"/"El gato y el ratón"

LITERACY

Focus

- Sing "Old MacDonald"/"El viejo MacDonald." Discuss the noise each animal makes. Tell the children that animal sounds have different human pronunciations and translations in different languages. Sing the song again, making the sound of the chicken in Japanese (plyo plyo), Turkish (cik cik), and Greek (ko-ko-ko-ko) or the cow in Danish (muh), Italian (muuuuu), and Thai (maw maw).
- Tell the children that they will continue to discuss sounds and movements. Today they will learn about animal sounds and movements.

Develop

One Way to Develop the Lesson

- Show Oral Language Cards 9 and 13–16. Invite them to demonstrate the sounds these animals make. *Why are animal sounds different from human sounds?*

  ¿Por qué los sonidos de animales son diferentes de los sonidos humanos?

  Discuss how people use their tongues and vocal chords to produce sound.
- Play a variation of Mother, May I?/Mamá, ¿puedo? Tell the children that instead of saying "Mother, may I?"/"Mamá, ¿puedo?" before moving, they must make animal sounds. Use Rafita and Pepita to give the commands.
- Sing "Sweetly Sings the Donkey"/"Dulcemente canta el burro" and "Hear the Lively Song"/"Oye la alegre canción." Discuss the animal sounds.

Another Way to Develop the Lesson

- Show Oral Language Cards 9 and 13–16. Encourage the children to demonstrate how each animal moves.
- Sing "Six White Ducks"/"Los seis patos blancos." Discuss the movement of the ducks. Ask a volunteer to demonstrate a duck walk. *Why do ducks waddle?*

  ¿Por qué los patos anadean?

  Ask all the children to squat, turn in their toes, and try to walk. *What happens when you walk this way?*

  ¿Qué pasa cuando caminan de esta manera?
- Invite the children to help you, Rafita, and Pepita make a list of animals and their movements. Ask volunteers to demonstrate the movements.

Practice

- Invite the children to match the animal patterns to the sounds on the cassette tape.
- Encourage the children to practice animal moves in the Gross Motor Center. They can fly like birds, slink like cats, waddle like ducks, gallop like ponies, jump like dogs, swim like fish, and hop like bunnies.
- Give them the animal Oral Language Cards 6–31. Have them sort the cards according to how the animals move (for example, whether they swim, fly, or walk).
- Place plastic animals in the Blocks Center. Encourage the children to imitate the sounds and movements the animals make.
- Fill the Library Center with books about animal sounds and movements.

Materials to Gather

- cassette tape of animal sounds
- plastic animals
- books about animal sounds and movements

Preparation

- Make a tape of animal sounds.
- Photocopy the animal patterns.

Scaffolding Strategies

More Help Display the Oral Language Cards depicting the more familiar animals first.

Extra Challenge Encourage the children to make up new sounds for animals or to create imaginary animals and their sounds.

Second Language Learners

As you sing the sounds of the animals in different languages, try to include animal sounds from the children's native languages. Ask the parents ahead of time to tell you the sounds, or ask the children as they are singing the song. Compare and contrast the animal sounds in English and the children's native languages.

DAY 2

Letter Knowledge

English

- Read "Lily Lee" from the *SRA Alphabet Book.*

Spanish

- Read "En el río" from *Los niños alfabéticos.*

Suggested Reading

The Cat in the Hat by Dr. Seuss
Salsa by Lillian Colon-Vila
Lo que escuchas by Allan Fowler

Technology Support

Have the children listen to the sounds made with the sense of hearing illustrations on the *SRA Photo Library* software in the Human Body category.

Anthology Support

"Los pollitos"
"The Baby Chicks"
"Three White Mice"
"Los tres ratones blancos"
"Five Huge Dinosaurs"
"Cinco enormes dinosaurios"
"In the Woods"
"En el bosque"

Reflect/Assess

- *Can you think of two animals that make similar sounds?*
  ¿Pueden pensar en dos animales que produzcan sonidos parecidos?
- *What sounds do the animals at your house or in your neighborhood make?*
  ¿Qué sonidos producen los animales en sus casas o en sus vecindarios?

Literacy Circle

Storytime 1

- Read *The Farm/La granja.* Discuss the animal sounds in the story. *Do the chickens make the same sound in English as they do in Spanish?*
  ¿Los pollos producen el mismo sonido en inglés y en español?

Storytime 2

- Read "Cat and Mouse"/"El gato y el ratón." *How did the cat use its voice to fool the mice?*
  ¿Cómo usó su voz el gato para engañar a los ratones?

Content Connection

Fine Arts

Objective
To begin to engage in dramatic play with others

Vocabulary
animal sounds, animal movements
sonidos de animales, movimientos de animales

DLM Materials
Teacher's Resource Anthology
"Going on a Bear Hunt"/ "Vamos a cazar un oso"
animal mask patterns

Activity 1

- Invite the children to participate in the action story "Going on a Bear Hunt"/"Vamos a cazar un oso." Discuss the ways they can use their bodies to make the sounds in the story.

Activity 2

- Make animal masks.
- Encourage the children to select animal masks, put them on, and move and make sounds like the animals the masks represent.

DAY 2

Objectives

- To imitate pattern sounds and physical movement
- To recognize and reproduce simple patterns of concrete objects

Vocabulary

repeating pattern	patrón periódico
pattern core	centro del patrón

DLM Materials

- pattern blocks
- *Math Resource Guide* Pattern Strips (see Day 1)
- *DLM Math* software
- *Where Is Thumbkin?* CD
- *Four Baby Bumblebees* CD
- *Esta es mi tierra* CD

Materials to Gather

- stringing cubes

More Help Have the children lay the strip down repeatedly so they are continually copying the pattern from the strip.

Extra Challenge Give children more difficult patterns to copy or more attributes to consider for each element in the pattern.

MATH

Focus

- Reintroduce the dancing pattern from Day 1.
- Count from 1 to 20.

Develop

- Demonstrate an A-B pattern with the stringing beads, using only one shape in two colors. After showing the pattern three complete times, have the children help you decide which bead should come next. When demonstrating a pattern core to children, such as A-B, A-A-B, A-B-A, and so on, it is best to give children three complete repetitions. Repeat A-B patterns until children begin to understand patterning, but then move on to more difficult patterns so children will not think all patterns are A-B.
- Show another Pattern Strip. Ask children to describe the pattern. Then ask them to continue, or keep going with, the pattern. *What shape would come next? Next?*

  ¿Qué figura vendría ahora para seguir con el patrón? ¿Después?

  Chant the pattern from the beginning while pointing. Repeat with other Pattern Strips.
- Reintroduce Build Stairs, Level 1 and Memory—Number, Level 1.

Practice

- Provide pattern blocks and encourage the children to make their own patterns.
- Encourage the children to use the Pattern Strips to copy and extend the patterns.
- Children may work on Build Stairs, Level 1. When they finish, invite them to work on Memory—Number, Level 1.

Reflect/Assess

- *How did you figure out what the patterns were?*
  ¿Cómo determinaron qué eran los patrones?
- *How do you know what comes next?*
  ¿Cómo saben qué viene después?

Music and Movement

- Sing "Fiddle-I-Fee" from the *Where Is Thumbkin?* CD.
- Sing "Baby Bumblebee" from the *Four Baby Bumblebees* CD or "Juancho Pancho" from the *Ésta es mi tierra* CD.

Content Connection

Science

Objective
To compare objects and organisms and identify similarities and differences

Materials to Gather
nature items

Activity 1
- Take the children outside to look for patterns in nature.

Activity 2
- Encourage the children to collect items from outdoors to make nature patterns. They might use leaves of different colors, twigs, rocks, or flowers.

Suggested Reading

Spotted Yellow Frogs by Matthew Van Fleet
Lots and Lots of Zebra Stripes by Stephen R. Swinburne

Reflect on the Day

- *How are animal sounds like human sounds? How are they different?*
  ¿En qué se parecen los sonidos de los animales a los sonidos humanos? ¿En qué se diferencian?
- *What was your favorite activity? Why?*
  ¿Cuál fue su actividad favorita? ¿Por qué?

Home Connection

Remind the children that they need to bring something from home that makes a noise to class tomorrow.

What Research Suggests

The computer can help children build the understanding of the important *plus 1* pattern of counting by connecting different representations of counting and by giving feedback.

Begin the Day

- Sing "The Wheels on the Bus"/"Ruedas del bus." Discuss the sounds and movements used in the song. *How can we create the sounds? How can we imitate the movements?*
  ¿Cómo podemos crear los sonidos? ¿Cómo podemos imitar los movimientos?
- Use one of the suggestions for Morning Circle offered in the front of this *Teacher's Edition.*

Objectives

- To listen with increasing attention
- To begin to understand cause-and-effect relationships

Vocabulary

pleasant	agradable
unpleasant	desagradable
loud	fuerte
soft	suave

DLM Materials

- *Teacher's Resource Anthology*
  "Wheels on the Bus"/"Ruedas del bus"
  "Little Hunk of Tin"/"Un pedacito de hojalata"
  Red Light! Green Light!/¡Luz roja! ¡Luz verde!
  "Sing Me a Rainbow"/"Cántame un arco iris"
  "The Three Billy Goats Gruff"/"Los tres chivitos Gruff"

Materials to Gather

- ticking clock
- spray bottle
- cookie sheet
- blocks
- magazines

LITERACY

Focus

- Sing "Little Hunk of Tin"/"Un pedacito de hojalata." Discuss the sounds made by the car. *How can we imitate the sounds of the car?*
  ¿Cómo podemos imitar los sonidos del carro?
- Invite the children to show the items they brought from home. Discuss the sound each item makes and what causes each sound.

Develop

One Way to Develop the Lesson

- Discuss indoor sounds. Make a list of things that make sounds in the classroom or at home. Distinguish between machines that make independent mechanical sounds and objects that make sounds only when something is done to them (for example, a ticking clock versus a drum).
- Hide a ticking clock and have the children locate it by listening for the sound.
- Remind the children about the term *onomatopoeia*. Give them some examples. Have them offer examples of their own.

Another Way to Develop the Lesson

- Discuss outdoor sounds. Take a listening walk around the school or neighborhood, writing down any sounds the children hear.
- Discuss pleasant sounds such as birds singing or water running and unpleasant sounds such as people screaming or sirens blaring.
- Play Red Light! Green Light!/¡Luz roja! ¡Luz verde! Encourage the children to make car sounds in conjuntion with the game. *Does making the noise change the game?*

  ¿Hacer el sonido cambia el juego?

Practice

- Provide a spray bottle full of water that has a control allowing you to change the intensity of the spray. Give the children a cookie sheet and encourage them to spray water on the cookie sheet using variations of intensity. *How does the sound change with intensity?*

  ¿Cómo cambia el sonido según la intensidad?
- Encourage the children to build block towers on a carpet square and on the bare floor. Have them knock over the towers. *How is the noise made by falling blocks different on each surface?*

  ¿En qué se diferencia el sonido producido por los bloques al caerse en cada superficie?
- Invite the children to cut pictures from magazines of things that make noises. Encourage them to classify the sounds into pleasant and unpleasant sounds.
- Allow the children to illustrate the lists of indoor and outdoor sounds.
- Have the children draw pictures of things that make sounds. Encourage them to describe the sounds made by the objects in their pictures. Label their work with their permission.

Scaffolding Strategies

More Help Invite the children to walk around the classroom locating items that make noises.

Extra Challenge Invite the children to think of things that make sounds both indoors and outdoors, such as dogs barking or water dripping.

Second Language Learners

After singing, "Wheels on the Bus"/"Ruedas del bus," encourage children to think of other things they would find on the bus, and how they would go. Sing the new verses.

Anthology Support

"A Thunderstorm"
"Una tempestad"
"Clickety, Clickety, Clack"
"The Wind"
"El viento"
"Floppy Rag Doll"
"Pimpón"

DAY 3

Letter Knowledge

English

- Invite the children to make the letter *l* with play dough.

Spanish

- Invite the children to make the letter *r* with play dough.

Suggested Reading

Crash! Bang! Boom! by Peter Spier
Clap Your Hands by Lorinda Cauley
Mira qué pasó! by Anne-Claire Leveque

Reflect/Assess

- *What is your favorite pleasant sound? Where do you hear it?*
  ¿Cuál es su sonido agradable favorito? ¿Dónde lo oyen?
- *Which sounds do you dislike? Why?*
  ¿Qué sonidos no les gusta? ¿Por qué?

Literacy Circle

Storytime 1

- Present the "Sing Me a Rainbow"/"Cántame un arco iris" flannel board story. Discuss the sounds that might accompany some of the weather conditions described in the story.

Storytime 2

- Invite the children to act out "The Three Billy Goats Gruff"/ "Los tres chivitos Gruff." Select three children to provide the sounds of each goat crossing the bridge.

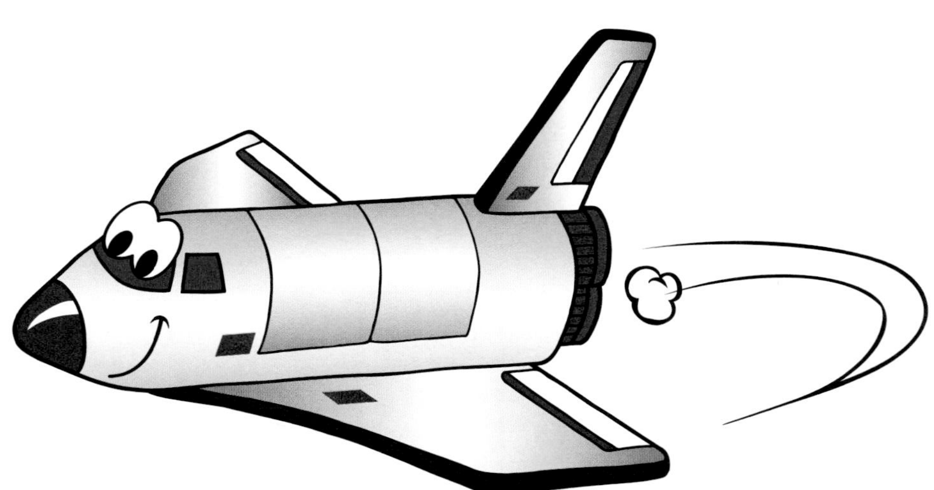

Content Connection

Health/Safety

Objectives

To know how to cross a street safely
To recognize the danger of fire and to learn to treat fire with caution

Vocabulary

listen
oír, escuchar

DLM Materials

- *Teacher's Resource Anthology*
  Stop, Look, and Listen/ Para, mira, y escucha

Activity 1

- Introduce Stop, Look, and Listen/ Para, mira, y escucha. If the children already know this safety rhyme, review it.
- Ask: *Why do you stop before crossing the street? What are you looking for? What are you listening for?*
  ¿Por qué se detienen antes de cruzar la calle? ¿En qué se fijan? ¿Qué escuchan?
  Go outdoors and practice, if possible.

Activity 2

- Discuss fire safety.
- Introduce Stop, Drop, and Roll/Detente, al suelo y revuélcate. Discuss how the actions of dropping and rolling will put out fire.

DAY 3

Objectives

- To recognize and reproduce simple patterns of concrete objects
- To begin to predict what comes next when patterns are extended

Vocabulary

repeating pattern	patrón periódico
pattern core	centro del patrón

DLM Materials

- pattern blocks
- *Math Resource Guide* Pattern Strips (see Day 1)
- *DLM Math* software
- *Diez deditos* CD
- *Teacher's Resource Anthology* Cooperative Musical Circle/Círculo musical cooperativo London Bridge/Este puente

Materials to Gather

- connecting cubes
- masking tape

Preparation

- Tape a large rectangle, square, or triangle on the floor.

MATH

Focus

- Introduce a new dancing pattern, such as slide, slide, stomp, stomp. Encourage children to use the dancing pattern with a familiar song.
- Discuss patterns in children's clothes.

Develop

- Put connecting cubes in the center of the circle area. Using two colors, build a tower of cubes, such as blue-blue-yellow. Have each child make a blue-blue-yellow tower. Have children link them all together. Have them chant the colors as you point to each cube in the long pattern. Repeat with a different pattern core.
- Have children march around the rectangle, square, or triangle taped on the floor while chanting a pattern, such as left-right-left-right or march-march-stop-march-march-stop. Identify these patterns as A-B (left, right) or A-A-B (march, march, stop). Most children won't know left and right, but naming them while you model the march is helpful.

Practice

- Challenge children to work in pairs or small groups to make cube patterns, following one of several models that you provide.
- Invite children to copy and extend Pattern Strips with pattern blocks.
- Children may work on Build Stairs, Level 1 or Memory—Number, Level 1.

Reflect/Assess

- Show the children a pattern. *What comes next in this pattern?* *¿Qué sigue en este patrón?*

Content Connection

Physical Development

Objectives
To begin to manipulate play objects that have fine parts
To begin to develop pincer control in picking up objects

Materials to Gather
construction paper, stringing beads

Activity 1

- Invite the children to make paper chains from 1" × 4" strips of construction paper. Encourage them to create patterns.

Activity 2

- Encourage the children to string beads in a pattern.

Music and Movement

- Invite the children to play Cooperative Musical Circle/Círculo musical cooperativo, or play "Las ruedas del camión" from the *Diez deditos* CD and encourage the children to sing along.
- Play London Bridge/Este puente. *What kind of noise would a falling bridge make?* *¿Qué tipo de sonido haría un puente cayéndose?*

Suggested Reading

Kente Colors by Deborah M. Newton Chocolate
Eight Hands Round: A Patchwork Alphabet by Ann Whitford Paul

Reflect on the Day

- *Are all inside noises soft and all outside noises loud? Why or why not?* *¿Todos los ruidos de adentro son suaves y los ruidos de afuera son fuertes? ¿Por qué sí o por qué no?*
- *What did you learn about sound and movement?* *¿Qué aprendieron sobre el sonido y el movimiento?*

Home Connection

Send home a note (located in the *Home Connections Resource Guide*) requesting family members who play musical instruments to come to school and play for the class next week, if possible.

Begin the Day

- Invite the children to participate in the action story "Mr. Wiggle and Mr. Waggle"/"Señor Wiggle y Señor Waggle." Discuss the sounds and movements in the story. *Why do the friends knock and call out loudly when they visit each other?*

  ¿Por qué los animales tocan y llaman con voz fuerte cuando se visitan?
- Use one of the suggestions for Morning Circle offered in the front of this *Teacher's Edition.*

Objectives

- To listen for different purposes
- To begin to understand cause-and-effect relationships

Vocabulary

loud	fuerte
soft	suave
fast	rápido
slow	despacio

DLM Materials

- *This Old Man Is Rockin' On/Este viejito tiene mucho ritmo*
- *Animal Orchestra/La orquesta de los animales*
- *Teacher's Resource Anthology*
  "Mr. Wiggle and Mr. Waggle"/ "Señor Wiggle y Señor Waggle"
  Hide and Seek/Esconde y busca
  "Head, Shoulders, Knees, and Toes"/ "Cabeza, hombros, rodillas y dedos"

Materials to Gather

- noisemakers
- beanbag or block
- music with different tempos
- lullaby music
- rock music
- straws
- pennies
- sandpaper
- rubber mat
- aluminum foil
- construction paper strips (1" × 12")
- small washers
- tongue depressors

LITERACY

Focus

- Display the noisemakers you have gathered. Name each item, showing the children how it makes noise.
- Tell the children they will be studying different kinds of sounds and movements.

Develop

One Way to Develop the Lesson

- Discuss soft and loud sounds and high and low sounds. Ask the children to describe the sounds most noisemakers make.
- Tell the children you are going to play a game of Hide and Seek/Esconde y busca in which they will use their voices to help friends find hidden objects. Show them a beanbag or a block that will serve as the first hidden object. Ask a volunteer to leave the room. Hide the beanbag or block. When the volunteer returns, tell him or her that you will sing loudly when he or she is close to the object and softly when he or she is far away from the object. Sing a familiar song with the class, adjusting the volume as the volunteer moves toward or away from the object. Play the game again using high and low voices.

Another Way to Develop the Lesson

- Discuss fast and slow sounds. Play music with a slow tempo and music with a fast tempo. Invite the children to move to each selection.
- Sing a song slowly and then speed it up. "Head, Shoulders, Knees, and Toes"/"Cabeza, hombros, rodillas y dedos" works well. Incorporate the movements.
- Discuss the differences between fast and slow sounds and the movements that go with them. *Can you move slowly to fast music? Try it.*

  ¿Pueden moverse lentamente cuando la música es rápida? Inténtenlo.

Practice

- Place lullaby music and rock music in the Listening Center. Invite the children to listen to both types of music and vote for the one they like best.
- Give the children straws and pennies. Invite them to rub the objects over a piece of sandpaper, a rubber mat, and a piece of aluminum foil. *What kind of sound does each object make on each surface?*

  ¿Qué tipo de sonido hace cada objeto en cada superficie?
- Invite the children to make clappers. Provide 1" × 12" strips of construction paper. Instruct the children to glue small washers to the ends of their strips. Fold the strips over tongue depressors and staple them in place. Invite the children to play their clappers by flipping them back and forth.
- Invite the children to explore the noisemakers you need in the lesson.
- Have the children fold pieces of paper in half. Encourage them to draw pictures on one side of things that make soft sounds and pictures on the other side of things that make loud sounds. Ask them to demonstrate the sounds.

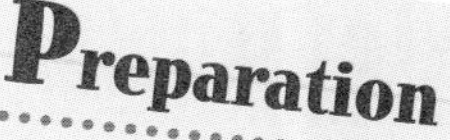

Preparation

- Gather noisemakers, such as whistles, bells, horns, and so on.

Scaffolding Strategies

More Help Invite the children to clap their hands slowly. Then have them clap their hands quickly. Encourage them to whisper their names and then shout their names.

Extra Challenge Invite the children to name some activities they might enjoy doing to fast-tempo music and some activities they might enjoy doing to slow-tempo music.

Second Language Learners

Read *The Farm*. Read a second time, and this time children make the animal noises. Note whether children are also beginning to repeat the patterned language of the book.

Anthology Support

"The Big Brass Drum"

"El tambor de hojalata"

"Family Fun"

"Diversión familiar"

DAY 4

Letter Knowledge

English

- Invite the children to make the letter *l* in a sand tray. Point out the letter *l* in *loud* and *lullaby*.

Spanish

- Invite the children to make the letter *r* in a sand tray. Point out the letter *r* in *radio, reloj,* and *rápido*.

Suggested Reading

Who Sank the Boat? by Pamela Allen
Hand Rhymes by Marc Brown
La cucaracha Martina: Un cuento folklórico del Caribe by Daniel Moreton

Reflect/Assess

- *Which tempo of music do you prefer?*

  ¿Qué compás musical prefieren?

- *What is the loudest noise you can think of? What is the softest noise you can think of?*

  ¿Cuál es el sonido más fuerte que se les ocurre? ¿Cuál es el sonido más suave que se les ocurre?

Literacy Circle

Storytime 1

- Read *This Old Man Is Rockin' On/Este viejito tiene mucho ritmo. What sounds do the instruments make?*

  ¿Qué sonidos hacen los instrumentos?

Storytime 2

- Read *Animal Orchestra/La orquesta de los animales.* Discuss the sound of each instrument introduced in the book. (Instrument sounds are located on the listening tape.)

Content Connection

Fine Arts

Objective
To begin to use art as a form of self-expression

Vocabulary
fast, slow
rápido, despacio

Materials to Gather
music (with varied tempos), tempera paint, clay

Activity 1

- Invite the children to paint to different tempos of music. *Do the tempos of the music change the way you paint?*
  ¿Los compases de la música cambian la manera en que pintan?

Activity 2

- Invite the children to create sculptures out of clay while listening to different tempos of music. *Do the tempos of the music have an effect on how quickly you work?*
  ¿Los compases de la música tienen un efecto sobre la rapidez con que trabajan?

DAY 4

Objectives

- To recognize and reproduce simple patterns of concrete objects
- To imitate sounds and physical movements

Vocabulary

repeating pattern	patrón periódico
pattern core	centro del patrón
vertical	vertical
horizontal	horizontal
slanted	inclinado (a)

DLM Materials

- pattern blocks
- *Math Resource Guide* Pattern Strips (see Day 1)
- *DLM Math* software
- *Making Music with Thomas Moore* CD

Materials to Gather

- connecting cubes
- masking tape
- building blocks
- straws

MATH

Focus

- Introduce a new dance pattern, such as swing left arm-swing right arm-turn around (an A-B-C pattern) or reintroduce any pattern from Days 1–3. Most children won't know left and right, but naming them while you model the dance pattern is helpful.
- March around a shape taped onto the floor. You may wish to use a different shape or a different pattern than you used on Day 3.

Develop

- Using only two colors of cubes, make towers with a new pattern.
- Introduce a Pattern Strip that has a positional pattern: vertical-vertical-horizontal-vertical-vertical-horizontal-vertical-vertical-horizontal. Name it as an A-A-B pattern. Have children use their arms to show each position as you point to it and chant it.
- Duplicate the pattern using building blocks, standing two building blocks vertically, then laying one down horizontally, and so on.

Practice

- Invite children to copy and extend any of the Pattern Strips with straws.
- Challenge children to make their own patterns with cube towers or building blocks.
- You may wish to practice patterns throughout the day by having children line up in a pattern. Call children by names to create a pattern, girl-boy-girl-boy (or A-A-B, depending on class ratios). If there are not enough children to finish the pattern core, ask what would come next.
- Have the children work on Build Stairs, Level 1 or Memory—Number, Level 1.

Reflect/Assess

- Show the children a cube tower that does not show a pattern. *Is there a pattern?*
  ¿Hay algún patrón?
- *How do you know?*
  ¿Cómo lo saben?

Music and Movement

- Invite the children to play their clappers to a selection of music from the *Making Music with Thomas Moore* CD.
- Encourage them to perform "Chicken Dance" from the *Making Music with Thomas Moore* CD. Discuss the increasing tempo of the music and the movements.

Content Connection

Social Studies

Objective
To identify common events and routines

Materials to Gather
paper

Activity 1

- Have children go for a walk and look for patterns in the neighborhood (or classroom).
- Encourage them to make a rubbing of a pattern that they find such as the brick on the building or boards on the floor.

Activity 2

- Discuss patterns in daily routines.
- Review the class schedule and point out the patterns.

Suggested Reading

Pattern Fish by Trudy Harris and Anne Canevari Green

Reflect on the Day

- *What was your favorite activity? Why?*
  ¿Cuál fue su actividad favorita? ¿Por qué?
- *Which animals make soft sounds? Which animals make loud sounds?*
  ¿Qué animales producen sonidos suaves? ¿Qué animales producen sonidos fuertes?
- *Pay attention to loud and soft sounds at your house tonight. We will talk about these sounds tomorrow.*
  Esta noche en sus casas, pongan atención a los sonidos fuertes y suaves. Hablaremos de estos sonidos mañana.

Home Connection

Tell children that their homework is to find patterns their families make, use, or have at home. Help them brainstorm ways they might use patterns. Send home take-home book packs with four children. You will find the directions and a recording sheet for this activity in the *Home Connections Resource Guide*.

Begin the Day

- Do the dance "Looby Loo" from the *Four Baby Bumblebees* CD or "El joky-poky" from the *Esta es mi tierra* CD. Discuss the relationships between the sound/music and the movements/dance.
- Use one of the suggestions for Morning Circle offered in the front of this *Teacher's Edition*.

Objectives

- To understand that reading and writing are ways to obtain information and knowledge, generate and communicate thoughts and ideas, and solve problems
- To express feelings through movement

Vocabulary

dance	bailar
shadow	sombra
tempo	compás

DLM Materials

- *Four Baby Bumblebees* CD
- *Esta es mi tierra* CD
- *This Old Man Is Rockin' On/Este viejito tiene mucho ritmo*
- *Humpty Dumpty Dumpty*
- *Teacher's Resource Anthology*
  "Hi, My Name Is Joe!"/"¡Hola, me llamo Joe!"
  "This Old Man Is Rockin' On"/"Un señor"
  "The Runaway Cookie Parade"/"El desfile de la galleta fugitiva" finger puppet patterns

Materials to Gather

- light source
- music (various tempos)
- washers
- paper plates
- crepe paper streamers

LITERACY

Focus

- Invite the children to perform "Hi, My Name Is Joe!"/"¡Hola, me llamo Joe!" Talk about the movements that go with the chant.
- Explain that sound and movement often go together. Ask the children to think of examples in which sound and movement go together, such as clapping their hands or stomping their feet.
- Tell the children that today they will learn about sounds and movements that go together.

Develop

One Way to Develop the Lesson

- Invite the children to get up and dance without music. After a minute or so, turn music on and encourage them to keep dancing.
- Ask the children if it was easier for them to dance with or without music. Explain that music helps people keep the rhythm or beat of their movements going.
- Invite the children to help you prepare a list of ways that sounds and movements go together. *Is it possible to make movements without making sounds? Can you clap your hands without making a sound?* *¿Es posible moverse sin hacer ruido? ¿Pueden aplaudir sin hacer ruido?*

Another Way to Develop the Lesson

- Provide a light source and music. Invite the children to dance between the light source and a wall. Encourage them to watch the movements of their shadows on the wall. *Do the shadows keep up with the beat of the music?*

  ¿Las sombras llevan el compás de la música?
- Change the tempo of the music and encourage the children to create faster- or slower-moving shadows.

Practice

- Place the "This Old Man Is Rockin' On"/"Un señor" flannel board story in the Language Center and encourage the children to retell the story or make up a new one using the flannel board pieces.
- Place the *This Old Man Is Rockin' On/Este viejito tiene mucho ritmo* book and listening tape in the Listening Center.
- Give the children washers to tape on the bottoms of their shoes. Have them try tap dancing.
- Give the children finger puppets. Show them how to make their puppets dance to music. Encourage them to color the costumes on their puppets.
- Give the children quarters of paper plates and crepe paper streamers. Show them how to glue the streamers to the edges of their plates to make dancing streamers. Tell them that they will use the streamers later, when they dance creatively to music.
- Make the light source available for the children to use to explore shadows they can make with their bodies. Have them cause their shadows to move quickly and slowly.

Preparation

- Make photocopies of the finger puppet patterns; then cut them out.
- Make the flannel board stories, if not already made.

Second Language Learners

Tell the "The Runaway Cookie Parade"/ "El desfile de la galleta fugitiva" flannel board story twice. First pantomime each activity in the story. Children can then pantomime the actions while you describe what they are doing. Be sure to use language from the story. Then tell the story using the flannel board figures.

Anthology Support

Bunny Hop
Salto de conejo
"Whose Dog Are Thou?"
"¿De quién son esos perros?"
"Inside Out"
"Adentro afuera"

DAY 5

Letter Knowledge

English

- Encourage the children to make the letter *l* with their bodies. Use the Think, Pair, Share game with this activity.

Spanish

- Encourage the children to make the letter *r* with their bodies. Use the Piensa, aparea, comparte with this activity.

Suggested Reading

Pigs Aplenty, Pigs Galore! by David McPhail
Flash, Crash, Rumble and Roll by Franklin M. Branley

Technology Support

Encourage the children to find the movement activities on the *SRA Photo Library* software in the Recreation category and the Occupation category. Have them dictate a couple of sentences comparing the skater and the ballerina in the Occupations category.

Reflect/Assess

- *Name some things other than dancing that people can do to music.*
  Nombren otras cosas aparte de bailar que la gente puede hacer con música.
  Remind the children about the songs you use at cleanup time.
- *How does music make you feel?*
  ¿Cómo los hace sentir la música?

Literacy Circle

Storytime 1

- Present the "The Runaway Cookie Parade"/"El desfile de la galleta fugitiva" flannel board story. Invite the children to form a line and dance like the runaway cookies. *Did the cookies make any sounds when they ran away?*
  ¿Las galletas hicieron ruido cuando se escaparon?

Storytime 2

- Read *Humpty Dumpty Dumpty*. Invite the children to perform the dance steps that Mr. Moore and the children perform in the book.

Content Connection

Fine Arts

Objectives

To participate in classroom music activities

To express feelings through movement

Vocabulary

square dance, promenade, partners

contradanza, pasear, compañeros

DLM Materials

- *Teacher's Resource Anthology*
  Square Dance/Baile de figuras
  "It's a Simple Dance to Do"/"Es un baile simple"

Activity 1

- Teach a simple Square Dance/Baile de figuras. Discuss moving to the music and the verbal directions.

Activity 2

- Introduce "It's a Simple Dance to Do"/"Es un baile simple." Discuss the movements of the dance.

DAY 5

MATH

Objectives

- To recognize and reproduce simple patterns of concrete objects
- To follow basic oral or pictorial cues for operating programs successfully

Vocabulary

repeating pattern	patrón periódico
pattern core	centro del patrón
vertical	vertical
horizontal	horizontal
slanted	inclinado (a)

DLM Materials

- rhythm band instruments
- *Math Resource Guide* Pattern Strips (see Day 1)
- *DLM Math* software
- *Making Music with Thomas Moore* CD

Materials to Gather

- connecting cubes
- masking tape
- streamers
- straws

Suggested Reading

The Maestro Plays by Bill Martin Jr
Jamberry by Bruce Degen
Chicka Chicka Boom Boom by Bill Martin Jr and John Archambault
Crash! Bang! Boom!: A Book of Sounds by Peter Spier

Focus

- March around a shape. Use a different shape or marching pattern than you used previously.
- Discuss patterns in children's clothes or in the classroom.

Develop

- Do another Pattern Strip with a positional pattern. Have children use their arms to illustrate horizontal and vertical.
- Have children copy the pattern with straws either on the strip or parallel with the strip.
- Work through a task from Build Stairs, Level 1 with the children.

Practice

- Invite the children to make their own cube patterns.
- Encourage the children to copy and extend any of the Pattern Strips with straws. Include strips with positional patterns.
- Challenge the children to make up their own dance patterns.
- Children may work on Build Stairs, Level 1 or Memory—Number, Level 1.

Reflect/Assess

- Give children connecting cubes. Have them show a pattern.
- Computer Show: *What work did you do on the computer? How did you do it?*
  ¿Qué trabajo hicieron en la computadora? ¿Cómo lo hicieron?

Music and Movement

- Encourage the children to use their dancing streamers to dance creatively to music from the *Making Music with Thomas Moore* CD.
- Give the children the rhythm band instruments. Encourage them to play the instruments along with music from the *Making Music with Thomas Moore* CD.

Content Connection

Science

Objective
To use one or more senses to observe and learn about objects, events, and organisms

Materials to Gather
rhythm band instruments

Activity 1

- Encourage the children to use their voices to make sound patterns, such as loud-soft-loud-soft-loud-soft or loud-soft-soft-loud-soft-soft-loud-soft-soft.

Activity 2

- Provide musical instruments to create patterns such as loud-soft-loud-soft or high-low-high-low. You may want to provide the musical terms.

Reflect on the Day

- *What have you learned about sound and movement this week?*
  ¿Qué aprendieron sobre el sonido y el movimiento esta semana?
- *How do sound and movement go together?*
  ¿Cómo se relacionan el sonido y el movimiento?

Home Connection

Remind the children to ask their family members about coming to class next week to play instruments.

Looking Ahead

Connecting to the Theme: Music

Building on the previous theme, **Sound and Movement,** children will explore rhythm, verse, tempo, and various musical instruments. Children should begin to understand that music is another form of expression. This week's lessons will invite the children to discriminate between different sounds, discuss instrument families (percussion, wind, and so on), and think about part-whole relationships.

	Objectives	DLM Materials	Materials to Gather
DAY 1	• To link new learning experiences and vocabulary to what is already known about a topic • To begin to play classroom instruments • To cooperate with others in a joint activity	• *Animal Orchestra/La orquesta de los animales* • *Teacher's Resource Anthology* • rhythm band instruments	• name puzzles • construction paper • yarn • marking pens • blocks
DAY 2	• To link new learning experiences and vocabulary to what is already known about a topic • To begin to sing a variety of simple songs • To participate in classroom music activities	• *Animal Orchestra/La orquesta de los animales* • *Listen to the Rain/Escucha la lluvia* • Oral Language Card 54 • *SRA Photo Library* software • rhythm band instruments • *Teacher's Resource Anthology*	• Musical Instrument Concentration • ankle bells • drum • empty pill or film canisters • sound makers • screen painting frames • old toothbrushes • tempera paint • tongue depressors or craft sticks
DAY 3	• To link new learning experiences and vocabulary to what is already known about a topic • To participate in classroom music activities • To begin to perform simple investigations	• *Animal Orchestra/La orquesta de los animales* • Oral Language Card 54 • *SRA Photo Library* software • rhythm band instruments • *Teacher's Resource Anthology*	• Musical Instruments Concentration • string instrument • tape of string music • box guitar • elastic
DAY 4	• To link new learning experiences and vocabulary to what is already known about a topic • To begin to distinguish among the sounds of several common instruments • To begin to perform simple investigations	• *Animal Orchestra/ La orquesta de los animales* • *This Old Man Is Rockin' On/Este viejito tiene mucho ritmo* • *Making Music with Thomas Moore* CD • Oral Language Card 54 • rhythm band instruments • *SRA Photo Library* software • *Teacher's Resource Anthology*	• Musical Instrument Concentration • wind instrument • waxed paper • paper-towel and toilet-paper tubes • tissue paper • crayons
DAY 5	• To link new learning experiences and vocabulary to what is already known about a topic • To understand that illustrations carry meaning but cannot be read • To become aware of routine healthy behaviors (e.g., brushing teeth)	• *This Old Man Is Rockin' On/Este viejito tiene mucho ritmo* • *Teacher's Resource Anthology*	• family tapes • musical note examples • dramatic-play props

(See individual lesson pages for complete lists of materials.)

Learning Centers

LISTENING

Music to My Ears

Objective
To begin to respond to music of various tempos through movement

Materials
several different types of music

Develop
Provide several different genres of music, such as blues, jazz, classical, and country. Invite the children to dance to it.

Reflect/Assess
Which types of music do you like best? Why?
¿Qué tipo de música les gusta más? ¿Por qué?
Why do you think blues is called blues?
¿Por qué creen que a los blues se les llama blues?

ART

Brush Strokes

Objective
To begin to use art as a form of self-expression

Materials
tempera paint, brushes, music with a variety of tempos

Develop
Play several different tempos of music and invite the children to paint to it.

Reflect/Assess
Which tempo made you want to paint the most?
¿Cuál ritmo los animó más a pintar?

CONSTRUCTION

Instrument Makers

Objective
To use different colors, surface textures, and shapes to create form and meaning

Materials
a variety of boxes, rubber bands, canisters, bells, sandpaper, toilet paper tubes, plastic bottles, seeds, pebbles, paper clips

Develop
Provide materials for children to use to make musical instruments of their own creation.

Reflect/Assess
How does your instrument work?
¿Cómo funcionan sus instrumentos?

What Research Suggests

There are a number of connections between music and brain development. Listening to music lowers anxiety and stimulates our emotions. Music instruction aids children's development of spatial relationship concepts. Music is filled with patterns and repetition, and patterns expand and organize our thinking. Repetition strengthens patterns.

Begin the Day

- Sing "Calliope Song." Point out the part each group plays in creating the effect of the whole song.
- Use one of the suggestions for Morning Circle offered in the front of this *Teacher's Edition.*

Objectives

- To link new learning experiences and vocabulary to what is already known about a topic
- To begin to play classroom instruments

Vocabulary

orchestra	orquesta
conductor	director
trombone	trombón
trumpet	trompeta
French horn	corno francés
violin	violín
drum	tambor, batería
double bass	contrabajo
flute	flauta
saxophone	saxofón
cymbals	platillos

Materials

DLM Materials

- *Animal Orchestra/La orquesta de los animales* book and tape
- rhythm band instruments
- *Teacher's Resouce Anthology*
  "Calliope Song"
  "Old MacDonald Has a Band"/ "El viejo MacDonald tiene una banda"
  "El circo"/"The Circus" flannel board story
  "The Traveling Musicians"/"Los músicos viajeros" flannel board story

Materials to Gather

- name puzzles
- construction paper
- yarn

LITERACY

Focus

- Sing "Old MacDonald Has a Band"/"El viejo MacDonald tiene una banda."
- Ask the children if they have ever seen an orchestra or band play, either in real life or on television. Encourage them to tell about their experiences.
- Describe the difference between an orchestra and a band, and tell the children that today we will be learning about orchestras and bands.

Develop

One Way to Develop the Lesson

- Show children the cover of the book *Animal Orchestra/La orquesta de los animales.* Point out the title and name of the author. Tell the children that the book is about a group of animals that all play instruments in an orchestra. Read the book and explain that each member of the orchestra makes a contribution to the way the music sounds when all the instruments are played together.
  El libro trata de un grupo de animales que tocan instrumentos en una orquesta. Cada miembro de la orquesta contribuye con el sonido de la música cuando todos los intrumentos se tocan a la vez.
- Give the children the rhythm band instruments and encourage them to play their instruments to a piece of classical music. Start by having them play only one type of instrument. Gradually add instruments until everyone is playing. Discuss how the sound of the instruments changed with each addition.

Another Way to Develop the Lesson

- Reread *Animal Orchestra/La orquesta de los animales*. Remind the children that the orchestra is made of many parts, like a puzzle, and that it takes all the pieces to make a whole puzzle.
- Use a name puzzle to show how children's names are made of several letters, like an orchestra is made of several instruments.

Practice

- Give the children their name puzzles to solve.
- Provide rhythm band instruments for children to explore in the Music Center. Encourage them to play the instruments two or three at a time.
- Give the children an 18-inch piece of yarn, a hole punch, and construction paper circles cut in 2-inch diameters. Have the children print one letter of their names on each circle and then string the circles onto the yarn to make name necklaces.
- Place the *Animal Orchestra/La orquesta de los animales* book and listening tape in the Listening Center.
- Invite the children to build a house in the Blocks Center. Can they build a house with one block?

Preparation

- Make "The Traveling Musicians"/"Los músicos viajeros" and "El circo"/"The Circus" flannel board stories.
- Make a name puzzle for each child by writing his or her name on a 4-inch by 10-inch piece of construction paper or tagboard. Make puzzle cuts between each letter.
- Prepare circles for name necklaces.

Second Language Learners

Tell "The Traveling Musicians"/"Los músicos viajeros" flannel board story. First, pantomime the story. Children can pantomime also as you describe their actions using story language. Then tell the story using flannel board figures. Place the flannel board and its figures in a center for the children to retell the story to a stuffed animal.

Anthology Support

"Family Fun"
"Diversión familiar"
"MacNamara's Band"
"Musical Instruments"
"Instrumentos musicales"

DAY 1

Letter Knowledge

English

- Introduce *m* using "Manuela" from the *English Phonics Resource Guide.* Point out that *music* begins with the letter *m.* Tell the children that the conductor of the orchestra is sometimes called a *maestro*, which also starts with *m*.

Spanish

- Introduce c using "El cumpleaños de la c" from the *Spanish Phonics Resource Guide.*

Suggested Reading

Dreamsong by Alice McLerran
Mañana es domingo by Alma Flor Ada
I Like Music by Leah Komaiko

Teacher's NOTE

If you have a family member playing an instrument this week, attempt to schedule the performance on the day that you are discussing the type of instrument he or she will play. Percussion instruments will be introduced tomorrow, string instruments on Wednesday, and wind instruments on Thursday.

Reflect/Assess

- *How are the instruments in the book like the letters in words?* For example, it takes several instruments to create a sound, and each instrument makes a specific sound.
  ¿En qué se parecen los instrumentos del libro a las letras de las palabras?
- *What is the role of the conductor in the orchestra?*
  ¿Qué papel cumple el director en la orquesta?
- *Which instrument in the story would you most like to play? Why?*
  ¿Cuál instrumento del cuento les gustaría tocar más? ¿Por qué?

Literacy Circle

Storytime 1

- Present the "El circo"/"The Circus" flannel board story. Discuss the whole/part relationships of the animals and the people who make up the circle.

Storytime 2

- Present "The Traveling Musicians"/"Los músicos viajeros" flannel board story. Point out that the traveling musicians are a band, not an orchestra.
- Discuss how many animals make up the band. *What does each animal add to the group/band?*
  ¿Con qué contribuyó cada animal al grupo/a la banda?

Content Connection

Social Studies

Objective
To cooperate with others in a joint activity

Vocabulary
team, teamwork
grupo, equipo; trabajo en equipo

Materials to Gather
blocks

Activity 1

- Play a team game, such as a relay race. Emphasize that every child is an important part/member of the team.

Activity 2

- Show children how to use a "water line" to pass blocks from one area of the room to another. *How does that approach make the work easier?*

  ¿Cómo esa técnica facilita el trabajo?

  Emphasize that everyone is working as a team to achieve a common goal. Ask the children what other things are easier to do in groups (for example, building a house, making a quilt, or playing baseball).

  ¿Qué otras cosas son fáciles de hacer en grupo?

DAY 1

Objectives

- To begin to predict what comes next when patterns are extended
- To start, use, and exit software programs

Vocabulary

pattern patrón

DLM Materials

- rhythm band instruments
- *Math Resource Guide* Build Stairs/Construye escaleras
- Pattern Strips (Levels 2 and 3)
- *DLM Math* software
- *Making Music with Thomas Moore* CD
- *Teacher's Resource Anthology* "Teddy Bear, Teddy Bear"/"Osito, osito"

Materials to Gather

- building blocks
- connecting cubes
- small toys

Teacher's NOTE

This week we will continue the type of patterns we did last week, but we will introduce a different type of pattern—N + 1. The N + 1 pattern is a growing pattern in which the next element is 1 more than the element before.

MATH

Focus

- Recite "Teddy Bear, Teddy Bear"/"Osito, osito" with the children. Pretend to climb the stairs as you count to 10.

Develop

- Demonstrate Build Stairs/Construye escaleras.
- As children watch, build two steps from connecting cubes. The first step is just one cube, and the second step is two cubes. Show them the two steps side by side. Ask them how many cubes you will need to finish making the next step.
- Introduce Build Stairs, Level 2 on the computer. Build Stairs, Level 2 focuses on the important N + 1 pattern. In this activity, Builder Betsy asks the child to put the steps in order to make stairs. When the children have finished, they may practice Memory—Number, Level 2.

Practice

- Invite children to make their own stairs with connecting cubes. Provide small toys, such as animals, that the children can use to climb the stairs and create a story.
- Have the children review copying and extending Pattern Strips.
- Children may start, use, and exit Build Stairs, Level 2, and Memory—Number, Level 2. The computer helps reinforce ideas and skills by giving children instant feedback on whether they are right or wrong.

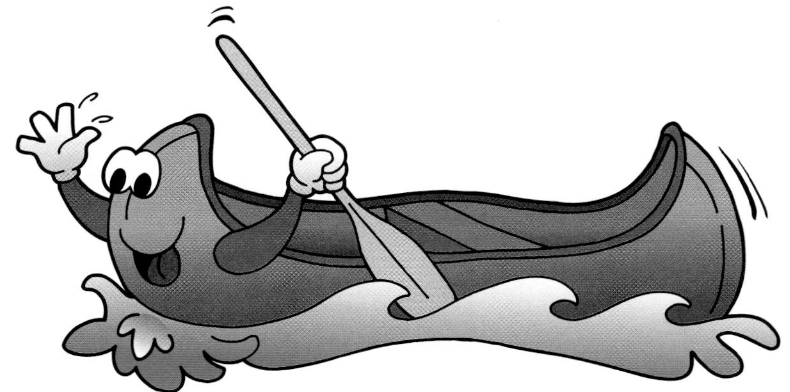

Reflect/Assess

- Pretend your fingers are walking up steps. Count up to 5 and stop. *What step comes next? How do you know?*
  ¿Qué paso sigue? ¿Cómo lo saben?

Music and Movement

- Play "De colores" from the *Making Music with Thomas Moore* CD. Ask the children to listen carefully to the song. *What causes the music to grow louder and fuller?*
- Let the children play rhythm band instruments to a favorite selection of music.

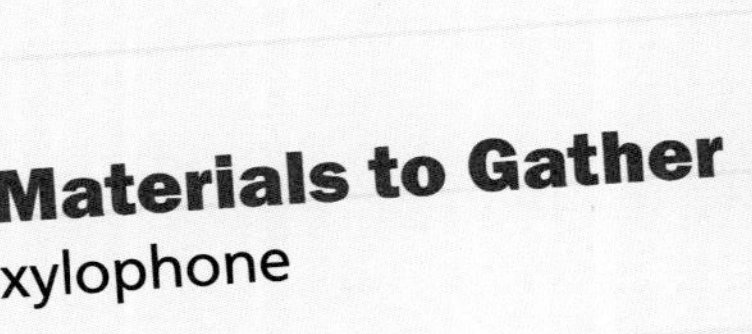

Content Connection

Fine Arts

Objectives
To participate in classroom music activities
To begin to respond to music of various tempos

Materials to Gather
xylophone

Activity 1

- Sing a song, such as "do, re, mi, . . ." that goes up and down a scale to reinforce the idea of steps. Play a xylophone and have children see and hear the step direction of the notes. For example, sing "go-ing up the stairs to the top" (one tone for each note—go back down as well).

Activity 2

- Continue dancing patterns with various musical styles. To emphasize strong patterns, do marches! Incorporate rhythm instruments and rhythmic counting!

Suggested Reading

Ten Black Dots by Donald Crews
1, 2, 3 Yippie by Lisa Jahn-Clough

Reflect on the Day

- *Which activity was your favorite today? Why?*
  ¿Cuál fue su actividad favorita de hoy? ¿Por qué?
- *What have you learned about the orchestra today?*
  ¿Qué aprendieron hoy sobre la orquesta?

Home Connection

Let families know that you will be collecting empty toilet-paper tubes for Thursday, and winter clothing items for the Dramatic Play Center for next week.

Begin the Day

- Teach the children the first verse to "The Big Bass Drum"/"El tambor de hojalata."
- Teach the children "Old MacDonald Has a Band"/"El viejo MacDonald tiene una banda," singing only the verse about the drum.
- Use one of the suggestions for Morning Circle offered in the front of this *Teacher's Edition.*

Objective

- To link new learning experiences and vocabulary to what is already known about a topic

Vocabulary

percussion instruments	instrumentos de percusión
rattle	cascabel
beat	ritmo

DLM Materials

- *Animal Orchestra/La orquesta de los animales*
- *Listen to the Rain/Escucha la lluvia*
- Oral Language Development Card 54
- Musical Instrument card patterns
- Musical Instrument Concentration game
- rhythm band instruments
- *SRA Photo Library* software
- *Teacher's Resource Anthology*
  "This Is the Way We Beat Our Drums"
  drumbeat rebus card
  drum puzzles
  "This Old Man Is Rockin' On"/"Un señor"
  "The Big Bass Drum"/"El tambor de hojalata"
  "Old MacDonald Has a Band"/"El viejo MacDonald tiene una banda"

Materials to Gather

- ankle bells, drum
- empty pill or film canisters
- small sound makers (such as seeds)
- screen painting frames
- old toothbrushes
- tempera paint

Focus

- Sing "This Is the Way We Beat Our Drums."
- Play a drum and ask the children to name the instrument. Tell them that the drum is a percussion instrument, and that today we will be discussing percussion instruments.

Develop

One Way to Develop the Lesson

- Show the children the percussion instruments in *Animal Orchestra/ La orquesta de los animales.* Explain that percussion instruments are instruments that we strike or shake to create a sound.
- Help the children create a list of percussion instruments. Encourage them to look at the rhythm band instruments and find the percussion instruments. If the instruments are on the list, point to the names of the instruments. If an instrument is not on the list, add it.
- Show the children Oral Language Card 54 (musical instruments). Ask a volunteer to point out the string instrument and the percussion instrument.

  ¿Quién quiere señalar el instrumento de cuerdas y el de percusión?
- Have the children listen to the sound of the drum in the Equipment category of the *SRA Photo Library* software.

Another Way to Develop the Lesson

- Play a piece of music or sing a simple song and invite the children to clap to the beat of the music. Remind them that their bodies are capable of making sounds. Ask volunteers to recall the sounds they made with their bodies last week. Explain that when the children were clapping to the music, they were using their hands as percussion instruments.
- Give each child a box or drum to play. Play the music again. This time, have the children join in with their drums a few at a time, until everyone is playing. Point out that they are all members of a group who are playing drums, and that the drums are just one part of the orchestra.

  Todos son miembros del grupo que toca tambor y los tambores son sólo una parte de la orquesta.

Practice

- Encourage the children to beat drums to music in the Music Center. Give them the Drumbeat Rebus Card to use to create their own music.
- Give the children ankle bells and invite them to make up a dance in the Gross Motor Center.
- Encourage the children to work the drum puzzles.
- Provide sound makers, such as gravel, sand, or seeds, and some empty film or pill canisters. Have the children make sound shakers and encourage them to make up shaking patterns or play their shakers to music.
- Have the children do some screen painting. Tell the children that the brush movement across the screen is a percussion movement. Tell them to listen to the sound as they paint.
- Have the children play the Musical Instruments Concentration game.

Preparation

- Photocopy and enlarge the drum from the musical instruments card patterns. Color it, laminate it, and cut it into puzzle pieces.
- Photocopy two copies of the musical instruments card patterns. Color them, cut them out, and laminate them to make a Musical Instrument Concentration game.
- Photocopy the drumbeat rebus card.
- Make ankle bells by sewing several jingle bells to an 8-inch strip of elastic and then sewing the ends of the elastic together to make a bracelet.
- Make a splatter paint screen.

Second Language Learners

Tell the "This Old Man Is Rockin' On"/"Un señor" story using the flannel board. Pantomime each activity. Have children follow along with you. Recite and audiotape the story as a group. Place story materials in a center for the children to sequence as they listen to the tape.

Anthology Support

"Jingle Bells"
"Ride a Cockhorse"
"Caballito de juguete"

DAY 2

Letter Knowledge

English

- Read "Molly's Glasses" from the *SRA Alphabet Book.*

Spanish

- Read "Cinco cerditos" from *Los niños alfabéticos.*

Suggested Reading

Conga Crocodile by Nicole Rubel
Grandpa's Song by Tony Johnston
Una extraña visita by Alma Flor Ada

Teacher's NOTE

People in different parts of the world beat out rhythms on drums unique to their culture. These drums include *congas, bongos,* Egyptian *darabukas,* Nigerian *balengos,* East Indian *tablas,* West Indian steel drums and Native American hand drums. Discuss the many different kinds of drums with the children.

Reflect/Assess

- *Do you know anyone who plays a percussion instrument? Who?*
  ¿Conocen a alguien que toca un instrumento de percusión? ¿Quién?
- *Which of the percussion instruments do you like best? Why?*
  ¿Cuál instrumento de percusión les gusta más? ¿Por qué?

Literacy Circle

Storytime 1

- Present the "This Old Man Is Rockin' On"/"Un señor" flannel board story. *Which of the instruments in the story is a percussion instrument?*
  ¿Cuál de los instrumentos del cuento es de percusión?

Storytime 2

- Read *Listen to the Rain/Escucha la lluvia. Is the rain a percussion instrument?*
  ¿La lluvia es un instrumento de percusión?

Content Connection

Fine Arts

Objective
To participate in classroom music activities

Vocabulary
percussion, beat, rhythm
percusión, ritmo, ritmo

Materials to Gather
tongue depressors or craft sticks

Activity 1

- Ask the children to brainstorm a list of percussion sounds they can make with their bodies (clapping, slapping knees, tapping feet).
- Encourage them to choose sounds they want to make, then have them play along with music from a favorite CD.

Elijan sonidos que quieran producir. Sigan la música.

Activity 2

- Use a tongue depressor or craft stick to tap out three or four beats. Encourage the children to copy your beats.

Imiten estos ritmos.

DAY 2

Objectives

- To recognize and reproduce simple patterns of concrete objects
- To begin to predict what comes next when patterns are extended

Vocabulary

pattern patrón

DLM Materials

- *Animal Orchestra/La orquesta de los animales*
- rhythm band instruments
- *Math Resouce Guide*
  Build Stairs/Construye escaleras
  Pattern Strips (Levels 2 and 3)
  Dot cards (1–5)
- *DLM Math* software
- *Four Baby Bumblebees* CD

Materials to Gather

- connecting cubes

What Research Suggests

Patterning is an important skill in itself, but patterning also supports children's learning of numbers, as with the *one more* pattern of counting.

MATH

Focus

- Read the first page of *Animal Orchestra/La orquesta de los animales.* Point to the numeral 1. *One is on this page. What number is on the next page?*

  ¿Qué número está en la próxima página?

  Slowly turn the page and share their happiness when they see they were correct. Count the animals on that page, reinforcing that there are two. Continue asking children to tell the next number. If they get stuck, lead them in counting from 1.

Develop

- Have Dot cards 1–5 laid out in order. Ask children to describe the pattern. Ask them what number would come next, continuing the pattern. Next? Chant the pattern (count 1, 2, 3, 4, 5) from the beginning while pointing.
- Reintroduce Build Stairs, Level 2.

Practice

- Challenge children to order the Dot cards from fewest to most.
- Play Build Stairs/Construye escaleras with connecting cubes.
- Have the children copy and extend Pattern Strips.
- Children may work on Build Stairs, Level 2 or Memory—Number, Level 2.

Reflect/Assess

- *How did you figure out what the patterns were?*
  ¿Cómo determinaron qué eran los patrones?
- *How do you know what comes next?*
  ¿Cómo saben qué viene después?

Music and Movement

- Have the children play drums (boxes) or shakers to music. Remind them that the percussion instruments keep the beat of the music.
  - Play "Clap Hands" from the *Four Baby Bumblebees* CD. *Which activities in the song are percussion activities?*
    ¿Qué actividades de la canción son de percusión?
  - Play "Green Bottles" from the *Four Baby Bumblebees* CD and invite the children to listen for the heavy drum beat in the music.

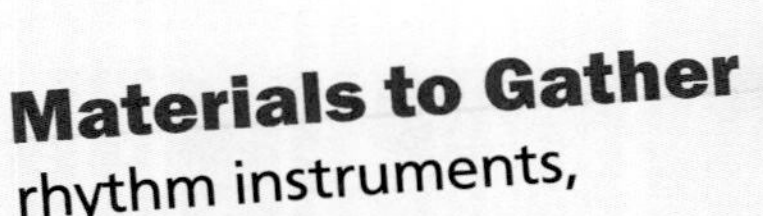

Content Connection

Fine Arts

Objectives

To begin to play classroom instruments

To use different colors, surface textures, and shapes to create form and meaning

Materials to Gather

rhythm instruments, colored acetate, overhead projector

Activity 1

- Encourage the children to practice making simple sound patterns with rhythm instruments. Invite them to try simple tone patterns using a xylophone, keyboard, or other musical instrument.

Activity 2

- Provide strips of colored acetate cut to the lengths of 1–5 cubes. Encourage the children to lay them on the overhead from shortest to longest. What happens?

Suggested Reading

Rooster's Off to See the World by Eric Carle

The Bear Under the Stairs by Helen Cooper

Reflect on the Day

- *How can we use our body as a percussion instrument?*
  ¿Cómo podemos usar nuestro cuerpo como un instrumento de percusión?
- *What was your favorite activity today? Why?*
  ¿Cuál fue su actividad favorita de hoy? ¿Por qué?

Begin the Day

- Teach the second verse to "The Big Bass Drum"/"El tambor de hojalata."
- Sing "Old MacDonald Has a Band"/ "El viejo MacDonald tiene una banda," adding the verse about the fiddle.
- Use one of the suggestions for Morning Circle offered in the front of this *Teacher's Edition.*

Objective

- To link new learning experiences and vocabulary to what is already known about a topic

Vocabulary

string instruments	instrumentos de cuerda
strike	tocar
strum	rasquear la guitarra

DLM Materials

- *Animal Orchestra/La orquesta de los animales* book and tape
- rhythm band instruments
- *SRA Photo Library* software
- *Teacher's Research Anthology*
  guitar puzzles
  "This Old Man Is Rockin' On"/"Un señor" flannel board story
  "Little Buckaroo"/"El pequeño domador" flannel board story
  "Frog Went a-Courtin'"/"El sapo fue a cortejar" flannel board story
  "Going On a Trail Ride"/"Vamos a un paseo por el camino"
  Musical Instruments Concentration game
  Musical Instruments card patterns
- Oral Language Development Card 54

Materials to Gather

- string instrument
- tape of string music

LITERACY

Focus

- Strum a ukulele, guitar, or other string instrument. If you don't have an actual instrument, make a box guitar. Ask the children to name the instrument. Explain that it is a string instrument.
- Tell children that today we will be discussing string instruments.

Develop

One Way to Develop the Lesson

- Show the children the string instruments in *Animal Orchestra/ La orquesta de los animales*. Explain that string instruments are instruments that we strum or play with a bow to create a sound. Help them create a list of string instruments.
- Encourage the children to look at the rhythm band instruments. *Are there any string instruments?*

  ¿Hay algún instrumento de cuerdas?

  (Children's rhythm band instruments usually include percussion instruments, not string instruments.) Remind them that the string instruments are only part of the orchestra or band. *Who can name another part of the orchestra or band we have learned about?*

  ¿Quién puede nombrar otra parte de la orquesta o banda que hayamos estudiado?
- Invite the children to listen to the sound of the piano in the Equipment category of the *SRA Photo Library* software.

Another Way to Develop the Lesson

- Review the string and percussion instruments. Ask the children to recall the instruments discussed yesterday. *Who can name some percussion instruments? Who can name some string instruments?*

  ¿Quién puede nombrar instrumentos de percusión? ¿Quién puede nombrar instrumentos de cuerdas?
- Show the children Oral Language Card 54 (musical instruments). Ask them to point out the string instrument and the percussion instrument.
- Show the children a string instrument and a percussion instrument. Ask them to close their eyes and listen. Play one of the instruments and ask them to identify which instrument you played.

  Cierren los ojos y escuchen. ¿Qué instrumento toqué?

Practice

- Place the *Animal Orchestra/La orquesta de los animales* book and listening tape in the Listening Center.
- Play some string music in the Listening Center. *Can you hear the string instruments singing?*

  ¿Pueden oír los instrumentos de cuerdas?
- Have the children work the guitar puzzles.
- Invite the children to play the Musical Instruments Concentration game.
- Place the "This Old Man Is Rockin' On"/"Un señor" flannel board story in the Language Center. Encourage the children to retell the story or to make up a new story. *Which of the instruments in the story are string instruments?*

  ¿Cuáles de los instrumentos del cuento son de cuerdas?

Preparation

- Gather boxes.
- Locate a string instrument.
- Make the "Little Buckaroo"/"El pequeño domador" flannel board story.
- Make the "Frog Went a-Courtin'"/"El sapo fue a cortejar" flannel board story.
- Photocopy and enlarge the guitar in the musical instruments card patterns to make guitar puzzles. Color them, laminate them, and cut them into puzzle pieces.
- Copy, color, laminate, and cut out the musical instruments card patterns to make a Musical Instruments Concentration game.

Second Language Learners

Perform the "Frog Went a-Courtin'"/"El sapo fue a cortejar" story using the flannel board. Pantomime each action. Have children repeat the actions. Then recite and audiotape the story together. Place the flannel board, its figures, and the tape in a center. Children can place the figures on the board corresponding with the tape.

Anthology Support

"Old King Cole"

"El rey Camilo"

DAY 3

Letter Knowledge

English

- Have the children form the letter *m* with play dough.

Spanish

- Have the children form the letter *c* with play dough.

Suggested Reading

Zin! Zin! Zin! A Violin by Lloyd Moss
Mama Rocks, Papa Sings by Nancy Van Laan
Tikki Tikki Tembo by Arlene Mosel

Teacher's NOTE

Different musical styles use different string instruments. For example, country and western musicians use steel guitars and fiddles. Bluegrass musicians play dobros, mandolins, and dulcimers. Classical music involves violins, cellos, violas, and harps. Jazz relies on a stringed bass and often a piano. Rock and roll relies largely on electric guitar.

Reflect/Assess

- *How are string and percussion instruments alike? How are they different?*
  ¿En qué se parecen los instrumentos de cuerdas y de percusión? ¿En qué se diferencian?
- *Which of the string instruments do you like best? Why?*
  ¿Cuáles instrumentos de cuerdas les gusta más? ¿Por qué?

Literacy Circle

Storytime 1

- Invite the children to participate in "Going on a Trail Ride"/"Vamos a un paseo por el camino." When you get to the part of the chant in which the children join the people on the wagon train, let them play their shoe box guitars and sing one of the western songs in the *Teacher's Resource Anthology,* such as "Oh, Susanna!" or "You Are My Sunshine"/"Tú eres mi sol."

Storytime 2

- Present the "Frog Went a-Courtin'"/"El sapo fue a cortejar" flannel board story. *Who plays a string instrument in the story?*
  ¿Quién toca un instrumento de cuerdas en el cuento?

Content Connection

Science

Objective
To begin to perform simple investigations

Vocabulary
stretch, high, low
estirar, alto, bajo

Materials To Gather
elastic

Activity 1

- Stretch three or four different widths of elastic bands between two chairs that are three feet apart. Ask the children to pluck the strings. *Which makes a higher sound?*

  Toquen las cuerdas. ¿Cuál produce un sonido más alto?

- Move the chairs together and retie the bands. *Is the sound the same?*

  ¿El sonido es el mismo?

Activity 2

- Tie a circle of elastic for each child. Ask the children to sit on the floor in a circle and stretch the elastic bands between their feet. Have them pluck and strum the bands. *What happens when you stretch the bands tighter?*

  ¿Qué pasa cuando estiran las cuerdas?

DAY 3

Objectives
- To recognize and reproduce simple patterns of concrete objects
- To predict what comes next when patterns are extended

Vocabulary
pattern patrón

DLM Materials
- *Math Resouce Guide*
  Build Stairs/Construye escaleras
  Pattern Strips (Levels 2 and 3)
  Dot cards (1–5)
- *DLM Math* software
- *Where Is Thumbkin?* CD

Materials to Gather
- connecting cubes
- box guitars

The Very Hungry Caterpillar by Eric Carle
1, 2, 3 to the Zoo: A Counting Book by Eric Carle

MATH

Focus
- Have children start in a crouching position and slowly rise to a standing position while counting with you up to 10. If you want to count higher than 10, children can slowly reach their hands toward the ceiling, eventually stretching on their tiptoes.

Develop
- Lay out Dot cards from 1 to 3 in a random order. Ask the children to arrange them from fewest to most. Then ask what comes next. Pass out the rest of the cards. Continue the pattern up to 10, allowing the children to add them to the set in the correct order.
- Some children may need to start back at 1 each time to figure out what comes next.

Practice
- Invite the children to order the Dot cards.
- Encourage the children to do the Build Stairs/Construye escaleras activity with connecting cubes.
- Have the children copy and extend Pattern Strips.
- Children may work on Build Stairs, Level 2 or Memory—Number, Level 2.

Reflect/Assess

- Show the children a pattern. *What do you think comes next in this pattern?*
  ¿Qué creen que sigue en este patrón?

Music and Movement

- Play "The Frog Went A-Courtin'" from the *Where Is Thumbkin?* CD. *What kind of instrument does the bumblebee play?/¿Qué tipo de instrumento toca la abeja?*
- Invite the children to play their box guitars to music. Remind them that the string instruments enhance the melody of the music.

Content Connection

Personal and Social Development

Objectives

To express interests and self-direction in learning

To begin to share and cooperate with others in group activities

Activity 1

- Encourage the children to arrange themselves in patterns when lining up to go to the restroom, outdoors, or to any place that requires a line.

Activity 2

- Create a pattern with color tiles or similar manipulatives, then remove random tiles. Have the children determine which tiles are missing.

Reflect on the Day

- *What did you learn about music today?*
  ¿Qué aprendieron hoy sobre la música?
- *Which instruments do you like best so far?*
  ¿Qué instrumento les gusta más hasta ahora?

Home Connection

Remind families that you are collecting empty toilet paper tubes for tomorrow and old winter clothing items for next week.

Begin the Day

- Teach the children the third verse to "The Big Bass Drum"/"El tambor de hojalata."
- Sing "Old MacDonald Has a Band"/ "El viejo MacDonald tiene una banda," adding the verse about the flute.
- Use one of the suggestions for Morning Circle offered in the front of this *Teacher's Edition.*

Objectives

- To link new learning experiences and vocabulary to what is already known about a topic
- To begin to distinguish among the sounds of several common instruments

Vocabulary

wind instruments	instrumentos de viento
blow	soplar

DLM Materials

- *Animal Orchestra/La orquesta de los animales*
- *This Old Man Is Rockin' On/Este viejito tiene mucho ritmo*
- rhythm band instruments
- Oral Language Development Card 54
- *Making Music with Thomas Moore* CD
- *SRA Photo Library* software
- *Teacher's Resource Anthology*
  horn puzzles
  "Little Boy Blue"/"Pequeño pastor"
  Musical Instruments Concentration game
  musical instruments card patterns

Materials to Gather

- paper towel tubes
- tissue paper
- wind instrument
- waxed paper

LITERACY

Focus

- Make up a song similar to "This Is the Way We Beat Our Drums" called "This Is the Way We Blow Our Horns."
- Blow a horn, harmonica, trumpet or other wind instrument. If you don't have an actual instrument, make a kazoo. Ask the children to name the instrument. Explain that it is a wind instrument.
- Tell the children that today we will be discussing wind instruments.

Develop

One Way to Develop the Lesson

- Show the children the wind instruments in *Animal Orchestra/La orquesta de los animales*. Explain that wind instruments are instruments that we blow or pump. Create a list of wind instruments.
- Encourage the children to look at the rhythm band instruments. *Are there any wind instruments?*
  ¿Hay algún instrumento de viento?
- You may want to add a harmonica to the instruments so wind instruments will be represented. Remind the children that the wind instruments are only one part of the orchestra.
- Have the children listen to the sound of the horn played by the musician in the Occupations category of the *SRA Photo Library* software.

Another Way to Develop the Lesson

- Whistle a tune. Tell the children that their mouths are wind instruments.
- Review the string, percussion, and wind instruments. Ask the children to recall the instruments discussed yesterday. *Who can name some string instruments? Who can name some percussion instruments?*

  ¿Quién puede nombrar algunos instrumentos de cuerdas? ¿Quién puede nombrar algunos instrumentos de percusión?
- Show the children Oral Language Card 54 (musical instruments). Ask a volunteer to point out the string instrument, the percussion instrument, and the wind instrument.
- Show the children three instruments: a string instrument, a percussion instrument, and a wind instrument. Ask them to close their eyes and listen while you play one of the instruments. Ask them to identify which instrument you played.

  ¿Qué instrumento toqué?

Practice

- Place the *Animal Orchestra/La orquesta de los animales* book and tape in the Listening Center. Are the children able to identify the wind instruments?
- Play the *Making Music with Thomas Moore* CD in the Listening Center. *Can you hear the saxophone?*
- Encourage the children to work the horn puzzles.
- Have the children play the Musical Instruments Concentration game.
- Show the children how to make kazoos. Give each of the children a toilet paper tube and encourage them to decorate it with crayons or tissue paper. Show them how to cover one end with a piece of waxed paper held in place with a rubber band. Encourage the children to play a familiar song with their kazoos.

Preparation

- Photocopy and enlarge the horn from the musical instruments card patterns. Color it, laminate it, and cut it into puzzle pieces.
- Make the Musical Instruments Concentration game by copying, coloring, laminating, and cutting out the musical instruments card patterns.

Second Language Learners

An English sound that does not occur in many other languages is the schwa (o in *other*). Children can practice the schwa sound by saying this song (tune of "This Is the Way We..."): *This is the way we beat our drum, beat our our drum, beat our drum. This is the way we beat our drum, pum, pum, pum, pum, pum.* Note their pronuciation of the schwa. If this is difficult, repeat the lines saying the schwa sound carefully.

Anthology Support

"I Have a Red Accordion"

"Tengo un acordeón rojo"

"Family Music"

"Familia musical"

DAY 4

Letter Knowledge

English

- Ask the children to make the letter *m* with their bodies. Use the Think, Pair, Share game with this activity.

Spanish

- Ask the children to make the letter *c* with their bodies. Use the Piensa, aparea, comparte game with this activity.

Suggested Reading

Ben's Trumpet by Rachel Isadora
Anna and the Bagpiper by Thomas Locker
Whistle for Willie by Ezra Jack Keats
Silba por Willie by Ezra Jack Keats

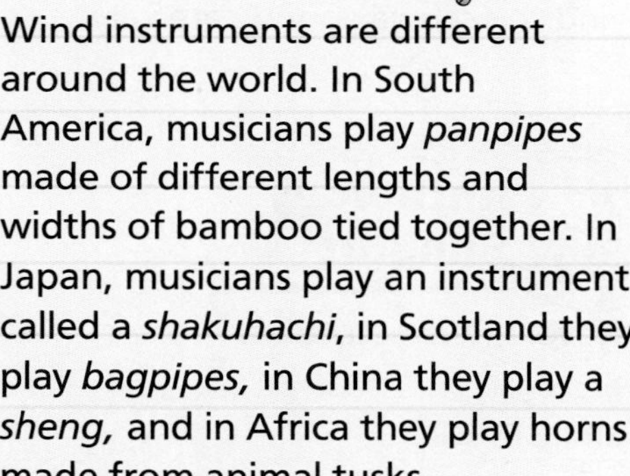

Teacher's NOTE

Wind instruments are different around the world. In South America, musicians play *panpipes* made of different lengths and widths of bamboo tied together. In Japan, musicians play an instrument called a *shakuhachi*, in Scotland they play *bagpipes,* in China they play a *sheng,* and in Africa they play horns made from animal tusks.

Reflect/Assess

- *Which wind instrument do you like best? Why?*

  ¿Qué instrumento de viento les gusta más? ¿Por qué?
- *Wind chimes make music when the wind blows. Are they a percussion instrument or a wind instrument?*

  Las campanitas hacen música cuando el viento sopla. ¿Son un instrumento de percusión o de viento?

Literacy Circle

Storytime 1

- Read *This Old Man Is Rockin' On/Este viejito tiene mucho ritmo. Which of the instruments in the story is a wind instrument?*

  ¿Cuál de los instrumentos del cuento es de viento?

Storytime 2

- Invite the children to act out "Little Boy Blue"/"Pequeño pastor." Have them try acting out some other nursery rhymes that have a musical instrument in them, such as "Old King Cole"/"El rey Camilo" or "Hey Diddle Diddle"/"¡Eh, chin, chin!"

Content Connection

Science

Objective
To begin to perform simple investigations

Vocabulary
breath, wind, sound
respirar, viento, sonido

DLM Materials
- *Teacher's Resource Anthology*
"Old MacDonald"/"El viejo MacDonald"

Materials to Gather
empty toilet paper tubes

Activity 1

- Read "The Wind"/"El viento." Discuss the sounds of the wind. Make a list of as many noises as the children can think of that involve the wind. *Is there a sound that wind makes by itself?*

  ¿Hay algún sonido que produzca el viento por sí solo?

Activity 2

- Encourage the children to experiment with their voices and their breath. *How many ways can you change your voice by changing the shape of your mouth? What if you cup your hands? Talk through a toilet paper tube? Hold your nose?*

  ¿De cuántas maneras pueden cambiar su voz al cambiar la forma de sus bocas? ¿Qué pasaría si pusieran sus manos en forma de taza sobre sus bocas? ¿Si hablaran a través de un tubo de papel de baño? ¿Si se taparan la nariz?
- Sing "Old MacDonald"/"El viejo MacDonald." Have the children sing while watching the mouth of a partner. *What happens to your mouth when you sing the E-I-E-I-O part of the song?*

  ¿Qué les pasa a sus bocas cuando cantan la parte de E-I-E-I-O?

DAY 4

Objectives

- To begin to predict what comes next when patterns are extended
- To recognize and reproduce simple patterns of concrete objects

Vocabulary

pattern patrón

DLM Materials

- pattern blocks
- *Math Resouce Guide*
  Build Stairs/Construye escaleras
  Dot cards (1–5)
  Pattern Strips (Levels 2 and 3)
- *DLM Math* software
- *Making Music with Thomas Moore* CD
- *Four Baby Bumblebees* CD

Materials to Gather

- connecting cubes
- kazoos

Suggested Reading

Pattern by Henry Pluckrose
Patterns by Karen Bryant-Mole

MATH

Focus

- Have steps made from 1, 2, and 3 connecting cubes laid out. Have the towers for 4 and 5 made but hidden from the children. Ask them to describe the pattern in steps 1, 2, and 3. Then encourage them to keep going. *How many cubes would we need for the next step to continue the pattern? Next?*

  ¿Cuántos cubos necesitaríamos para que el siguiente paso siga el patrón? ¿El próximo?

  Chant the pattern from the beginning while pointing.

Develop

- In a random order, lay out all the towers that make the steps. Ask children to help you put them in order again.
- Distribute Dot cards 1–5 to the children, each child getting one card. Encourage the children to put the numbers in order. Have the children hold out the cards in front so everyone can check.

Practice

- Invite children to order the Dot cards.
- Challenge children to make their own sets of stairs with connecting cubes. Invite them to make steps for an ant, a person, or a giant.
- Encourage children to copy and extend Pattern Strips.
- At the computer, children may work on Build Stairs, Level 2 or Memory—Number, Level 2.

Reflect/Assess

- *How did you fix the steps when they were all mixed up?*
  ¿Cómo arreglaron los pasos cuando se mezclaron?

Music and Movement

- Play "De colores" from the *Making Music with Thomas Moore* CD. Ask the children to listen for the bagpipes and the saxophone. Thomas plays the saxophone in most of the selections on this CD.
- Let them play their kazoos to music. Remind them that the wind instruments support the melody of the music. You may want to use "Whistle While You Work" from the *Four Baby Bumblebees* CD.

Content Connection

Social Studies

Objectives

To label common features in familiar environments

To identify common features in the home and school environments

Activity 1

- Have children go for a walk and look for patterns in the neighborhood, including steps.

Activity 2

- Encourage the children to build structures with steps in the Blocks Center.

Reflect on the Day

- *Who can describe the sound of the kazoo?*
  ¿Quién puede describir el sonido de la chicharra?
- *How are wind instruments like string instruments? How are they different?*
  ¿En qué se parecen los instrumentos de viento y los de cuerdas? ¿En qué se diferencian?

Home Connection

Ask the children to remind their families that you will need winter dress-up clothes next week.

Begin the Day

- Sing "Row, Row, Row Your Boat"/ "Rema, rema, tu canoa" in a round. Point out that each group's part contributed to the whole song.
- Use one of the suggestions for Morning Circle offered in the front of this *Teacher's Edition.*

Objectives

- To link new learning experiences and vocabulary to what is already known about a topic
- To understand that illustrations carry meaning but cannot be read

Vocabulary

hootenanny domingada
minstrels trovadores

DLM Materials

- *This Old Man Is Rockin' On/Este viejito tiene mucho ritmo* book and tape
- *Teacher's Resource Anthology*
  "Frosty the Snowman"/"Frosty, el muñeco de nieve" flannel board story
  "The Traveling Musicians"/"Los músicos viajeros" flannel board story
  "Head, Shoulders, Knees, and Toes" rebus card
  Musical Instruments Concentration game
  musical instruments card patterns

Materials to Gather

- family tapes
- examples of musical notes
- dramatic-play props such as microphones, headphones, and sheet music

LITERACY

Focus

- Remind the children that their bodies are musical instruments. Sing "If You're Happy and You Know It"/"Si estás contento." Call attention to the fact that clapping and stomping are percussion activities. Invite them to think of other percussion responses, such as tapping and snapping, and use them in the song.
- Tell the children that today we will be talking about music we can make with our bodies.

Develop

One Way to Develop the Lesson

- Tell the children that their voices are musical instruments. Have a hootenanny—a group sing-along. Sing two or three of the children's favorite songs.
- Show the children examples of musical notes. Emphasize that when you are just learning a new song you have never heard before, you will need to read both the musical notes and the words. The notes and words are parts that make up the whole song.
- Show the children the rebus directions for singing "Head, Shoulders, Knees, and Toes"/"Cabeza, hombros, rodillas y dedos." Invite them to read the pictures to sing the song. Point out that the tune is one they already know.
  La música es una que ya conocen.

Another Way to Develop the Lesson

- Tell the children that songs are used for many purposes, such as celebrations ("Happy Birthday"/"Feliz cumpleaños"), ceremonies, and holidays. Other songs teach lessons, provide directions, and tell stories. Write song purposes at the top of a piece of chart paper and ask the children which songs are sung for each purpose.
- Tell the children that you are going to tell them a story that is also a song. Present the "Frosty the Snowman"/"Frosty, el muñeco de nieve" flannel board story.
- Explain that long ago, stories weren't written down like they are today, because most people couldn't read or write. Instead, stories were enjoyed through songs. The people who sang the story songs were called *minstrels*.

  Las personas que cantaron las canciones se llamaban trovadores.

Practice

- Place the rebus directions for "Head, Shoulders, Knees, and Toes"/"Cabeza, hombros, rodillas y dedos" in the Music Center.
- Place the family tapes in the Listening Center.
- Place the *This Old Man Is Rockin' On/Este viejito tiene mucho ritmo* book and listening tape in the Listening Center.
- Provide props for the Dramatic Play Center such as headphones, a microphone, sheet music, and rhythm band instruments.
- Invite the children to draw a picture of something from one of their favorite songs. With their permission, label the work.

Preparation

- Make the "Frosty the Snowman"/"Frosty, el muñeco de nieve" flannel board story.
- Photocopy the "Head, Shoulders, Knees, and Toes" rebus card.
- Find examples of musical notes. *Wordsong/Canto de palabras* has musical notes on the cover and on page 26.
- Copy, color, laminate, and cut out the musical instruments card patterns to make the Musical Instruments Concentration game.

Second Language Learners

As children retell stories, they may repeat words, pause, or use a place marker such as *um* repeatedly. They may also use circumlocutions such as *that thing you put on your neck.* This is no reason for alarm, as it takes time to remember new vocabulary. Major story events, story sequencing cards, or props may help children remember words. Make comments to incorporate new vocabulary as children recall stories.

Anthology Support

"Three Bears Rap"
"El rap de los tres osos"
"Itsy Bitsy Spider"
"La araña pequeñita"
"There Was an Old Woman Who Swallowed a Fly"
"Había una anciana que se tragó una mosca"

DAY 5

Letter Knowledge

English

- Have the children find and circle the letter *m* in magazines and newspapers.

Spanish

- Invite the children to find and circle the letter *c* in magazines and newspapers.

Suggested Reading

Los cinco patitos by Pamela Paparone
The Happy Hedgehog Band by Martin Waddell
Music, Music for Everyone by V. Williams
Arroz con leche by Lulu Delacre

Technology Support

Review parts of the computer with the children. Allow them to type their names using the keyboard.

Reflect/Assess

- *Which story song is your favorite? Why?*
  ¿Cuál canción fue su favorita? ¿Por qué?
- *How does singing make you feel?*
  ¿Cómo se sienten al cantar?

Literacy Circle

Storytime 1

- Present "The Traveling Musicians"/"Los músicos viajeros" flannel board story. *Which of the animals wants to sing?*
  ¿Cuál animal quiere cantar?

Storytime 2

- Read any book in the program that is both a song and a story, such as *The Itsy Bitsy Spider/La araña pequeñita, The Farm/La granja,* or *The Little Ants/Las hormiguitas.*

Content Connection

Health/Safety

Objective
To become aware of routine healthy behaviors

Vocabulary
lesson, reminder
lección, recordatorio

Materials
Teacher's Resource Anthology
"This Is the Way We Clean Our Teeth"/"Así nos limpiamos los dientes"
"Drink, Drink, Drink Your Milk"/"Toma, toma tu leche"

Activity 1

- Remind the children that songs can be used to teach a lesson. Tell them that you are going to sing a song with them that reminds them how to brush their teeth.
- Sing "This Is the Way We Clean Our Teeth"/"Así nos limpiamos los dientes." Invite them to change the words to the song to reflect another lesson, such as caring for their ears or washing their hands.

  Cambien la letra de la canción para que hablemos de otra lección.

Activity 2

- Explain that some songs provide directions, such as "This Is the Way We Clean Our Teeth"/"Así nos limpiamos los dientes," while others just serve as reminders.
- Teach the children "Drink, Drink, Drink Your Milk"/"Toma, toma, toma tu leche." Invite them to change the words to the song to serve as another reminder (for example, to look both ways before they cross the street).

  Cambien la letra de la canción para que sirva de recordatorio.

DAY 5

Objectives

- To begin to predict what comes next when patterns are extended
- To follow basic oral or pictorial cues for operating programs successfully

Vocabulary

pattern patrón

DLM Materials

- pattern blocks
- *Math Resouce Guide*
  Build Stairs/Construye escalares
  Pattern Strips (Levels 2 and 3)
  Dot cards (1–5)
- *DLM Math* software
- *Four Baby Bumblebees* CD
- *Teacher's Resource Anthology*
  "This Old Man"/"Este viejito"

Materials to Gather

- connecting cubes
- building blocks

MATH

Focus

- Sing "This Old Man"/"Este viejito." Call attention to the N + 1 pattern.

Develop

- Reintroduce Build Stairs/Construye escaleras. Make steps (connecting cube towers) containing 1 to 10 cubes. Show children the steps that range in height from 1 to 5 connecting cubes laid out in a random order. Ask children to help you put them in order. *How many cubes would we need for the next step to continue the pattern? Next?*

  ¿Cuántos cubos necesitaríamos para que el próximo paso siga el patrón? ¿El próximo?

  Then lay out the towers containing 6 to 10 cubes and challenge the children to keep going.

Practice

- Invite the children to order the Dot cards from 1 to 5.
- Challenge the children to continue the N + 1 pattern while making steps with more than 10 connecting cubes.
- Encourage children to make their own patterns with paper blocks or building blocks.
- Have the children copy and extend Pattern Strips.
- Children may work on Build Stairs, Level 2 and Memory—Number, Level 2.

Reflect/Assess

- Computer Show *What work did you do? How did you do it?*
  ¿Qué trabajo hicieron? ¿Cómo lo hicieron?
- *How did you get the steps in the correct order?*
  ¿Cómo siguieron los pasos en el orden correcto?

Music and Movement

- Play "Do-Re-Mi" from the *Four Baby Bumblebees* CD. Have the children sing along.
- Sing "Who's Afraid of the Big Bad Wolf" from the *Four Baby Bumblebees* CD. *Which story is the song telling?*
  ¿Qué historia cuenta la canción?

Content Connection

Social Studies

Objectives
To share ideas and take turns listening and speaking
To identify common features in the local landscape

Activity 1

- Invite the children to play a game with a partner such as Tic Tac Toe. Call attention to the pattern of *your turn, my turn, your turn, my turn.*

Activity 2

- Ask students if they have ever ridden on an elevator instead of walking up stairs. Discuss the pattern of the floors when going up (N + 1).

Suggested Reading

On the Stairs by Julie Hofstrand Larios
Elevator Magic by Stuart J. Murphy

Reflect on the Day

- *What have you learned about music this week?*
  ¿Qué aprendieron esta semana sobre la música?
- *Which of the songs that we sang today do you like best? Why?*
  ¿Cuál de las canciones que cantamos hoy les gusta más? ¿Por qué?

Home Connection

Remind families to bring in winter clothes for Monday.

Looking Ahead

Connecting to the Theme: Winter

We do not experience seasons the same way wherever we live. Through the children's recognition of people's varied seasonal impressions, they can begin to think about different places in our world. This week's lessons will allow the children to make a winter word web, paint and create with winter colors, and sequence story events.

	Objectives	DLM Materials	Materials to Gather
DAY 1	• To begin to engage in conversation and follow conversational rules (e.g., staying on topic and taking turns) • To begin to dictate words, phrases, and sentences to an adult recording on paper (e.g., "letter writing," "story writing") • To use one or more senses to observe and learn about objects, events, and organisms	• Rafita and Pepita puppets • *Flannel Kisses/Besos de franela* • Oral Language Cards 58–59 • *Teacher's Resource Anthology* • *SRA Photo Library* software	• chart paper • felt • paintbrushes • tempera paint • winter books • bare branch • masking tape
DAY 2	• To begin to identify rhymes and rhyming sounds in familiar words, participate in rhyming games, and repeat rhyming songs and poems • To begin to retell the sequence of a story • To use one or more senses to observe and learn about objects, events, and organisms • To begin to perform simple investigations	• *Flannel Kisses/Besos de franela* • *Teacher's Resource Anthology*	• winter scene book • chart paper • "Frosty the Snowman" clothing items • plastic bag of ice • shaving cream
DAY 3	• To begin to retell the sequence of a story • To begin to predict what will happen next in a story • To use a variety of materials (e.g., crayons, paint, clay, markers) to create original work	• *The Color Bear/El oso de colores* • *Teacher's Resource Anthology*	• Rhyming Word Concentration • blue construction paper • chart paper • old magazines • shaving cream • play dough • puff paint • decorations
DAY 4	• To begin to break words into syllables or clap along with each syllable in a phrase • To use language to express common routines and familiar scripts • To begin to recognize that living things have similar needs for water, food, and air	• *Flannel Kisses/Besos de franela* • *The Color Bear/El oso de colores* • *The Tortilla Factory/La tortillería*	• chocolate syrup • hot plate • milk • rebus for making hot chocolate • assorted nuts
DAY 5	• To enjoy listening to and discussing storybooks and information books read aloud • To describe similarities and differences between objects • To recognize changes in the environment over time (e.g., growth, seasonal changes)	• *Teacher's Resource Anthology* • *SRA Photo Library* software • Oral Language Cards 58 and 59	• summer clothing • tracing paper • winter books • chart paper

(See individual lesson pages for complete lists of materials.)

Learning Centers

SCIENCE

Observing Winter

Objective
To gather information using simple tools such as a magnifying lens and an eyedropper

Materials to Gather
berries, magnifying lenses, pinecones, winter observation bottles, winter pictures

Develop
Prepare the winter observation bottles. Fill the Science Center with winter pictures and winter items. Provide magnifying lenses for up-close looks. During the week, add different berries and change the items in the observation bottles. Be sure to explain that the berries are not edible.

Reflect/Assess
What was your favorite thing to observe in the winter observation bottles?
¿Cuál fue su cosa favorita en las botellas de observación de invierno?

DRAMATIC PLAY

Winter Dress-Up

Objective
To begin to engage in dramatic play with others

Materials to Gather
winter clothes

Develop
Provide a variety of winter clothing. Encourage the children to experiment with everything from sweaters and coats to mittens and socks. Discuss what causes people to change the clothing they wear between autumn and winter.

Reflect/Assess
Which pieces of clothing are the warmest?
¿Qué ropa es la más cálida?

ART

Expressing Winter

Objective
To use a variety of materials to create original work

Materials to Gather
chalk, construction paper, crayons, markers, tempera paint in winter colors

Develop
Challenge the children to use different art materials each day. Encourage them to focus on winter colors. Display all of the children's winter pictures using a Winter Wonderland Wall.

Reflect/Assess
What was your favorite way to make a picture? Why?
¿Cuál fue su forma de pintar favorita? ¿Por qué?

What Research Suggests

People have a tendency to become more sedentary during the winter months because the weather inhibits many outdoor activities. However, it is important to exercise in the winter. People's brains need plenty of oxygen to remain alert no matter what time of the year it is.

Begin the Day

- Teach the children "The North Wind Doth Blow"/"El viento del norte soplará" or "Invierno."
- Use one of the suggestions for Morning Circle offered in the front of this *Teacher's Edition.*

Objectives

- To begin to engage in conversation and follow conversational rules
- To begin to dictate words, phrases, and sentences to an adult recording on paper

Vocabulary

bare	descubierto
barren	árido, deslucido
brown	marrón, café
cold	frío
frost	helada, congelación, escarcha
white	blanco
winter	invierno

DLM Materials

- Rafita and Pepita puppets
- *Flannel Kisses/Besos de franela*
- Oral Language Development Cards 58 and 59
- *Teacher's Resource Anthology* winter card patterns Winter Concentration game
- *SRA Photo Library* software

Materials to Gather

- chart paper
- felt
- paintbrushes
- plastic bag book
- tempera paint
- winter books
- craft sticks
- powdered drink mix

LITERACY

Focus

- Teach the children "Winter Is Coming"/"Ya viene el invierno." Ask: *What winter things are mentioned in the song?*
  ¿Qué cosas de invierno se mencionan en la canción?
- Tell the children that we will be learning about winter this week.

Develop

One Way to Develop the Lesson

- Help children create a word web about winter. Start by writing the word *winter* in the center of a sheet of chart paper. Draw a circle around it. As the children tell you what they know about winter, write their responses on lines drawn around *winter*.
- Discuss the signs of winter. Let Rafita and Pepita lead the discussion. Ask: *What do the trees look like? What does the weather feel like? What activities can we do in the winter?*
  ¿Cómo son los árboles? ¿Cómo se siente el clima? ¿Qué actividades podemos hacer en el invierno?
- Add notes to the winter word web during your discussion. Keep the web available so you can add any new discoveries the children make about winter throughout the week. Explain to the children that they will be studying winter all week.
- Have the children explore the Earth category on the *SRA Photo Library* software and find winter scenes. Encourage the children to dictate a description of their favorite scene.

Another Way to Develop the Lesson

- Show Oral Language Card 59. Use the suggestions on the back of the card to prompt further discussion about the signs of winter. You may want to use Oral Language Card 58 for contrast.

Practice

- Provide white, blue, gray, and brown tempera paint for the children to paint a winter scene. After they have finished painting, challenge the children to dictate a sentence about winter for you to print on their paintings. If they are reluctant to have you write on their paintings, write the sentence on the back or on a sentence strip. Collect the paintings and place them in a plastic bag book. You now have a class winter scene book to share tomorrow.
- Fill the Library Center with books about winter.
- Cut out white patterns and small dots for snow, brown tree trunks and branches, and other winter felt pieces appropriate for your part of the country. Help the children create a winter scene on the flannel board.
- Have the children play the Winter Concentration game.
- Give the children ice cubes on craft sticks and powdered drink mix. Encourage them to paint pictures using these materials.

Preparation

- Create the Winter Concentration game by copying, coloring, laminating, and cutting out the winter card patterns.
- Cut the felt pieces for a winter scene.
- Assemble a plastic bag book to hold the class winter scene pictures.
- Place water in an ice tray, put a craft stick in the center of each cube, and freeze.

Scaffolding Strategies

More Help Ask the children leading questions about winter. For example, *How does the weather feel when you go outdoors?*
¿Cómo se siente el clima cuando salen?

Extra Challenge Help the children make a second word web that is more specific (for example, *winter animals*).

Second Language Learners

Take a nature walk outdoors. Audiotape children's comments about trees, grass, plants, clothing, and so on. Discuss winter activities. If possible, have another adult photograph what the children discuss. Return to your room and use the audiotape and photos to start your winter word web.

DAY 1

Letter Knowledge

English

- Introduce the letter *n* using the story "Nicole" from the *English Phonics Resource Guide*.

Spanish

- Introduce the letter *q* using the story "Queta cumple quince años" in the *Spanish Phonics Resource Guide*.

Suggested Reading

Snowy, Flowy, Blowy by Nancy Tafuri
Polar Bear, Polar Bear by Bill Martin Jr.
The Hat/El sombrero by Jan Brett

Anthology Support

"This Is the Way We Dress for Winter"
"Así nos vestimos en invierno"
"I'm a Frozen Icicle"
"Soy un carámbano congelado"
"Cap, Mittens, Shoes, and Socks"
"Gorra, mitones, zapatos y medias"
"Diez niños felices"

Reflect/Assess

- *What is your favorite thing about winter?*
  ¿Qué cosa les gusta más del invierno?
- *How is winter like fall? How is it different?*
  ¿En qué se parecen el invierno y el otoño? ¿En qué se diferencian?

Literacy Circle

Storytime 1

- Read *Flannel Kisses/Besos de franela.*

Storytime 2

- Read the listening story "The Ant and the Grasshopper"/"La hormiguita y el grillo." Ask: *Which animal was preparing for winter?*
  ¿Qué animal se preparaba para el invierno?

Content Connection

Science

Objective
To use one or more senses to observe and learn about objects, events, and organisms

Vocabulary
berries, brown, pinecones, winter
moras; marrón, café; piñas del pino; invierno

Materials to Gather
bare branch, masking tape

Activity 1

- Lead the children on a nature walk. Look for signs of winter. Have them pick up items for the Science Center. Remind them not to bring any insects or animals indoors and to be careful.
- Help the children make nature bracelets. Loosely wrap a strip of masking tape, sticky side out, around each child's wrist. Have them stick any small winter items they find to their "bracelets."

Activity 2

- Place a large, bare branch in your Science Center. Encourage the children to examine it. They can measure it, build with it, look at it with a magnifying lens, attach pictures to it, make crayon rubbings of it, and so on.

DAY 1

Objectives

- To begin to recognize, describe, and name shapes
- To start, use, and exit software programs

Vocabulary

trapezoid	trapecio
rhombus	rombo
hexagon	hexágono
triangle	triángulo
square	cuadrado
rectangle	rectángulo
circle	círculo
diamond	diamante

DLM Materials

- pattern blocks
- *Math Resource Guide*
  Guessing Bag
  Shape Book
- *DLM Math* software
- *Where Is Thumbkin?* CD
- *Making Music with Thomas Moore* CD

Materials to Gather

- three-dimensional object
- magazines and newspapers
- plastic bags
- streamers (blue, white, brown, gray)

Preparation

- Place a 3-dimensional geometric shape in the Guessing Bag.
- Write children's names on the plastic bags they will use for storing the shapes they find.

MATH

Focus

- Use the pattern blocks to reintroduce shapes to children.
- Tell the children that this week we will be looking for shapes in things like street signs, toys, and so forth.

Develop

- Tell the children they will be creating a Shape Book this week.
- Show the children the magazines and newspaper ads. Explain that they will look for and cut out pictures such as street signs, toys, and so on that contain shapes they have been learning about. Ask children to trace over each shape they find with a crayon before cutting. You may wish to have children glue the picture onto a book page and have them store their pages or pictures in the plastic bags.
- Demonstrate Mystery Toys, Level 4 to the children. They will choose the shape the character requests from a larger set of shapes, including rhombuses, half-circles, trapezoids, and hexagons.

Practice

- Encourage children to continue to find pictures of shapes in magazines and newspapers. They will trace over the outline of the shapes with crayon, cut out the whole picture, glue it onto a book page, and save it for their Shape Book.
- Invite the children to sort pattern blocks.
- Encourage the children to feel the object in the Guessing Bag and look around the room for something they think resembles it.
- Have the children work on Mystery Toys, Level 4.

Reflect/Assess

- *How is the new shape like any of the other shapes you know?*
  ¿En qué se parece la figura nueva a cualquier otra figura que conozcan?

Music and Movement

- Play "Jingle Bells" from the *Where Is Thumbkin?* CD. Ask the children to sing along.
- Supply the children with streamers in the wintry colors of blue, white, brown, and gray. Have the children dance creatively to music from the *Making Music with Thomas Moore* CD.

Content Connection

Science

Objectives

To use one or more senses to observe and learn about objects, events, and organisms

To describe observations

Materials to Gather

bowl, ice

Activity 1

- Challenge children to feel the object in the Mystery Box over the next couple of days and guess what it might be, using the shape, as well as the weight, and so on. Encourage them to discuss their observations

Activity 2

- Freeze a shape in a bowl of ice. Dump the large cube of ice in a dish and encourage the children to identify the shape of the object in the ice before it melts. Ask the children to describe what they see as the ice melts.

Suggested Reading

Circles, Triangles, and Squares by Tana Hoban
So Many Circles, So Many Squares by Tana Hoban
The Shape of Things by Dayle Ann Dodds
The Wing on a Flea: A Book About Shapes by Ed Emberley

Reflect on the Day

- *What are three things that we learned about winter today?*
  ¿Cuáles son tres cosas que aprendimos hoy sobre el invierno?
- *Which winter color is your favorite?*
  ¿Qué color de invierno es su favorito?

Begin the Day

- Sing "Frosty the Snowman"/"Frosty, el muñeco de nieve" with the children. Find out what the children know about Frosty. Ask: *Have you heard this song before? Have you seen the movie?*

  ¿Han oído esta canción antes? ¿Han visto la película?
- Use a suggestion for Morning Circle offered in the front of this *Teacher's Edition*.

Objectives

- To begin to identify rhymes and rhyming sounds in familiar words, participate in rhyming games, and repeat rhyming songs and poems
- To begin to retell the sequence of a story

DLM Materials

- *Flannel Kisses/Besos de franela*
- *Teacher's Resource Anthology* "Frosty the Snowman"/"Frosty, el muñeco de nieve" flannel board story

Materials to Gather

- winter scene book (created with Day 1 winter pictures)
- Rhyming Word Concentration game
- chart paper
- "Frosty the Snowman" clothing items (see Practice)
- plastic bag of ice
- shaving cream

Preparation

- Make a copy of the rhyming word picture cards from the *English or Spanish Phonics Resource Guide* to create a Rhyming Word Concentration game.
- Make the flannel board story.
- Freeze water in a plastic bag to make ice.

LITERACY

Focus

- Teach the children "Five Little Snowmen"/"Cinco muñecos de nieve."
- Encourage the children to talk about their experiences with snow. If you live in an area of the country where children seldom see snow, bring in some pictures of snow to share.
- Tell the children we will be learning about snow and ice today.

Develop

One Way to Develop the Lesson

- Present the "Frosty the Snowman"/"Frosty, el muñeco de nieve" flannel board story.
- Help the children retell the events of the story. Ask: *What happened first? What caused Frosty to come to life? What did Frosty do? What happened when Frosty went to town?*

  ¿Qué sucedió primero? ¿Qué hizo que Frosty recobrara la vida? ¿Qué hizo Frosty? ¿Qué pasó cuando Frosty fue al pueblo?
- Place the flannel board pieces on the board as the children retell the story's events.

Another Way to Develop the Lesson

- Write the word *snow/nieve* on chart paper or on the board.
- Ask the children to think of words that rhyme with *snow/nieve*. For *snow,* they might say *go, row, toe, show, know,* and so on. For *nieve,* the children might say *nueve, llueve,* or *breve*.
- Challenge the children to complete a rhyming couplet. Provide them with the first line (for example, *Winter brings a blanket of snow* and, for Spanish, *El invierno trae una colcha de nieve*). Encourage the children to add the second rhyming line.

Practice

- Place the "Frosty the Snowman"/"Frosty, el muñeco de nieve" flannel board story in the Language Center. Encourage the children to retell the story.
- Post a chart of the rhyming couplet in the Writing Center. Invite the children to copy the couplet and then illustrate it.
- Give the children the Rhyming Word Concentration game. Have them play a game of Concentration or match rhyming pairs and pictures.
- In the Art Center, cover a table with shaving cream. Ask the children to write or draw pictures in the "snow."
- Place a hat, scarf, gloves, and corncob pipe in the Dramatic Play Center. Invite the children to dress up and re-create Frosty's story.
- Put a bag of ice in the Science Center. Encourage the children to observe the ice as it melts. Be sure to address any questions.

Scaffolding Strategies

More Help Have the children find a word that rhymes with their names.

Extra Challenge Encourage the children to look around the room for something that rhymes with *snow/nieve*.

Second Language Learners

Read rhyming couplets to help children identify rhyming words. Read all of the first line. Pause to help the children identify the couplet's last word. For example: *It was such an icy day, I could not go out to (play). I stayed warm inside to play with the blocks, I took off my boots and wore just my (socks).* Use pictures of rhyming words if possible.

Anthology Support

"Winter Is Coming"
"Ya viene el invierno"
"Jingle Bells"
"Tilín, tilín"
"Diez niños felices"

DAY 2

Letter Knowledge

English

- Read "Norman Says Nelly Is Noisy" from the *SRA Alphabet Book*.

Spanish

- Read "Quinto" from *Los niños alfabéticos.*

Suggested Reading

Frozen Noses by Jan Carr
Snowsong Whistling by Karen Lotz
Un día feliz by Ruth Krauss
First Snow by Emily Arnold McCully

Reflect/Assess

- *What caused Frosty to melt?*
  ¿Qué hizo que Frosty se derritiera?
- *Who can think of a word that rhymes with* ice?
  ¿Quién puede pensar en una palabra que rime con hielo?

Literacy Circle

Storytime 1

- Read the winter scene book created with the children's winter paintings. Invite each child to discuss his or her contribution.

Storytime 2

- Reread *Flannel Kisses/Besos de franela.*

Content Connection

Science

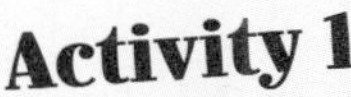

Objectives

To use one or more senses to observe and learn about objects, events, and organisms

To begin to perform simple investigations

Vocabulary

friction, warm

fricción, tibio

Activity 1

- Ask the children if they can think of ways to tell if it is cold outside without going outdoors. Help the children think of answers such as checking how people are dressed outside or touching the windowpane to see how cold it is.
- Have the class look outside a window for clues about how cold it might be. Have volunteers touch the window to check the temperature.

Activity 2

- Ask the children how to stay warm on a cold day (for example, sitting by a fire in a fireplace, covering up with a blanket, eating warm soup, or drinking hot chocolate or tea). Let them share their experiences and generate a list of their ideas.
- Have the children blow into their hands. Ask them if their breath makes their hands warm. Explain that the oxygen in our bodies is warm, so we can use it to warm other parts of our bodies.
- Have the children rub their hands together. Ask: *What happens?*

  ¿Qué pasa?

  Explain that rubbing our hands together causes friction. Friction creates heat that we can use to stay warm.

DAY 2

Objectives

- To begin to recognize, describe, and name shapes
- To begin to use words that indicate where things are in space

Vocabulary

trapezoid	trapecio
rhombus	rombo
hexagon	hexágono
triangle	triángulo
square	cuadrado
rectangle	rectángulo
circle	círculo
diamond	diamante

DLM Materials

- *Math Resource Guide*
  Guessing Bag
  Shape Book
- *DLM Math* software
- *Making Music withThomas Moore* CD
- *Teacher's Resource Anthology*
  "If You're Happy & You Know It"/
  "Si estás contento"

Materials to Gather

- 3-dimensional object
- magazines and newspapers

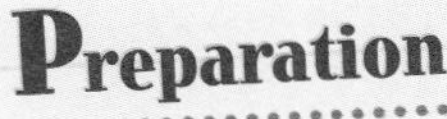

- Fill Guessing Bag.

MATH

Focus

- Count in groups of 3 from 1 to 30, pointing to shapes in the room with each count.
- Sing "If You're Happy & You Know It"/"Si estás contento." Substitute pointing to various shapes for "clap your hands," "stomp your feet," and so forth.

Develop

- Take a shape walk through the school or outside. Have children take crayons and paper on the walk and look for objects with the shapes you have been studying. Ask them to draw what they see. As children name the shape they see, label it for them. These will be used in their Shape Books.
- Back in the room, discuss the shapes they found. Ask why the things are the shape they are. *Why are wheels round? Why are roads often straight lines?*

  ¿Por qué las ruedas son redondas? ¿Por qué los caminos a menudo son líneas rectas?
- The Shape Book is the first of several math books the children will be making during the year.

Practice

- Encourage children to continue to find pictures of shapes in magazines and newspapers. They will trace over the outline of the shapes with crayon, cut out the whole picture, glue it onto a book page, and save it for their Shape Book.
- Invite children to feel the object in the Guessing Bag.
- Have children work on Mystery Toys, Level 4.

Reflect/Assess

- *What shapes did you find today?*
  ¿Qué figuras encontraron hoy?

Content Connection

Social Studies

Objective
To begin to understand cause-and-effect relationships

Materials to Gather
building blocks

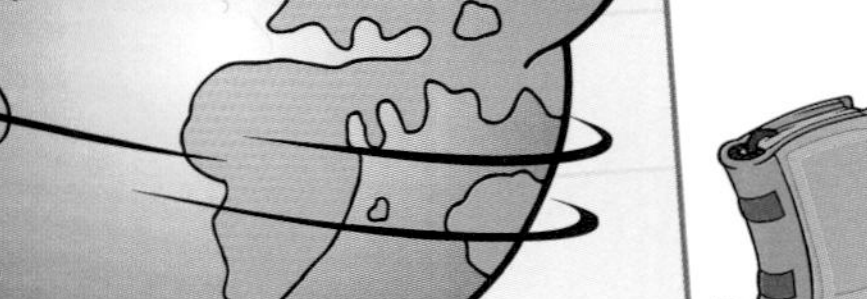

Activity 1

- Ask children questions about why things are shaped as they are. Why is a spoon shaped differently from a fork or knife? Why is a bowl round rather than shaped like a box?

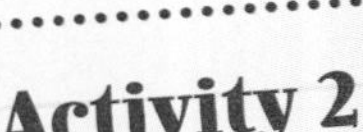

Activity 2

- Challenge the children to build a circular house in the Blocks Center. Lead the children into a discussion about how they would furnish their house.

Music and Movement

- Teach the children to do some exercises. Explain that exercising helps keep us warm in the wintertime.
- Play an instrumental selection from the *Making Music with Thomas Moore* CD. Invite the children to pretend to be snowflakes.

Suggested Reading

Shapes in Nature by Judy Feldman
Shape by Henry Pluckrose
If You Look Around You by Fulvio Testa

Reflect on the Day

- *What did you learn about snow today?*
  ¿Qué aprendieron hoy sobre la nieve?
- *Which activity did you most enjoy today?*
  ¿Qué actividad disfrutaron más hoy?

What Research Suggests

Another advantage of the computer is that it helps children focus their attention on *learning* and it increases *motivation.*

Begin the Day

- Sing "Winter Is Coming"/"Ya viene el invierno" with the children.
- Use one of the suggestions for Morning Circle offered in the front of this *Teacher's Edition*.

Objectives

- To begin to retell the sequence of a story
- To begin to predict what will happen next in a story

Vocabulary

black	negro
brown	marrón, café
glass	vidrio, vaso
grass	césped, pasto
green	verde
honey	miel
orange	anaranjado
purple	morado
red	rojo
snow	nieve
white	blanco
yellow	amarillo

DLM Materials

- *The Color Bear/El oso de colores* book and listening tape
- *Teacher's Resource Anthology*
  "Frosty the Snowman"/"Frosty, el muñeco de nieve" flannel board story
  Winter Concentration game (see Day 1)

Materials to Gather

- Rhyming Word Concentration game (see Day 2)
- chart paper
- old magazines
- shaving cream

LITERACY

Focus

- Do the "Five Little Snowmen"/"Cinco muñecos de nieve" finger play. Ask the children: *Do you think these snowmen knew the story of Frosty? Why or why not? Who remembers what happened to Frosty?*

  ¿Creen que estos hombres de nieve sabían el cuento de Frosty? ¿Por qué sí o por qué no? ¿Quién recuerda lo que le pasó a Frosty?
- Tell the children we will continue to discuss winter weather today.

Develop

One Way to Develop the Lesson

- Tell the children that you have another story about snow to share with them. Show the cover of *The Color Bear/El oso de colores*. Ask them if they remember hearing this story before. Ask: *Does anyone remember how snow is involved in the story?*

  ¿Quién recuerda el papel de la nieve en el cuento?
- Read *The Color Bear/El oso de colores*.
- Discuss what happened first in the story. Ask the following questions: *What did the bear do when the snow started to fall? What did the snow cover first? Next? And so on? Where was the bear when the snow melted?*

  ¿Qué hizo el oso cuando comenzó a caer nieve? ¿Qué cubrió primero la nieve? ¿Después? ¿Y así sucesivamente? ¿Dónde estaba el oso cuando la nieve se derritió?

Another Way to Develop the Lesson

- Help the children think of words that rhyme with *bear/oso*. Since the focus is on listening, words that are spelled differently are allowed (for example: *chair, care; oso, cariñoso).*
- Make a list of the children's rhyming words on chart paper. Remind them that words that sound alike are called *rhyming words*.

Practice

- Place the Rhyming Word picture cards in the Language Center. Provide old magazines for the children to search through. Have them look for items that rhyme with one of the picture cards.
- Put *The Color Bear/El oso de colores* book and listening tape in the Listening Center. Ask children to listen for rhyming words.
- Invite the children to play the Rhyming Word Concentration game.
- Cover a table in the Art Center with shaving cream. Encourage the children to continue drawing or writing on it.
- Invite the children to play the Winter Concentration game.

Preparation

- Photocopy the Rhyming Word picture cards and cut them out.

Scaffolding Strategies

More Help Allow the children to sequence the story by reviewing the book's illustrations.

Extra Challenge Give the children squares of construction paper. Ask them to lay down the colored squares in the sequence in which they disappeared in the story.

Second Language Learners

As children are making snowmen, encourage them to ask other children for materials out of their reach: *Please pass the twigs.* If they do not know the material's name, they can describe it: *That brown thing.*

Anthology Support

"I'm a Frozen Icicle"
"Soy un carámbano congelado"
"Diez niños felices"
"Invierno"
"Jack Frost"
"Raindrop Song"
"Canción gotas de lluvia"

DAY 3

Letter Knowledge

English

- Have the children make the letter *n* with play dough.

Spanish

- Have the children make the letter *q* with play dough.

Suggested Reading

The Snowman by Raymond Briggs
The First Snowfall by Anne and Harlow Rockwell
White Snow, Bright Snow by Alvin Tresselt
El pingüino Pedro by Marcus Pfister

Reflect/Assess

- *What are some activities that you like to do in the winter?*
  ¿Cuáles son algunas actividades que les gusta hacer en el invierno?
- *Can you remember a pair of rhyming words that we learned today?*
  ¿Pueden recordar un par de palabras que rimen que hayamos aprendido hoy?

Literacy Circle

Storytime 1

- Ask the children to participate in telling the action story "Going on a Bear Hunt"/"Vamos a cazar un oso." Ask: *When do bears sleep in their caves? What time of year do you think it was in the story?*
  ¿Cuándo duermen los osos en sus cuevas? ¿Qué época del año era en el cuento?

Storytime 2

- Tell the listening story "Canelita."

Content Connection

Fine Arts

Objective
To use a variety of materials (e.g., crayons, paint, clay, markers) to create original work

Vocabulary
construct, snowy
construir, hacer; nevoso, nevado(a)

DLM Materials
Teacher's Resource Anthology
play dough, puff paint

Materials to Gather
blue construction paper, various decorations

Activity 1

- Prepare the puff paints and mix the play dough.
- Give the children white play dough. Provide scraps of construction paper, wallpaper samples, twigs, sequins, and other craft decorations. Encourage the children to make and decorate snowmen.

Activity 2

- Supply the children with white puff paint and blue construction paper. Encourage them to create a snowy scene.

DAY 3

Objectives

- To begin to recognize, describe, and name shapes
- To start, use, and exit software programs

Vocabulary

trapezoid	trapecio
rhombus	rombo
hexagon	hexágono
triangle	triángulo
square	cuadrado
rectangle	rectángulo
circle	círculo
diamond	diamante

DLM Materials

- Oral Language Development Cards 41–44
- *SRA Photo Library* software
- *Math Resource Guide*
  Guessing Bag
  Shape Book
  Memory Game: Geometry version/ Juego de memoria: versión geométrica
  Memory Game: Geometry cards (Sets C1 and C2)
- *DLM Math* software
- *Where Is Thumbkin?* CD

Materials To Gather

- 3-dimensional object
- magazine and newspaper ads

MATH

Focus

- Invite the children to share the shapes they have found for their Shape Books.

Develop

- Show the children Oral Language Development Cards 41–44. Encourage them to discuss the shapes they see on each card.
- Review Memory Game: Geometry version/Juego de memoria: versión geométrica with the children.
- Introduce and demonstrate Memory—Geometry, Level 4. Ask children to help you as you match shapes to real-world objects such as street signs and toys.

Practice

- Encourage children to continue to find pictures in magazines and newspaper ads that show shapes.
- Invite children to feel the object in the Guessing Bag.
- Have the children play Memory Game: Geometry version/Juego de memoria: versión geométrica
- Invite the children to search for photos in the Earth category on the *SRA Photo Library* software for examples of shapes that occur in nature.
- Have the children work on Memory—Geometry, Level 4.

Reflect/Assess

- *What shapes did you find on the shape walk?*
  ¿Qué figuras hallaron en el recorrido de figuras?

Music and Movement

- Play "Gray Squirrel" from the *Where Is Thumbkin?* CD. Have the children act out the song. Discuss what squirrels do in the wintertime.
- Ask the children to take off their shoes and try some sock skating to simulate ice-skating. Remind them to be careful and mindful of others.

Content Connection

Fine Arts/Social Studies

Objectives

To begin to engage in dramatic play
To begin to understand cause-and-effect relationships

DLM Materials

Teacher's Resource Anthology
"Going on a Bear Hunt"/
"Vamos a cazar un oso"

Activity 1

- Play Going on a Shape Hunt. Using the traditional "Going on a Bear Hunt"/ "Vamos a cazar un oso" activity, lead children on a "shape hunt." You might specify areas of the classroom and give details of what shapes to find there. For example, the face of the paint cup lids in the Art Center would be "circles." Have the children echo each line as you chant,
  "We're going on a shape hunt."
  "It's a good day for a shape hunt."
  "Over in the Art Center. . .
  Try to find a circle."
- Discuss how the shape of the object is related to its use.

Activity 2

- Investigate the materials in one center. Classify the items in that center by their shapes. Discuss how the shape of the object makes it easy or difficult to use.

Suggested Reading

The Shape of Things by Dayle Ann Dodds

Reflect on the Day

- *Which story from today was your favorite?*
  ¿Qué historia de hoy les gustó más?
- *Which animals do you think are considered winter animals?*
  ¿Qué animales creen que se consideran animales de invierno?

Home Connection

Send home the 2D Shape Hunt page from the *Home Connections Resource Guide.*

Begin the Day

- Sing "When I'm Chilly"/"Cuando tengo frío" with the children.
- Use one of the suggestions for Morning Circle offered in the front of this *Teacher's Edition*.

Objectives

- To begin to break words into syllables or clap along with each syllable in a phrase
- To use language to express common routines and familiar scripts

Vocabulary

chocolate	chocolate
hot	caliente
soup	sopa
syllables	sílabas
tea	té
warm	tibio

DLM Materials

- *Flannel Kisses/Besos de franela* book and tape
- *The Color Bear/El oso de colores*
- *The Tortilla Factory/La tortillería*
- *Teacher's Resource Anthology*
  making hot chocolate rebus
  Winter Concentration game (see Day 1)
  "When I'm Chilly"/"Cuando tengo frío"
  "Drink, Drink, Drink Your Milk"/"Toma, toma tu leche"
  "Chocolate Rhyme"/"Rima de chocolate"

Materials to Gather

- chocolate syrup (Allergy Warning)
- hot plate (Safety Warning)
- milk (Allergy Warning)

LITERACY

Focus

- Sing "Drink, Drink, Drink Your Milk"/"Toma, toma, toma tu leche." Ask: *Do you like milk? When do you drink milk?*

  ¿Les gusta la leche? ¿Cuándo toman leche?

  Keep in mind that some children may have dairy-related allergies.
- Explain that today you are going to talk about wintertime foods and how they are different from summertime foods. During the lesson, encourage the children to think about when they eat certain foods.

Develop

One Way to Develop the Lesson

- Read "Chocolate Rhyme"/"Rima de chocolate" from the chart paper. Ask the children to say it with you. You may want to show the rhyme in English and in Spanish. Then read it in both languages.
- Clap out the syllables of the word *chocolate*. Explain that each syllable works on its own to make the sound of the whole word. Call attention to the rhyme again. Point out the way the word *chocolate* is broken into syllables. Replace *chocolate* in the rhyme with *strawberry*. Ask: *Which word has more syllables,* strawberry *or* chocolate?

  ¿Cuál palabra tiene más sílabas refrescos *o* chocolate*?*
- Invite the children to discuss their experiences with chocolate. (Be sensitive to chocolate allergies.) Ask: *Have you ever tried chocolate pie, pudding, or ice cream? Have you ever had chocolate milk or chocolate chip cookies?*

  ¿Alguna vez han probado pastel, pudín o helado de chocolate? ¿Alguna vez han tomado leche achocolatada o comido galletas con chispas de chocolate?

Another Way to Develop the Lesson

- Sing "When I'm Chilly"/"Cuando tengo frío" again. Ask the children to name some of their favorite winter foods.
- Discuss the foods we eat in the wintertime. Help the children think about fruits and nuts that we eat during this time of the year. Talk about warm foods, such as soups, oatmeal, and teas.
- Make a list of foods that the children associate with winter.
- Briefly discuss different fruits and vegetables that are not usually available during the winter season, and why.

Preparation

- Photocopy the making hot chocolate rebus.
- Write the "Chocolate Rhyme"/"Rima de chocolate" on chart paper.
- Gather the ingredients for hot chocolate.

Practice

- Place the "Chocolate Rhyme"/"Rima de chocolate" chart paper in the Writing Center. Encourage the children to copy part of the rhyme.
- Have the children follow the rebus directions for making hot chocolate. Discuss how hot chocolate feels on a frosty day.
- Ask the children to look through old magazines for pictures of wintertime foods and for foods usually available in the other seasons. Have them cut out the pictures and sort them into two piles.
- Place the *Flannel Kisses/Besos de franela* book and listening tape in the Listening Center. Let the children listen to and review the story.
- Allow the children to play the Winter Concentration game.

Scaffolding Strategies

More Help Teach the rhyme orally before children attempt to read it.

Extra Challenge Print the word *chocolate* on a sentence strip. Help the children cut it into the correct syllables.

Second Language Learners

Clap out syllables of familiar story words: *Fros-ty the Snow-man, flan-nel, choc-o-late,* and *win-ter.* If possible, have pictures that represent each word. Do a Word Puzzle (pronounce a word without clapping). Have the children say the puzzle more rapidly until they figure out the word. This indicates how they blend syllables, an important prereading skill.

Anthology Support

"Winter Is Coming"
"Ya viene el invierno"
"Invierno"

DAY 4

Letter Knowledge

English

- Help the children think of foods that begin with the letter *n*.

Spanish

- Help the children think of foods that begin with the letter *q*.

Suggested Reading

Lucky Pennies and Hot Chocolate by Carol Diggory Shields
Sadie and the Snowman by Allen Morgan
The Jacket I Wear in the Snow by Shirley Neitzel
It's Snowing! It's Snowing! by Jack Prelutsky

Scaffolding Strategies

More Help If a child is using an object for a shape that seems unconventional, ask him or her to use his or her finger and trace the shape to help them understand it.

Extra Challenge Invite children to make theme shape books by asking them to make one for food, nature/natural things, or things in school.

Reflect/Assess

- *How do we make hot chocolate?*
  ¿Cómo hacemos chocolate caliente?
- *What is your favorite food to eat in the winter?*
  ¿Cuál es su comida favorita en el invierno?

Literacy Circle

Storytime 1

- Read *The Tortilla Factory/La tortillería*. Discuss how the land looks in the winter.

Storytime 2

- Reread *The Color Bear/El oso de colores*.

Content Connection

Science

Objective
To begin to recognize that living things have similar needs for water, food, and air

Vocabulary
light, sunlight, water
luz, luz solar, agua

Materials to Gather
assorted nuts (Allergy Warning)

Activity 1

- Discuss what fruits and vegetables need to be able to grow. Ask: *What is lacking in the winter that makes it difficult for fruits and vegetables to grow?* *¿Qué hace falta en el invierno que dificulta el cultivo de frutas y vegetales?*

Activity 2

- Ask the children to sort a tray of nuts (almonds with almonds, peanuts with peanuts, and so on). Allow them to sample the nuts, making sure that none of the children have nut product allergies.

DAY 4

Objective

- To begin to recognize, describe, and name shapes

Vocabulary

trapezoid	trapecio
rhombus	rombo
hexagon	hexágono
triangle	triángulo
square	cuadrado
rectangle	rectángulo
circle	círculo
diamond	diamante

DLM Materials

- *Math Resource Guide*
  Guessing Bag
  Shape Book
  Memory Game: Geometry version/ Juego de memoria: versión geométrica
  Memory Game: Geometry cards (Sets C1 and C2)
- *DLM Math* software
- *Teacher's Resource Anthology*
  "Raindrop Song"/"Canción gotas de lluvia"

Materials to Gather

- objects and corresponding construction paper shapes
- newspapers and magazines
- 3-dimensional object

Preparation

- Gather objects that match shapes. Cut paper shapes the same size.
- Make plastic bag books.

MATH

Focus

- While marching, count from 1 to 30. Turn after every 5 counts.

Develop

- Hold a shape in front of an object, such as a circle shape in front of a dinner plate. Ask children what you could be hiding. After they guess, reveal the object. Repeat with other shapes and objects.
- Have the children share what they have found for their Shape Books. Ask if anyone has found rhombuses. Repeat with other shapes. Any shapes the children cannot find may be drawn.
- Reintroduce and discuss the computer game, Mystery Toys, Level 4 and Memory—Geometry, Level 4.

Practice

- Encourage children to continue to look for pictures to finish their Shape Books.
- Using the plastic bag book directions, help children put together their Shape Books as they finish finding pictures. Label the shapes as children tell you what they are.
- Invite children to feel the object in the Guessing Bag.
- Have the children play Memory Game: Geometry version/Juego de memoria: versión geométrica.
- Have children work on Mystery Toys, Level 4 or Memory—Geometry, Level 4.

Reflect/Assess

- *What was the hardest shape to find for your Shape Book?*
  ¿Cuál fue la figura más difícil de encontrar para tu libro de figuras?

Content Connection

Health and Safety

Objectives

To begin to recognize and select healthy foods

To recognize the symbol for poison

To recognize the danger of poisonous substances, including drugs

Materials to Gather

food items, pictures of food

Activity 1

- Use "food riddles" to have children guess the food or food picture you have. For example, suggest a food that is round (or a sphere) and its name is its color (an orange). Discuss each food as to its health value.

Activity 2

- Review the symbol for poisonous substances used on containers. What shape is the symbol?
- Discuss the danger of poisonous substances.

...d ...nt

...ivide children... ...eate two lines ... Place half of ... e first line and the othe... f at the second line. Give each team a pinecone. Have a team member roll the pinecone to the opposite line and hand it to the next player. That player will roll it back. Repeat for each child.

- Invite the children to sing and act out the "Raindrop Song"/ "Canción gotas de lluvia."

Suggested Reading

The Shape of Things by Dayle Ann Dodds

Reflect on the Day

- *What did you learn about winter foods today?*
  ¿Qué aprendieron hoy sobre las comidas de invierno?
- *Which activity was your favorite today and why?*
  ¿Qué actividad de hoy fue su favorita y por qué?

Home Connection

- Send a note home to families indicating that next week the class will be studying workers in the community. Invite family members to volunteer to talk to the class about their jobs.
- Send four children home with take-home book packs. You will find the directions and a recording sheet for this activity in the *Home Connections Resource Guide*.

Begin the Day

- Sing "Cap, Mittens, Shoes, and Socks"/"Gorra, mitones, zapatos y medias." Help the children make up new verses using winter clothing items.
- Use a suggestion for Morning Circle found in the front of this *Teacher's Edition.*

Objectives

- To enjoy listening to and discussing storybooks and information books read aloud
- To describe similarities and differences between objects

Vocabulary

cool fresco
sweaters suéteres
vest chaleco

DLM Materials

- *Teacher's Resource Anthology*
  "Dress-Me-Bears for Winter"/ "Vísteme para el invierno" flannel board story
  "Dress-Me-Bears for Summer"/ "Vísteme para el verano" flannel board story
  "Cap, Mittens, Shoes, and Socks"/ "Gorra, mitones, zapatos y medias"
  "This Is The Way We Dress for Winter"/"Así nos vestimos en invierno"
  "Weather"/"El tiempo"
  Think, Pair, Share/Piensa, aparea, comparte
  Winter Concentration game (see Day 1)
- *SRA Photo Library* software

Materials to Gather

- summer clothing
- tracing paper
- winter books

Literacy

Focus

- Sing "This Is the Way We Dress for Winter"/"Así nos vestimos en invierno" with the children.
- Discuss the kind of clothes the children wear in the winter. Ask: *What happens to the weather? How does the weather affect the clothes you choose to wear?*
  ¿Qué le pasa al clima? ¿Cómo afecta el clima la ropa que nos ponemos?

Develop

One Way to Develop the Lesson

- Present the "Dress-Me-Bears for Winter"/"Vísteme para el invierno" flannel board story. Discuss the clothing that the bears chose to wear.
- Encourage the children to look at the Clothing category of the *SRA Photo Library* software and pick the items that might be worn in the winter.

Another Way to Develop the Lesson

- Present the "Dress-Me-Bears for Summer"/"Vísteme para el verano" flannel board story. Discuss how the summer clothing is different from the winter clothing.

Practice

- Give the children the "Dress-Me-Bears for Winter"/"Vísteme para el invierno" and the "Dress-Me-Bears for Summer"/"Vísteme para el verano" flannel board stories. Invite them to retell the stories or to tell new ones.
- Add summer clothing to the Dramatic Play Center. Have the children sort the clothing into a summer pile and a winter pile.
- Fill the Library Center with books about winter. Suggest that the children pay attention to what the book characters are wearing.
- Provide children with the patterns for the "Dress-Me-Bears for Winter"/"Vísteme para el invierno" flannel board story and tracing paper. Have them create their own Dress-Me-Bears.
- Invite the children to play the Winter Concentration game.

Preparation

- Make the flannel board stories.

Second Language Learners

Audiotape the children's retelling of the "Dress-Me-Bears for Winter"/"Vísteme para el invierno" and "Dress-Me-Bears for Summer"/"Vísteme para el verano" stories. Note fluency and sequencing ability. Overgeneralization may occur as native speakers learn a new language: *He putted on his boots.* This indicates that the speaker is internalizing the new language's rules. Correct them gently and restate: *Yes, he put on his boots.*

Anthology Support

"Winter Is Coming"
"Ya viene el invierno"
"Jack Frost"
"Invierno"
"Diez niños felices"

DAY 5

Letter Knowledge

English

- Use the Think, Pair, Share game as you allow the children to shape their bodies into the letter *n*.

Spanish

- Use the Piensa, aparea, comparte game as you allow the children to shape their bodies into the letter *q*.

Suggested Reading

Caps, Hats, Socks, and Mittens by Louise Borden
Weather by Pasquale De Bourgoing
Look! Snow! by Kathryn O. Galbraith
Froggy se viste by Jonathan London

Reflect/Assess

- *How do you dress differently in the winter than in other seasons?*

  ¿En qué se diferencia la ropa que se ponen en invierno de la que se ponen en otras estaciones?
- *What is your favorite thing to wear in the summer?*

  ¿Qué ropa les gusta ponerse más en el verano?

Literacy Circle

Storytime 1

- Reread *Flannel Kisses/Besos de franela.* Ask the children to pay special attention to how characters are dressed.

Storytime 2

- Invite the children to participate in the "Weather"/"El tiempo" action story.

Content Connection

Social Studies

Objective
To recognize changes in the environment over time

Vocabulary
seasons, summer, winter
estaciones, verano, invierno

DLM Materials
Oral Language Development Cards 58 and 59

Materials to Gather
chart paper

Activity 1

- Make two separate word webs on a piece of chart paper or on the board. Write the word *winter* and draw a circle around it. Repeat for the word *summer*.
- First, encourage the children to tell you what they know about winter. Then discuss what they know about summer. Prompt the children with suggestions (for example: clothing, food, animals, activities, weather, and so on). Record responses on the webs.
- After both word webs are done, help the children draw conclusions about the similarities and differences between summer and winter.

Activity 2

- Show the children Oral Language Cards 58 and 59. Use the suggestions on the back of the cards to discuss each season.
- Once you have finished discussing summer and winter, review the likenesses and differences of the two seasons with the children.

DAY 5

Objectives
- To recognize, describe, and name shapes
- To use a variety of software packages with audio, video, and graphics to enhance learning experiences

Vocabulary
trapezoid	trapecio
rhombus	rombo
hexagon	hexágono
triangle	triángulo
square	cuadrado
rectangle	rectángulo
circle	círculo
diamond	diamante

DLM Materials
- *Math Resource Guide*
  Guess My Rule/Adivina mi regla
  Shape Set
- See Day 4
- *DLM Math* software
- *Teacher's Resource Anthology*
  The Statues of Marfil/La estatuas de Marfil
  Drop the Handkerchief/Suelta el pañuelo

Materials to Gather
- See Day 4

Preparation
- Cut pictures from magazines or newspapers that contain shapes.
- Photocopy Shape Sets.

MATH

Focus
- Have children tell what they think the object in the Guessing Bag is and why they think that. After everyone has contributed, reveal the object.

Develop
- Hold a shape in front of an object, such as a circle shape in front of a dinner plate. Ask children what you could be hiding. After they guess, reveal the object. Repeat with other shapes and objects.
- Play Guess My Rule/Adivina mi regla with the Shape Set. Repeat with a new shape. (See Nursery Rhymes, Day 3.)
- Complete a task from Mystery Toys, Level 4 and Memory—Geometry, Level 4, with the children. Talk about the various shapes in the pictures.

Practice
- Have the children share their Shape Books.
- Encourage children to play Guess My Rule/Adivina mi regla with pictures or Shape Sets.
- Have the children play Memory Game: Geometry version/Juego de memoria: versión geométrica.
- Have children work on Mystery Toys, Level 4 or Memory—Geometry, Level 4. Remember, if you sign in as yourself at the computer, you can go directly to any activity and level by pressing command–control–A.

Reflect/Assess

- *How did you figure out my rule?*
  ¿Cómo descubrieron mi regla?
- *What shapes are you using to build designs or pictures?*
  ¿Qué figuras usan para hacer diseños o dibujos?

Music and Movement

- Play The Statues of Marfil/ Las estatuas de Marfil.
- Play Drop the Handkerchief/ Suelta el pañuelo.

Content Connection

Social Studies/Fine Arts

Objectives
To identify common features of local landscape
To begin to show interest in the artwork of others

Materials to Gather
pictures of houses

Activity 1
- Brainstorm with children the shapes they see in various kinds of houses. Provide books, photographs, or postcards with different houses to facilitate conversation.

Activity 2
- Take a look at the books in the Library Center. Sort the books into shapes.

Suggested Reading

Buildings That Changed the World by Klaus Reichold and Bernhard Graf
The Shape of Things by Dayle Ann Dodds

Reflect on the Day

- *What are five things you learned about winter this week?*
  ¿Cuáles son cinco cosas que aprendieron esta semana sobre el invierno?
- *How is winter different from fall? Spring? Summer?*
  ¿En qué se diferencia el invierno del otoño? ¿De la primavera? ¿Del verano?

Home Connection

Remind the children to ask their family members about volunteering to speak to the class next week about where they work.

Assessment in the Prekindergarten Classroom

Performance Assessment Checklist

The objectives in ***The DLM Early Childhood Express*** cover a wide range of skills that young children develop. Of course, all children do not acquire these skills in the same manner or in the same time frame. It is, however, reasonable to assume that over the course of a school year, most of the objectives will have been accomplished.

You informally observe your children every day. You know what each child is able to do. In order to help you turn the knowledge you gain from observing the children into a tangible assessment of the skills development of each child, the objectives from ***The DLM Early Childhood Express*** are arranged in a Performance Assessment Checklist. You can use this checklist to fit your needs. For example, combined with samples of children's work and/or your anecdotal notes, it can provide parents with specific information about their children's skills-development progress.

It is recommended that you observe each child over three time spans during the year. You do not necessarily have to look for each skill on the same day; the observation period can cover whatever time span you desire. Allow enough time between observations so that growth can be seen, possibly observing at the beginning, in the middle, and toward the end of the school year.

To use the checklist, make a copy for each child. You might choose to keep each child's checklist in a separate folder. You might want to divide the list into smaller sections, such as Literacy, Math, and so on, and keep those lists in notebooks near the places you are most likely to observe the children interacting with the various content areas.

Enter each child's name on his or her Performance Assessment Checklist(s), and note the dates of the observation period(s). For the skills being assessed, indicate a child's progress using the following scale. Once a skill has been mastered, no further observation for that particular skill is required.

N: not currently performing

O: occasionally performing

C: consistently performing

Portfolio Assessment

In addition to observing children's performances on an informal and ongoing basis, many teachers want to provide documentation of the children's progress. Keeping a portfolio for each child is a wonderful way to document progress for parents. You can use the contents of the portfolio to support the Performance Assessment Checklist. The article following the checklist will help you understand and set up a portfolio assessment system that works for you and your class.

OBSERVATION PERIODS			
1st	Fall	______	to ______
2nd	Winter	______	to ______
3rd	Spring	______	to ______

KEY
N: not currently performing
O: occasionally performing
C: consistently performing

NAME ____________________

Literacy

I. LANGUAGE AND EARLY LITERACY DEVELOPMENT

A. Listening Comprehension

		1st	2nd	3rd
1.	Listens with increasing attention			
2.	Listens for different purposes (e.g., to learn what happened in a story, to receive instructions, to converse with an adult or a peer)			
3.	Understands and follows simple oral directions			
4.	Enjoys listening to and responding to books			
5.	Listens to and engages in several exchanges of conversations with others			
6.	Listens to tapes and records, and shows understanding through gestures, actions, and/or language			
7.	Listens purposefully to English-speaking teachers and peers to gather information and shows some understanding of the new language being spoken by others (ESL)			

B. Speech Production and Speech Discrimination (Oral Language Development)

		1st	2nd	3rd
1.	Perceives differences between similar sounding words (e.g., "coat" and "goat," "three" and "free," [Spanish] "juego" and "fuego")			
2.	Produces speech sounds with increasing ease and accuracy			
3.	Experiments with new language sounds			
4.	Experiments with and demonstrates growing understanding of the sounds and intonation of the English language (ESL)			

C. Vocabulary (Oral Language Development)

		1st	2nd	3rd
1.	Shows a steady increase in listening and speaking vocabulary			
2.	Uses new vocabulary in everyday communication			
3.	Refines and extends understanding of known words			
4.	Attempts to communicate more than current vocabulary will allow, borrowing and extending words to create meaning			
5.	Links new learning experiences and vocabulary to what is already known about a topic			
6.	Increases listening vocabulary and begins to develop a vocabulary of object names and common phrases in English (ESL)			

D. Verbal Expression (Oral Language Development)

		1st	2nd	3rd
1.	Uses language for a variety of purposes (e.g., expressing needs and interests)			
2.	Uses sentences of increasing length (three or more words) and grammatical complexity in everyday speech			
3.	Uses language to express common routines and familiar scripts			
4.	Tells a simple personal narrative, focusing on favorite or most memorable parts			
5.	Asks questions and makes comments related to the current topic of discussion			
6.	Begins to engage in conversation and follows conversational rules (e.g., staying on topic and taking turns)			
7.	Begins to retell the sequence of a story			
8.	Engages in various forms of nonverbal communication with those who do not speak his/her home language (ESL)			
9.	Uses single words and simple phrases to communicate meaning in social situations (ESL)			
10.	Attempts to use new vocabulary and grammar in speech (ESL)			

PERFORMANCE ASSESSMENT CHECKLIST

Name ______________________

E. Phonological Awareness

		1st	2nd	3rd
1.	Becomes increasingly sensitive to the sounds of spoken words			
2.	Begins to identify rhymes and rhyming sounds in familiar words, participates in rhyming games, and repeats rhyming songs and poems			
3.	Begins to attend to the beginning sounds in familiar words by identifying that the pronunciations of several words all begin the same way (e.g., "dog," "dark," and "dusty," [Spanish] "casa," "coche," and "cuna")			
4.	Begins to break words into syllables or claps along with each syllables in a phrase			
5.	Begins to create and invent words by substituting one sound for another (e.g., bubblegum/gugglebum, [Spanish] calabaza/balacaza)			

F. Print and Book Awareness

		1st	2nd	3rd
1.	Understands that reading and writing are ways to obtain information and knowledge, generate and communicate thoughts and ideas, and solve problems			
2.	Understands that print carries a message by recognizing labels, signs, and other print forms in the environment			
3.	Understands that letters are different from numbers			
4.	Understands that illustrations carry meaning but cannot be read			
5.	Understands that a book has a title and an author			
6.	Begins to understand that print runs from left to right and top to bottom			
7.	Begins to understand some basic print conventions (e.g., the concept that letters are grouped to form words and that words are separated by spaces)			
8.	Begins to recognize the association between spoken and written words by following the print as it is read aloud			
9.	Understands that different text forms are used for different functions (e.g., lists for shopping, recipes for cooking, newspapers for learning about current events, letters and messages for interpersonal communications)			

G. Letter Knowledge and Early Word Recognition

		1st	2nd	3rd
1.	Begins to associate the names of letters with their shapes			
2.	Identifies 10 or more printed alphabet letters			
3.	Begins to notice beginning letters in familiar words			
4.	Begins to make some letter/sound matches			
5.	Begins to identify some high-frequency words (age 4)			

H. Motivation to Read

		1st	2nd	3rd
1.	Demonstrates an interest in books and reading through body language and facial expressions			
2.	Enjoys listening to and discussing storybooks and information books read aloud			
3.	Attempts to read and write independently			
4.	Shares books and engages in pretend-reading with other children			
5.	Enjoys visiting the library			

I. Developing Knowledge of Literary Forms

		1st	2nd	3rd
1.	Recognizes favorite books by their cover			
2.	Selects books to read based on personal criteria			
3.	Understands that books and other print resources (e.g., magazines, computer-based texts) are handled in specific ways			
4.	Becomes increasingly familiar with narrative form and its elements by identifying characters and predicting events, plot, and the resolution of a story			
5.	Begins to predict what will happen next in a story			
6.	Imitates the special language in storybooks and story dialogue, and uses it in retellings and dramatic play (such as "Once upon a time…")			
7.	Asks questions and makes comments about the information and events from books			
8.	Connects information and events in books to real-life experiences			
9.	Begins to retell some sequences of events in stories			
10.	Shows appreciation of repetitive language patterns			

NAME ______________________

J. Written Expression

		1st	2nd	3rd
1.	Attempts to write messages as part of playful activity			
2.	Uses known letters and approximations of letters to represent written language (especially meaningful words like his/her name and phrases such as "I love you" or [Spanish] "Te quiero")			
3.	Attempts to connect the sounds in a word with its letter forms			
4.	Understands that writing is used to communicate ideas and information			
5.	Attempts to use a variety of forms of writing (e.g., lists, messages, stories)			
6.	Begins to dictate words, phrases, and sentences to an adult recording on paper (e.g., "letter writing," "story writing")			

Math

II. MATHEMATICS

A. Number and Operations

		1st	2nd	3rd
1.	Arranges sets of concrete objects in one-to-one correspondence			
2.	Counts by ones to 10 or higher			
3.	Counts concrete objects to five or higher			
4.	Begins to compare the numbers of concrete objects using language (e.g., "same" or "equal," "one more," "more than," or "less than")			
5.	Begins to name "how many" are in a group of up to three (or more) objects without counting (e.g., recognizing two or three crayons in a box)			
6.	Recognizes and describes the concept of zero (meaning there are none)			
7.	Begins to demonstrate part of and whole with real objects (e.g., an orange)			
8.	Begins to identify first and last in a series			
9.	Combines, separates, and names "how many" concrete objects			

B. Patterns

		1st	2nd	3rd
1.	Imitates pattern sounds and physical movements (e.g., clap, stomp, clap, stomp,...)			
2.	Recognizes and reproduces simple patterns of concrete objects (e.g., a string of beads that are blue, blue, yellow, blue, blue)			
3.	Begins to recognize patterns in their environment (e.g., day follows night, repeated phrases in storybooks, patterns in carpeting or clothing)			
4.	Begins to predict what comes next when patterns are extended			

C. Geometry and Spatial Sense

		1st	2nd	3rd
1.	Begins to recognize, describe, and name shapes			
2.	Begins to use words that indicate where things are in space (e.g., "beside," "inside," "behind," "above," "below")			
3.	Begins to recognize when a shape's position or orientation has changed			
4.	Begins to investigate and predict the results of putting together two or more shapes			
5.	Puts together puzzles of increasing complexity			
6.	Puts together shapes to make new shapes and designs			
7.	Identifies horizontal and vertical lines			

D. Measurement

		1st	2nd	3rd
1.	Covers an area with shapes (e.g., tiles)			
2.	Fills a shape with solids or liquids (e.g., ice cubes, water)			
3.	Begins to make size comparisons between objects (e.g., taller than, smaller than)			
4.	Begins to use tools to imitate measuring			
5.	Begins to categorize time intervals and uses language associated with time in everyday situations (e.g., "in the morning," "after snack")			
6.	Begins to order two or three objects by size (seriation) (e.g., largest to smallest) (age 4)			

NAME ______________________

E. Classification and Data Collection

		1st	2nd	3rd
1.	Matches objects that are alike			
2.	Describes similarities and differences between objects			
3.	Sorts objects into groups by an attribute and begins to explain how the grouping was done			
4.	Participates in creating and using real and pictorial graphs			

III. SCIENCE

A. Science Processes

		1st	2nd	3rd
1.	Begins to demonstrate safe practices and appropriate use of materials			
2.	Asks questions about objects, events, and organisms			
3.	Shows an interest in investigating unfamiliar objects, organisms, and phenomena			
4.	Uses one or more senses to observe and learn about objects, events, and organisms			
5.	Describes observations			
6.	Begins to perform simple investigations			
7.	Gathers information using simple tools such as a magnifying lens and an eyedropper			
8.	Explores by manipulating materials with simple equipment (e.g., pouring from a cup and using a spoon to pick up sand or water)			
9.	Uses simple measuring devices to learn about objects and organisms			
10.	Compares objects and organisms and identifies similarities and differences			
11.	Sorts objects and organisms into groups and begins to describe how groups were organized			
12.	Begins to offer explanations, using his or her own words			
13.	Predicts what will happen next based on previous experience			
14.	Solves simple design problems (e.g., making a box into a little house for a storybook character, toy, or pet)			
15.	Participates in creating and using simple data charts			
16.	Shares observations and findings with others through pictures, discussions, or dramatizations			

B. Science Concepts

		1st	2nd	3rd
1.	Observes and describes properties of rocks, soil, and water			
2.	Describes properties of objects and characteristics of living things			
3.	Begins to observe changes in size, color, position, weather, and sound			
4.	Identifies animals and plants as living things			
5.	Groups organisms and objects as living or nonliving and begins to identify things people have built			
6.	Begins to recognize that living things have similar needs for water, food, and air			
7.	Begins to identify what things are made of (e.g., distinguishing a metal spoon from a plastic spoon)			
8.	Uses patterns (such as growth and day following night) to predict what happens next			
9.	Identifies similarities and differences among objects and organisms			
10.	Begins to use scientific words and phrases to describe objects, events, and living things			

NAME ____________________

Social Studies

IV. SOCIAL STUDIES

A. Individual, Culture, and Community

		1st	2nd	3rd
1.	Shares ideas and takes turns listening and speaking			
2.	Cooperates with others in a joint activity			
3.	Identifies and follows classroom rules			
4.	Participates in classroom jobs and contributes to the classroom community			
5.	Identifies similarities among people like himself/herself and classmates as well as among himself/herself and people from other cultures			
6.	Begins to examine a situation from another person's perspective			

B. History

		1st	2nd	3rd
1.	Identifies common events and routines (e.g., snack time, storytime)			
2.	Begins to categorize time intervals using words (e.g., "today," "tomorrow," "next time")			
3.	Recognizes changes in the environment over time (e.g., growth, seasonal changes)			
4.	Connects past events to current events (e.g., linking yesterday's activity with what will happen today)			
5.	Begins to understand cause-and-effect relationships (e.g., if one goes outside in the rain, one will get wet)			

C. Geography

		1st	2nd	3rd
1.	Identifies common features in the home and school environment (e.g., the library, the playground)			
2.	Creates simple representations of home, school, or community through drawings or block constructions			
3.	Begins to use words to indicate relative location (e.g., "front," "back," "near," "far")			
4.	Identifies common features of the local landscape (e.g., houses, buildings, streets)			
5.	Labels common features in familiar environments			

D. Economics

		1st	2nd	3rd
1.	Understands the basic human needs of all people for food, clothing, and shelter			
2.	Understands the roles, responsibilities, and services provided by community workers			
3.	Becomes aware of what it means to be a consumer			

Fine Arts

V. FINE ARTS

A. Art

		1st	2nd	3rd
1.	Uses a variety of materials (e.g., crayons, paint, clay, markers) to create original work			
2.	Uses different colors, surface textures, and shapes to create form and meaning			
3.	Begins to use art as a form of self-expression			
4.	Shares ideas about personal artwork			
5.	Begins to show interest in the artwork of others			

B. Music

		1st	2nd	3rd
1.	Participates in classroom music activities			
2.	Begins to sing a variety of simple songs			
3.	Begins to play classroom instruments			
4.	Begins to respond to music of various tempos through movement			
5.	Begins to distinguish among the sounds of several common instruments			

NAME ________________

C. Dramatic Play

		1st	2nd	3rd
1.	Expresses feelings through movement			
2.	Begins to create or re-create stories, moods, or experiences through dramatic representations			
3.	Begins to engage in dramatic play with others			

Health/Safety

VI. HEALTH AND SAFETY

A. Health

		1st	2nd	3rd
1.	Becomes aware of routine healthy behaviors (e.g., brushing teeth)			
2.	Begins to follow health-promoting routines (e.g., washing hands)			
3.	Begins to understand the need for exercise and rest			
4.	Refines use of eating utensils			
5.	Begins to recognize and select healthy foods			
6.	Prepares simple healthy snacks			
7.	Demonstrates an understanding of basic health and safety rules			

B. Safety

		1st	2nd	3rd
1.	Recognizes the danger of fire and learns to treat fire with caution			
2.	Responds appropriately during a fire drill			
3.	Knows how to seek help in an emergency			
4.	Knows how to cross a street safely			
5.	Recognizes the symbol for poison			
6.	Knows never to eat substances that are not food			
7.	Recognizes the danger of poisonous substances, including drugs			
8.	Knows not to talk to, accept rides from, or take treats from strangers			
9.	Knows how to get help from a parent and/or trusted adult when made to feel uncomfortable or unsafe by another person/adult			
10.	Knows never to take medicine unless it is administered by a trusted adult			
11.	Knows about safe behavior around bodies of water (e.g., pools, lakes)			
12.	Knows about safe behavior around bugs and insects			
13.	Understands about safe behavior in potentially dangerous places			

Personal/Social

VII. PERSONAL AND SOCIAL DEVELOPMENT

A. Personal Development

		1st	2nd	3rd
1.	Develops a sense of personal space			
2.	Expresses interest and self-direction in learning			
3.	Begins to show self-control by following classroom rules			
4.	Begins to be responsible for individual behavior and actions			
5.	Begins to show greater ability to control intense feelings (e.g., anger)			

B. Social Development

		1st	2nd	3rd
1.	Begins to share and cooperate with others in group activities			
2.	Respects other people's space and personal belongings			
3.	Begins to develop friendships with others			
4.	Begins to express thoughts, feelings, and ideas through language as well as through gestures and actions			
5.	Responds to the suggestions of others			

Physical

VIII. PHYSICAL DEVELOPMENT

A. Physical Movement

		1st	2nd	3rd
1.	Explores moving in space			
2.	Shows an awareness of name, location, and relationship of body parts			
3.	Moves within a space of defined boundaries, changing body configurations to accommodate the space			
4.	Becomes more able to move from one space to another in different ways (e.g., running, jumping, hopping, skipping)			
5.	Becomes more able to move in place (e.g., axial movements such as reaching, twisting, turning, and bending)			
6.	Begins to move in rhythm			
7.	Begins to participate in group games involving movement (e.g., Duck, Duck, Goose)			

B. Gross-Motor Development

		1st	2nd	3rd
1.	Begins to throw or kick an object in a particular direction			
2.	Begins to play catch with a bean bag or a large ball			
3.	Bounces a large ball and catches it			
4.	Begins to coordinate arms and legs (e.g., swinging, stretching)			

C. Fine-Motor Development

		1st	2nd	3rd
1.	Begins to develop pincer control in picking up objects (e.g., weaving, touching small objects)			
2.	Begins to practice self-help skills (e.g., zipping, buttoning)			
3.	Begins to hold writing tools with fingers instead of with a fist			
4.	Begins to manipulate play objects that have fine parts			
5.	Begins to use scissors			
6.	Begins to coordinate finger activities and clapping exercises			

Technology

IX. TECHNOLOGY APPLICATIONS

		1st	2nd	3rd
1.	Starts, uses, and exits software programs			
2.	Uses a variety of input devices, such as mouse, keyboard, voice/sound recorder, or touch screen			
3.	Begins to use technical terminology, such as "mouse," "keyboard," "printer," "CD-ROM"			
4.	Follows basic oral or pictorial cues for operating programs successfully			
5.	Enjoys listening to and interacting with storybooks and information texts (e.g., multimedia encyclopedia) in electronic forms			
6.	Uses a variety of software packages with audio, video, and graphics to enhance learning experiences (e.g., improving vocabulary, increasing phonological awareness)			

Promoting Authentic Assessment:

Portfolios in Early Childhood Education

Beverly J. Irby, Ed.D., Professor
Genevieve Brown, Ed.D., Professor

Department of Educational Leadership and Counseling
Sam Houston State University
Huntsville, Texas

Student assessment and evaluation are too often based on standardized tests. These assessment or evaluation measurements are limited and provide little information that teachers, parents, and students can use to gain a comprehensive picture of academic, linguistic, social, or developmental progress. Recognizing the limitations of such assessment methods, teachers have begun to restructure student assessment to include authentic, or performance-based, methods in which students actively participate in assessing their own learning.

Using the portfolio process facilitates authentic assessment and provides multiple opportunities for learning. The portfolio is a collection of thoughtfully selected work samples, or artifacts, and accompanying reflections indicative of the child's learning experiences, effort, and progress toward and/or attainment of established curriculum goals. As children choose work samples for their portfolios, they become involved in their own learning and assessment. They begin to have a notion of evaluating their own work, thus initiating the development of reflective, self-assessment skills.

How Can Portfolios Help?

One of the greatest advantages of the portfolio is that using it allows teachers, parents, and children to follow the children's progress in order to identify areas of growth and necessary improvement. Through reviewing children's portfolio artifacts and listening to children's reflections on their work, teacher are able to:
(1) keep track of children's accomplishments,
(2) address state and local accountability factors, (3) align instruction and assessment, and (4) facilitate parent-teacher conferences.

According to teachers, portfolios are beneficial to children in the following ways. Using portfolios:

- Involves children in the learning process
- Highlights student strengths as opposed to weaknesses
- Initiates the skill of reflective practice among children
- Encourages curiosity and creativity
- Promotes organizational skills
- Motivates children as they review their own progress
- Promotes oral language development as they articulate their reflections
- Enhances children's self-confidence
- Addresses learning styles, language proficiencies, and ethnic backgrounds of students

Not only does the use of portfolios benefit children, but teachers also report benefits. They say that the portfolio process helps them to:

- Promote reflection on classroom pedagogy among teachers
- Maintain a focus on student performance
- Provide concrete examples of the child's work to pass on to special teachers or to the next year's teacher
- Offer an easily understood document for parents as teachers conduct parent-teacher conferences
- Promote authentic assessments based on classroom experiences
- Plan curriculum that is individualized and developmentally appropriate for each child
- Assist in identification of needed curriculum resources
- Capitalize on teacher observations of children in daily classroom activities

- Document each child's actual learning based upon developmental and academic benchmarks
- Share information with parents about their child's learning behavior, attitudes, and development
- Assess their own pedagogical practices in relation to students' learning and understanding
- Record and aggregate specific details related to a child's skills and accomplishments

What Should Be Included in the Young Child's Portfolio?

Determining the physical and organizational structure of the assessment portfolio is the first step. Teachers have reported using a variety of means to store the contents of the assessment portfolio:

- Expandable file folders
- File folders color coded to curriculum areas
- Large manilla or colored envelopes coded to curriculum or skill areas
- Three-ring binders.

Although the exact contents of each child's assessment portfolio may vary, most of them include at least two broad sections. Most teachers have a section for representative student work and a section for their personal observations and other documentation of the child's progress. A third section that we suggest is a parent section.

Student work section. Prior to beginning an assessment portfolio, teachers must be clear on how to organize or arrange the students' work. Teachers report that the most common arrangement is by curriculum area subdivided by goals and including samples demonstrating student progress arranged chronologically under each goal.

Specific student work samples that might be included in the assessment portfolio are:

- Drawings or paintings
- Emergent writing samples
- Recorded readings or reflections
- Video tapes of musical or physical performances
- Teacher-made photographs of the students working together/social interactions.

At the heart of the assessment portfolio is the critical piece called reflection. Without reflective work with the child, the portfolio is nothing more than a scrapbook. The young child can be assisted in the development of self-assessment through use of the Reflection Question Model. This model is designed to help the teacher elicit each child's "new learnings" and to clarify and reinforce their "new understandings." The three steps for initiating self-assessment and reflection are Select, Interpret, and Describe.

As teachers guide the children through the three steps of reflection during a portfolio conference, they may ask all or some of the questions listed at each step. Children's responses, or reflections, may be audio recorded or may be recorded by the teacher onto a printed form listing the three steps and the accompanying questions. The questions are designed to encourage the child to articulate what he/she has learned, to enhance motivation for learning, and to build confidence related to his/her progress. Guiding prekindergarten children to engage in self-reflection takes time. Teachers report, however, that when children become accustomed to this reflective process, they are usually realistic and able to make appropriate comments and suggestions. Because time to sit down with children to lead them through the Model and record their responses is limited, some teachers have trained parent volunteers or teacher assistants to record responses.

STEP 1. Select. The teacher should guide the child to select the artifacts that represent his/her best work. In this step, the teacher will ask the following or similar questions:

- Which work sample you are most proud of?
- Which example would you most like to show your parents or friends?
- Which example would you most like to talk about with me or with our class?

STEP 2. Describe. In this step the teacher will guide the student to recall the situations or activities related to the learning experience.

- What can you tell me about this project?
- What do you like about this work sample (or specific product—drawing, recording, book)?

- Where were you when you worked on this project?
- Who helped you with this project?
- How did you make this project/sample/drawing…?
- How did you know how to do the project…?

Step 3. Interpret. The child has now described the project. Step three represents the actual self-assessment or reflection. The following questions may be used as a guide:

- Why do you want to share this work with others?
- Why do you think you did such a good job on this work?
- What was the hardest thing about this work?
- What was the best part of doing this project?
- Is there something that you need help with?
- What else do you want to know about this?
- Is there something else you would like to tell me about this?

Teacher reporting section. This section contains documentation of the child's work via various measures as observed by the teacher. This documentation may include:

- Observational checklist taken over time (developmental, state or district developed, teacher-developed, criterion-referenced)
- Norm-referenced test results
- Conference interview notes
- Goals and objectives checklist
- Reading log entries
- Benchmark tests
- Rating scales
- Video or audio tapes
- Photographs
- Parent-teacher conference notes
- Anecdotal notes

Parent section. This section is usually not as detailed or extensive as the previous two sections of the portfolio. The teachers will need to solicit items for this section and should encourage parents to take an active role in extending the child's learning and in recording observations of the child's learning. Some teachers hold workshops at the beginning of the year on how parents might participate in the portfolio process. The entire portfolio should be reviewed with a parent or family member at least twice a year. Included in this section of the portfolio might be:

- Parent observations regarding their child's work
- Summaries of parent-teacher conferences from the parent's perspective
- Records or logs of home readings/activities
- Records of family experiences related to learning goals (photos, brochures, library card, event tickets).

How Is the Portfolio of the Young Child Evaluated?

The portfolio, by definition, advances the notion that it is a thoughtful and purposeful collection of artifacts used to demonstrate progress toward a set of established criteria or goals; therefore, it is the goals and objectives of the child's program that should be kept at the front of the evaluation process. The teacher can review the evidence in each child's portfolio as it aligns with academic and developmental goals or objectives. A summary statement for each child that provides a holistic view of the child's progress should be developed by the teacher and included in the completed portfolio.

The portfolio process is time-consuming and requires commitment. However, our work with teachers indicates that (1) when they believe portfolio development will make a difference in their children's performance and in their own performance, (2) when teachers, parents, and children have ownership in the process, (3) when there is a supportive environment in which to use portfolios, and (4) when necessary resources exist, teachers are willing to commit to the process and invest the time and energy required. In summary, teachers say that their own classroom practices have been positively affected by the incorporation of the portfolio process and that they are better able to assess and meet the developmental needs of all the children they serve.